Atkins for Life Low-Carb Cookbook

Shrimp and Avocado Salad with Lemon and Cilantro, page 332

Atkins *for* Life
Low-Carb Cookbook

More than 250 recipes for every occasion

Veronica Atkins

with Stephanie Nathanson and The Atkins Kitchen

Photography by Ben Fink

ST. MARTIN'S PRESS
New York

ATKINS FOR LIFE LOW-CARB COOKBOOK. Copyright © 2004 by Atkins Nutritionals, Inc. All rights reserved. Printed in the United States of America. No part of this book may be used or reproduced in any manner whatsoever without written permission except in the case of brief quotations embodied in critical articles or reviews. For information, address St. Martin's Press, 175 Fifth Avenue, New York, N.Y. 10010.

Photographs copyright © 2004 by Ben Fink
Design by Vertigo Design, Inc.   www.vertigodesignnyc.com

www.stmartins.com
www.atkins.com

Library of Congress Cataloging-in-Publication Data available upon request
ISBN 0-312-33125-8
EAN 978-0312-33125-2

First Edition: November 2004
10 9 8 7 6 5 4 3 2 1

To the memory of my dear husband, Robert, whose dream it was to change the way the world eats so that people everywhere would enjoy better health. This dream starts in the kitchen, where he enjoyed nothing more than a home-cooked low-carb meal.

Contents

day by day

on the weekend

party and holiday menus

low-carb cooking for life

Congratulations for choosing the cookbook that will give you the solutions you need to follow a controlled-carb eating plan for life—and welcome to my kitchen! I am excited about this publication because it is an enjoyable way for me to communicate the delicious pleasures, as well as the health and weight-loss benefits, of low-carb meals. I'm also delighted to be able to share the secrets I have learned during my many years as a devotee of the Atkins Nutritional Approach. And I should know— Dr. Atkins loved to eat, and I found great joy in creating wonderful dishes that we could both savor.

While we dined out regularly and had our favorite restaurants, most nights we ate in. I have always loved to cook, and once I met the man who was to become my husband, I joined his crusade to change people's eating habits and incorporated its tenets into our life together. I was his partner in every aspect of this important work, so at home I turned my culinary skills to developing delicious and filling meals that balanced a variety of protein sources and healthy natural fats with a wealth of vegetable options. Although this way of cooking was initially new to me, I immediately adapted to it and found that cooking the low-carb way evoked my creative side whenever I stepped into the kitchen. With this book, you'll also soon see that low-carb cooking and eating can be both exciting and delicious.

At Our Dinner Table

If you're already doing Atkins, you know that variety and good taste are essential to your commitment to stay with it for a lifetime. I have always been inspired by vegetables, which Dr. Atkins absolutely adored. The bitter greens, such as kale and chard, as well as tomatoes (technically a fruit) and garlic, which are all rich in cancer-fighting antioxidants, were among his favorites. (I used a head of garlic almost every night!) These items were the recurring stars of our dinner plates, but I value fresh produce above all else, which usually meant I bought and served whatever was in season.

Aside from ensuring the freshest-tasting produce, shopping in season also made it easier for us to enjoy as much variety as possible in our meals. Each night we enjoyed a vegetable side and a huge salad alongside our main dish. The salad often included another of Dr. Atkins' much-loved choices, the avocado (like tomatoes and olives, it is botanically a fruit). The one vegetable that was never on the menu, however, was the white potato—which is higher on the glycemic index than table sugar. I did regularly include other root vegetables such as turnips, parsnips, and sweet potatoes in our meals.

When it came to the entrées I prepared, Dr. Atkins preferred pork, lamb, chicken, and especially duck. Of course, he was famous for his love of beef. About once a week, we had steak for dinner or even a juicy burger. And he enjoyed fish, made with a crispy crust of chopped nuts such as pecans. His top choices were Chilean sea bass and shad, but even more, he favored lobster, shrimp, and scallops.

Thanks to the meals we shared, we never felt that living a controlled-carb lifestyle deprived us of luxurious foods. We knew that we could even guiltlessly relish a sweet ending, which was usually mixed fresh berries, melon, or papaya, or another fruit with a dollop of whipped cream.

Choosing the Best Ingredients

When it came to selecting the foods that we ate, my European heritage—I was born in Russia and lived in many other countries before immigrating to the United States—established grocery shopping as an everyday ritual for me. Mostly, I went to the nearest grocery store, but when we were at our country house I took advantage of the seasonal farmers' markets. I also grow my own watercress and arugula—more of those nutritious bitter greens. Their bright, vivid flavor has always said "health" to me—and indeed, they are loaded with cancer-fighting antioxidants and carotenoids. Both greens contribute lovely flavor to salads, but are also delightful when cooked in soups and other dishes. Fortunately, most supermarkets now make this kind of produce readily available, so there's no need to have a green thumb!

Living in New York City, where the tradition of a neighborhood butcher shop prevails, I have also had the luxury of building a relationship with my butcher. Such specialty vendors have long-standing suppliers who can vouch for the quality of the meat. My butcher knows what I like and often puts something aside for me or recommends a certain cut when I haven't any specific ideas in mind. Likewise, I always buy fish from a fishmonger.

Does that mean this is the only way to get the freshest meats and seafood? Not at all. But do seek out the freshest ingredients to which you have access. Most supermarkets still have butchers on duty during daytime hours, so ask to have meat ground and large cuts sliced into steaks, rather than picking up cellophane-wrapped packages that may have been sitting around for days. When it comes to fresh fish, don't be shy—ask whoever is working behind the fish counter to let you smell that day's catch! It should have the scent of the ocean. And take advantage of specials and sales—you can always freeze what you don't use immediately. Throughout this book we have provided you with many more helpful tips for choosing the highest-quality foods.

Atkins for Your Life

As you can tell, Dr. Atkins and I were easily able to fit the Atkins Nutritional Approach into our style of eating and our way of life, and I have no doubts that you can use the solutions in this book to adapt to your needs as well. If the foods I've talked about make your mouth water, I'm quite certain you'll be pleased with this cookbook. It's absolutely bursting with recipes that make use of such delights, as well as your other favorite foods. I also suspect that you'll find it to be the kind of cookbook you can curl up with in bed. There are countless bits of wisdom for making cooking and preparation easier and more enjoyable! Quite simply, this book was designed to make doing Atkins a permanent part of your life.

As with *Atkins for Life*, which spent 50 weeks at or near the top of the bestseller list, this book is written primarily for people who are at or close to their goal weight and are living the Atkins lifestyle. This cookbook will introduce you to all the wonderful meals you can be eating for the rest of your life. That said, there are plenty of main dish and other recipes that are suitable for people just starting Atkins, whether in the Induction or Ongoing Weight Loss phases. (For a brief recap of the four phases of the Atkins Nutritional Approach, see pages xi–xii. For more detailed information, see *Atkins for Life* or *Dr. Atkins' New Diet Revolution* or go to www.atkins.com.)

We know you have a busy life, so to give you the information you need at a glance, each recipe includes complete nutritional information per serving, including Net Carbs—the only carbs you need to count when you do Atkins (see What Are Net Carbs? on page xiv). Total carbohydrate, Net Carbs, protein, fiber, and fat content are expressed in grams, rounded to the nearest 0.5. Calories are rounded to the nearest whole number. Icons identify the phases of Atkins for which a recipe is appropriate. Cook times and prep times are provided to help you plan your meal preparation. When appropriate, we have also given times for chilling or marinating. Slow cooker recipes provide times for slow and extra-slow simmering.

Finally, throughout this book you will find numerous tips for success in the kitchen and to help you move toward your weight-loss and -maintenance goals. However, let me take the opportunity to add some additional advice that has served me well and may be of assistance for your waistline and your health.

- **Practice portion control.** Although doing Atkins does not require you to count calories and you can eat protein foods until you feel satisfied, be careful not to stuff yourself.

- **Be moderate.** The way to take permanent control of your weight is to eat moderate amounts of food. If you make Atkins a lifestyle, you will find that you are satiated more quickly.

- **Focus on whole foods.** By concentrating on carbohydrate foods such as vegetables, berries, legumes, and whole grains that are full of nutrients but do not wreak havoc with your blood sugar levels, you will find that you are in control of your appetite, rather than vice versa.

- **Follow serving sizes carefully.** If you eat larger portions, your carb counts can change significantly.

- **Know your limits.** This cookbook is full of delectable dishes. Understand that there should be a difference between the way you eat day to day and the occasional treat.

Here's to a happy and healthy low-carb life!

—*Veronica Atkins*

how to use this book

To make it crystal clear that you can do Atkins easily whatever your lifestyle—and whatever the demands on your time—the recipes in this book are organized into three sections: Day by Day, which focuses on the busy workweek, On the Weekend, and Party and Holiday Menus, which are further divided into chapters based on situations and occasions. Day by Day includes Speedy Weeknight Suppers, With Budget in Mind, and Brown-Bag Lunches, which place a premium on convenience, ease of preparation, and time. The On the Weekend chapters such as Breakfasts and Brunches and Delectable Desserts assume that you may have more time and may be cooking for relaxation. Finally, Party and Holiday Menus focuses on entertaining, with thirteen different holidays and occasions throughout the year, starting with Thanksgiving and ending with Halloween.

As you immerse yourself in these recipes, you will find solid evidence that controlling carbs works in virtually every situation, whether you're having a casual dinner with the family or hosting a dinner party, when you're in a hurry or when you are spending the day creating delicacies in your kitchen. Whether you love to cook or you eat to live, if you like to take shortcuts or you enjoy starting from scratch, if you tinker in the kitchen mostly on the weekends or cook every day, here are recipes that suit your lifestyle. Thanks to the structure of the book, it's worth pointing out that you will find entrées, side dishes, and desserts in several chapters. Remember that if you are interested in checking out every dessert, for example, the index lists them alphabetically under the "Desserts" heading.

Understanding Recipe Coding

Each recipe is coded with numbers in colored boxes to indicate which of the four phases of Atkins for which it is appropriate, as follows:

PHASE **1:** Induction

PHASE **2:** Ongoing Weight Loss (OWL)

PHASE **3:** Pre-Maintenance

PHASE **4:** Lifetime Maintenance

In general, three factors determine the phase coding:

- the number of grams of Net Carbs per serving
- whether the recipe is a main dish or a side, snack, or dessert
- the ingredients in the recipe

Net Carb Counts per serving for Main Dishes:

- Induction: 0 to 7 grams
- Ongoing Weight Loss: 0 to 12 grams
- Pre-Maintenance/Lifetime Maintenance: 0 to 18+ grams

Net Carb Counts per serving for Side Dishes, Snacks, or Desserts:

- Induction: 0 to 3 grams
- Ongoing Weight Loss: 0 to 9 grams
- Pre-Maintenance/Lifetime Maintenance: 0 to 10+ grams

Typically, recipes suitable for Induction do not contain any of these ingredients:

- Fruit
- Fruit juices other than lemon and lime
- Nuts or seeds
- Milk or yogurt (reduced-carb, whole-milk dairy beverages are acceptable)
- Grains (including flour)
- Starchy vegetables
- Legumes
- Alcohol

After eating your vegetables, you can have one or two servings of low-carb convenience foods suitable for Induction so long as they do not provide weight gain or stimulate cravings for sweets or starchy foods. You are allowed to eat one slice of low-carb bread (with no more than 3 grams of Net Carbs) a day during Induction. Atkins Quick Quisine Bake Mix is a suitable ingredient in Induction, as are low-carb shake mixes. Atkins Endulge products and low-carb soy chips, which are used as ingredients in this book, are not suitable for Induction and the recipes that include them are coded for Ongoing Weight Loss or beyond.

In general, recipes suitable for Ongoing Weight Loss (OWL) can contain berries, nuts, seeds, and alcohol.

Recipes coded for Pre-Maintenance and Lifetime Maintenance contain fruit other than berries and moderate amounts of legumes, starchy vegetables, and grains. Because Pre-Maintenance is like a training program for Lifetime Maintenance, there is no difference in coding between the two, but if you are in the early stages of Pre-Maintenance you might want to wait to try some of the higher-carb recipes.

There are occasional exceptions to these guidelines, such as when amounts of ingredients are too small to affect blood sugar. So one carrot in a salad that serves four may mean that a recipe is coded for OWL if the Net Carb count is no more than 9 grams. Similarly, a splash of orange juice in a salad dressing might not keep a recipe within the correct Net Carb range from being coded for OWL.

NOTE: Just because you are in one phase of Atkins does not mean that every recipe is suitable for you. For example, a dessert that contains 20 grams of Net Carbs per serving may not be right for you if you are in Lifetime Maintenance but you are able to maintain your weight only by staying under 50 grams of Net Carbs a day. Similarly, if you find you are losing weight easily doing Atkins, while you are still in OWL you may be able to occasionally eat dishes coded for later phases.

Low-Carb Cooking Techniques

There are no major differences between "regular" cooking and low-carb cooking. To a large extent, it is a matter of getting out of certain habits. For example, learn how to sauté properly so that there is no need to bread fish, poultry, or meat. Just be sure to use an oil with a high smoke point so that it does not burn. Also, learn how to sear meat over a high heat, which creates a naturally crispy crust.

When making stew, be sure not to dredge meats in flour. Instead, purée a few cups of the fluid and vegetables as a natural thickener. When it comes to sauces, have no fear: You will still be able to have them. Basically, there are several options. One is to use a special low-carb thickener (as explained on page xv) instead of the usual white flour. Another option is to make butter- or cream-based sauces (an example is Pan-Seared Steak with Mustard Sauce on page 12). Dipping sauces—try mustard mixed with no-sugar-added jam—and salsa are appropriate with pork and poultry dishes, among others. When making soups, simply adjust the ratio of low-glycemic vegetables such as green beans, tomatoes, and cabbage to high-glycemic vegetables such as sweet potatoes, carrots, and parsnips so that you use all or mostly the former. Cut back on (or eliminate altogether) starches such as barley, brown rice, or whole-wheat pasta. Never thicken soups with bleached flour.

Making low-carb salad dressings is a cinch so long as you stay away from sugar, honey, or maple syrup. Feel free to use olive oil, nut or seed oils, and an array of vine-

what are carbs?

Carbohydrate, along with protein and fat, is one of the three macronutrients that supply our bodies with the calories they need to function. Although fat and protein can be measured with assays, any macronutrient component that is not fat or protein is considered a carbohydrate (food also contains water, minerals, and vitamins.) In the simplest terms carbohydrate foods include sugars and starches, so in addition to fruits, grains, and potatoes, any vegetable contains carbohydrates. But most foods contain either two or three of the macronutrients in varying amounts. Lentils and milk, for example, both contain carbohydrate, fat, and protein.

The Atkins Nutritional Approach stresses the consumption of the carbohydrates that are richest in nutrients, while eliminating refined carbohydrates such as sugar and bleached white flour that are deficient in vitamins and minerals. When you eat foods high in refined, poor-quality carbs they can rapidly raise your blood sugar and insulin to higher than normal levels. Over time excessive sugar in the blood damages the body. Excessive insulin promotes fat storage leading to obesity, Type 2 diabetes, and cardiovascular disease.

gars. It is advisable to avoid balsamic vinegar in Induction. Only balsamic vinegars that have been aged for years are made without added sugar. If you do like a touch of sweetness, add a pinch of the noncaloric sweetener sucralose to your own vinaigrette.

Low-carb baked goods are unquestionably different from comparable cakes and cookies made with sugar and bleached white flour. Light and airy they are not, but they make up for it with richer, more complex flavor. Without as much gluten as white-flour products, baked goods tend to be crumbly and delicate.

In desserts, blending more than one type of sweetener tends to give a better flavor and mitigate any bitter aftertaste. Another way we sweeten some recipes is with sugar-free syrups. Yet another Atkins trick is to use the natural fructose in fresh fruit—Very Berry Bran Coffee Cake (see page 171) is an example—for added sweetness. The goal is always for the sweetness to be subtle enough to take a backseat to the flavor of the chocolate or the strawberry or the mango.

Low-Carb Ingredients

With a few exceptions, notably sugar, honey, molasses, and all other caloric sweeteners, bleached white flour, cornstarch, and margarine and other hydrogenated oils, there are very few foods that are verboten when it comes to cooking the Atkins way. However, that does not mean that ingredients such as whole-wheat flour, apples, or navy beans are suitable in the earlier weight-loss phases of Atkins.

Here is one of the delicious ironies about cooking the low-carb way. Sugar dulls your palate, so when you eliminate it and its sweet cousins, your palate becomes more sensitive to flavors. Many of the foods that people eat who have been following a low-fat program use sugar to make up for the fat, which carries flavor. Ditch the sugar and all the foods that contain it, and make room in your palate for new flavors that can range from the vivid—think of spice rubs redolent of cumin, saffron, cinnamon, cayenne, coriander, and ginger—to the more subtle delights of sweet paprika, lemongrass, celery leaves, citrus zest, and toasted nuts. After you have been on Atkins for a while, your palate is likely to change so that you are satisfied with less sweetness.

what are net carbs?

When you do Atkins, you count only grams of Net Carbs. Fiber is the indigestible part of plant foods such as vegetables, and therefore it does not impact blood sugar. The Net Carb content of a food represents the grams of total carbs minus grams of fiber. There are a few other categories in foods that are also considered carbohydrates but likewise do not impact blood sugar in most people. Used primarily in low-carb foods, they include glycerine and sugar alcohols. While these must be listed on food labels as carbohydrates, they too can be subtracted from the total carb count to yield Net Carbs.

In addition, there are a number of products specifically designed to make it easier to cook low carb:

Sugar substitutes: Sugar in its myriad forms is never acceptable on Atkins. Instead use sucralose (brand name Splenda), which comes in a pourable granulated form, as well as packets, and can be heated without losing its sweetness. Saccharin (brand name Sweet'N Low) can be used to sweeten drinks. Some of our recipes use Atkins Endulge chocolate bars, which are sweetened with the sugar alcohol maltitol, in addition to or instead of sucralose.

Flours: Bleached white flour is not allowed on Atkins. Instead, our baked goods rely on Atkins Quick Quisine Bake Mix, soy flour, soy protein isolate, vital wheat gluten (which keeps the protein and does away with most of the carb content) and whole-wheat flour and whole-wheat pastry flour. In European-style desserts such as tortes, we rely primarily on nut flours. Ground nuts can also make a delicious crumbly crust or can be mixed with whole-wheat pastry flour to make pie crusts and other desserts.

Dairy. Milk is not acceptable in the first two phases of Atkins, nor is yogurt, because of their high-carb count, coming primarily from lactose (milk sugars). Whole milk and full-fat yogurt are fine in the two later phases. You can substitute a half measure of cream blended with an equal amount of water or one of the new reduced-carb dairy beverages that have about one-quarter of the carbs and more protein than milk. Hood makes an Atkins-approved product, and there are other brands available as well.

Thickeners: For soups, stews, and dessert sauces, two low-carb thickeners are invaluable. ThickenThin not/Starch and Thick-It Up! are available at www.atkins.com/shop.

Recipe ingredients key. The Atkins Test Kitchen uses whole-food ingredients whenever possible and generic brands unless a brand-name product is the only one available. However, there are occasions when the use of low-carb products allows us to create a recipe that would otherwise be too high in carbs or certain unacceptable ingredients—or improve taste immeasurably. When an Atkins-brand product is available, we use it to develop and test the recipe, so our nutrition analysis is based on the nutrient content of our own products, which do not contain added sugars, bleached white flour, or hydrogenated oils. So, if you choose to use another low-carb brand, keep in mind that we cannot guarantee the accuracy of the provided nutrition information or the recipe's successful outcome (ingredients in low-carb products can vary drastically). To help you choose a low-carb product that does not exceed the Net Carb count in a recipe, use the following key:

- Low-carb bread: 3 grams of Net Carbs or less per slice
- Low-carb tortilla: 3 grams of Net Carbs or less per tortilla wrap
- Low-carb pasta: 5 grams of Net Carbs or less per serving
- Low-carb ice cream: 3 to 4 grams of Net Carbs or less per ½ cup
- Low-carb pancake syrup: 0 grams of Net Carbs per 2-ounce serving
- Low-carb sandwich roll: 6 grams of Net Carbs or less per roll
- Low-carb soy chips: 4 grams of Net Carbs or less per ounce

day by day

we all want to feed our families well, but resolve can weaken after a long day on the job or ferrying kids to and fro. Zipping through the drive-thru might seem like a temptingly convenient alternative to making dinner at home, but can be expensive, both in dollars and in terms of compromising your health. Here are 23 ultra-fast, ultra-tasty recipes for main dishes and sides you can have on the table before the pizza would be delivered. Some are simple, while others appeal to more sophisticated palates, but all are sure to win raves.

Shrimp and Broccoli Rabe, page 6

speedy *weeknight* suppers

on many busy weeknights, I had to get

dinner on the table for Dr. Atkins and myself in half an hour or less. Many of the entrées in the following pages, like Extra-Crispy Fish with Lemon-Dill Dip (page 8) and Cheesy Chicken Cutlets with Arugula (page 21), were lifesavers on those hectic days. Over the years, I also turned to certain tried-and-true time-savers. For example, try washing and spin-drying enough salad greens for three days. Use what you need that night, and then refrigerate the remainder right in the salad spinner (or a zip-close plastic bag). On the next few evenings, simply take out what you need, add tomatoes, cucumbers, and avocado, and toss with dressing. This simple routine meant Dr. Atkins and I could enjoy a wonderfully fresh salad with our entrée every night of the week.

To save time prepping veggies like carrots, onions, and squash, wash, trim, and cut them up over the weekend or the night before and pop them in those handy zip-close bags. Fresh vegetables are incomparable, but blanched spinach, sweet peas, baby lima beans, and corn kernels all freeze well. Frozen fruit is also quite versatile, particularly out-of-season varieties. Be sure to purchase the kind without added sugar. Keep an array of other ingredients, such as lower sodium chicken and beef broth, canned chickpeas, and unsweetened coconut milk (great for curries) in your pantry. Flavor boosters like olives and capers keep for months in the refrigerator (once opened). Combine them with garlic, olive oil, and low-carb pasta and you've got a meal!

My freezer is filled with nuts (the low temperature keeps them from getting rancid). A must in the low-carb kitchen, they add crunch to salads, and, when finely chopped, crispy coatings to fish and chicken.

With these items on hand, you'll surprise yourself with the variety of meals you can produce—in a flash.

Blackened Fish with Salsa Verde

1 2 3 4 Per serving: **NET CARBS: 2 GRAMS** ▪ Carbohydrates: 2.5 grams ▪ Fiber: 0.5 gram ▪ Protein: 31.5 grams ▪ Fat: 22 grams ▪ Calories: 345 ▪ **PREP TIME: 5 MINUTES** ▪ **COOK TIME: 14 MINUTES** ▪ **SERVINGS: 4**

A quick tour of the supermarket's spice aisle reveals a variety of Cajun spice blends. Each has a distinct nuance, but most include onion, garlic, pepper, and often dried chili peppers; all are fairly to quite spicy.

4 (6- to 8-ounce) catfish fillets,
  patted dry

2 tablespoons Cajun seasoning

2 tablespoons canola oil

¾ cup mild salsa verde

½ cup chopped fresh cilantro

tip

Salsa verde, also know as green salsa, is made from tomatillos. Like tomato-based salsas, it usually contains jalapeños and can vary considerably in heat level. You'll get plenty of spice from the Cajun seasoning, so look for a milder salsa.

1 Sprinkle fish on both sides with seasoning.

2 Heat oil in a large nonstick skillet over medium-high heat. Add half of the fillets and cook until lightly browned, about 3 minutes. Turn and cook until just opaque, 2 to 3 minutes longer. Transfer to plates. Repeat with remaining fish.

3 Meanwhile, combine salsa and cilantro. Serve fish, topped with the salsa.

Shrimp and Broccoli Rabe

Per serving: **NET CARBS: 15 GRAMS** ■ Carbohydrates: 17.5 grams ■ Fiber: 2.5 grams ■ Protein: 35 grams ■
Fat: 8.5 grams ■ Calories: 282 ■ **PREP TIME: 20 MINUTES** ■ **COOK TIME: 10 MINUTES** ■ **SERVINGS: 4**

3 4

Greens and beans are a classic Italian combination—creamy cannellini beans temper the bitterness of broccoli rabe. Add shrimp and red pepper flakes for an elegant meal. For photo, see page 3.

2 (¾-pound) bunches broccoli
   rabe, trimmed

1 tablespoon extra virgin olive oil

4 garlic cloves, minced
   (2 teaspoons)

1 cup lower sodium chicken broth

¼ teaspoon salt

½ teaspoon red pepper flakes

1½ pounds extra-large shrimp,
   peeled and deveined (about 30
   shrimp)

¾ cup canned cannellini beans,
   rinsed and drained

1 Fill a large saucepan two-thirds full with water and bring to a boil; add broccoli rabe, return to a boil, and cook until bright green but still firm, 3 to 5 minutes. Drain well in a colander.

2 Wipe out saucepan. Add oil and heat over medium-high heat. Add garlic and cook, stirring, until it just begins to color, about 30 seconds. Add broth, salt, and red pepper flakes; bring to a boil. Cook until reduced by half, about 4 minutes. Add shrimp and cook until shrimp just begin to curl. Add broccoli rabe and beans, and cook until heated through, 1 to 3 minutes. Season to taste with salt.

tip

Larger shrimp typically cost more than smaller ones, but it's less time-consuming to peel a pound of extra-large shrimp than a pound of medium shrimp. Look for "easy peel" shrimp that are slit along the back. You can simply grab the legs and tail and pull—the shell pops off.

Chicken Thighs alla Puttanesca

1 2 3 4 Per serving: **NET CARBS: 4.5 GRAMS** ■ Carbohydrates: 7 grams ■ Fiber: 2.5 grams ■ Protein: 46.5 grams ■ Fat: 11.5 grams ■ Calories: 324 ■ **PREP TIME: 10 MINUTES** ■ **COOK TIME: 25 MINUTES** ■ **SERVINGS: 4**

Chicken thighs have a richer flavor than breasts and are better able to stand up to the bold sauce. If you can't find boneless thighs, use bone-in ones rather than boneless breasts, but increase the cooking time to 40 minutes.

8 (4-ounce) boneless, skinless chicken thighs

¼ teaspoon pepper

20 pitted kalamata olives

1 (14½-ounce) can crushed fire-roasted tomatoes in purée

2 garlic cloves, minced (1 teaspoon)

1 tablespoon coarsely chopped fresh oregano leaves or 1 teaspoon dried oregano

2 tablespoons capers, rinsed and drained

1 Heat oven to 425°F. Put chicken in a 1½-quart baking dish; season with pepper and scatter olives on top.

2 Combine tomatoes, garlic, and oregano in tomato can. Spoon over chicken to cover. Bake until chicken is just cooked through, about 25 minutes.

3 Transfer chicken and sauce to a platter; sprinkle with capers and serve.

Extra-Crispy Fish with Lemon-Dill Dip

2 **3** **4** Per serving: **NET CARBS: 3 GRAMS** ■ Carbohydrates: 5 grams ■ Fiber: 2 grams ■ Protein: 51 grams ■ Fat: 32.5 grams ■ Calories: 520 ■ **PREP TIME: 5 MINUTES** ■ **COOK TIME: 14 MINUTES** ■ **SERVINGS: 4**

This dish works best with a mild, slightly sweet fish such as scrod, pollock, whiting, haddock, or hake.

2 (1-ounce) bags low-carb soy chips, finely ground

4 (8-ounce) fish fillets, about ½ inch thick

2 tablespoons canola oil, divided

½ cup mayonnaise

3 tablespoons chopped fresh dill

2 teaspoons grated lemon zest

¼ teaspoon pepper

1 Spread ground chips on a piece of waxed paper or paper plate. Dredge fillets in chips to coat on both sides.

2 Heat 1 tablespoon of the oil in a large nonstick skillet over medium heat. Add half the fish and cook until just opaque inside and golden brown outside, 3 to 4 minutes per side. Carefully transfer to plates and tent with foil to keep warm. Repeat with remaining tablespoon oil and fish.

3 Combine mayonnaise, dill, and zest in a small bowl. Season with pepper and serve alongside fish.

tip

The ground chips make for a somewhat fragile coating, so turn the fish fillets carefully. If you don't have a long fish spatula, you may want to use two spatulas, or a spatula and a wooden spoon.

Scallops with Lemon-Chive Sauce

1 2 3 4 Per serving: **NET CARBS: 3.5 GRAMS** ■ Carbohydrates: 5.5 grams ■ Fiber: 2 grams ■ Protein: 21 grams ■ Fat: 15 grams ■ Calories: 238 ■ **PREP TIME: 10 MINUTES** ■ **COOK TIME: 10 MINUTES** ■ **SERVINGS: 4**

Sea scallops can measure up to two inches across. They tend to be chewier than the smaller bay scallops; take care not to overcook them lest they become rubbery. Pat them thoroughly dry before cooking—if they are damp, they won't brown properly.

2 pounds sea scallops, patted dry (28 scallops)

⅛ **teaspoon salt**

¼ **teaspoon pepper**

3 tablespoons unsalted butter, divided

1 garlic clove, minced (½ teaspoon)

1 (10-ounce) bag baby spinach

1½ tablespoons fresh lemon juice

2 tablespoons chopped fresh chives

2 teaspoons grated lemon zest

1 Season scallops with salt and pepper.

2 Melt 1 tablespoon of the butter in a large nonstick skillet over medium-high heat. Add garlic and cook, stirring, until fragrant, about 30 seconds. Add spinach and stir until wilted. Transfer spinach to a platter and cover loosely with foil to keep warm.

3 Wipe out skillet and return it to stove over medium-high heat. Add remaining 2 tablespoons butter. When butter is melted and begins to sizzle, add half of the scallops and cook until browned, about 2 minutes; turn and cook until just opaque, 1 to 2 minutes longer. Transfer to platter and cover loosely with foil to keep warm. Repeat with remaining scallops.

4 Carefully add lemon juice to the skillet, as butter may splatter. Use a wooden spoon to scrape up any brown bits from bottom of pan. Remove from the heat; stir in chives and zest. Pour over scallops and serve.

tip

You use the lemon juice in this recipe before you need the zest, but be sure to remove the zest (that is, the colored part of the peel) from the lemon before you juice it. Once you've cut the lemon it's nearly impossible to zest it.

Pan-Seared Steak with Mustard Sauce

1 2 3 4 Per serving: **NET CARBS: 0.5 GRAM** ▪ Carbohydrates: 0.5 gram ▪ Fiber: 0 grams ▪ Protein: 46 grams ▪ Fat: 44 grams ▪ Calories: 592 ▪ **PREP TIME: 5 MINUTES** ▪ **COOK TIME: 15 MINUTES** ▪ **SERVINGS: 4**

To turn this dish into company fare, add two tablespoons of brandy or cognac to the hot pan after removing the steaks but before adding the broth.

1 tablespoon canola oil

4 (8-ounce) sirloin steaks, about 1 inch thick

½ teaspoon salt

¼ teaspoon pepper

½ cup lower sodium beef broth or water

2 slices bacon, cooked and crumbled

1 tablespoon coarse-grain Dijon mustard

1 tablespoon unsalted butter

1 Heat a large skillet over medium-high heat. Add oil to pan and season steaks with salt and pepper. When skillet is very hot, add steaks and cook until done to taste, 4 to 6 minutes per side for medium-rare. Transfer to a plate and cover loosely with foil to keep warm.

2 Pour broth into skillet, scraping up browned bits from bottom of pan. Add bacon, mustard, and any accumulated juices from the steak, stirring to combine. Bring to a boil. Whisk in butter until blended. Serve sauce over steak.

tip

If you can't find 8-ounce steaks, buy two 1-pound steaks. Cut them in half before cooking and serve a half steak per person, or cook the steaks whole (you may need to increase the cooking time slightly), then slice before serving.

Pork, Spinach, and Noodle Soup

2 Per serving: **NET CARBS: 7 GRAMS** ▪ Carbohydrates: 10 grams ▪ Fiber: 3 grams ▪ Protein: 38.5 grams ▪
3 4 Fat: 23 grams ▪ Calories: 395 ▪ **PREP TIME: 15 MINUTES** ▪ **COOK TIME: 15 MINUTES** ▪ **SERVINGS: 4** (2 cups each)

This is a hearty main-dish soup. Look for presliced 10-ounce packages of cremini mushrooms in your grocery store. They are sometimes called "Baby Bella" mushrooms, as they are younger versions of the popular portobello.

2 tablespoons canola oil

2 garlic cloves, minced
(1 teaspoon)

1 tablespoon dried lemongrass

4 ounces sliced cremini
mushrooms

3 (14½-ounce) cans lower
sodium chicken broth, plus
1 can water

4 ounces low-carb spaghetti

1 pound thin boneless pork chops,
cut into strips

1 medium carrot, grated (¾ cup)

1 (10-ounce) bag baby spinach
(4 cups packed)

1 tablespoon tamari sauce

½ teaspoon dark sesame oil

tip Dried lemongrass often has a woody texture that some people can find off-putting. Put it in a tea ball or tie it in cheesecloth to allow the flavor to infuse the soup, then remove before serving. (If you opt to infuse, add the lemongrass with the broth instead of with the garlic.)

1 Heat canola oil in a large saucepan over medium-high heat. Add garlic and lemongrass; cook, stirring, until fragrant, 15 to 30 seconds. Add mushrooms and cook until most of the liquid has evaporated, about 5 minutes. Remove and reserve.

2 Bring broth and water to a boil. (To save time, heat broth and water in the microwave so it will come to a boil quickly.)

3 Break spaghetti into 2- to 4-inch lengths; stir into boiling broth and cook 5 minutes less than package directions. Add pork and carrot and simmer until pork is just cooked through, 4 to 5 minutes. Stir in mushroom mixture, spinach, tamari, and sesame oil.

4 Use tongs to divide pasta, pork, and vegetables among bowls. Top with hot broth and serve.

Pasta with Gorgonzola and Walnuts

Per serving: **NET CARBS: 6.5 GRAMS** ▪ Carbohydrates: 9.5 grams ▪ Fiber: 3 grams ▪ Protein: 25 grams ▪ Fat: 54.5 grams ▪ Calories: 616 ▪ **PREP TIME: 10 MINUTES** ▪ **COOK TIME: 14 MINUTES** ▪ **SERVINGS: 4**

Gorgonzola is one of Italy's premier cheeses. Made of cow's milk, it's fairly mild among blue cheeses, though it makes for a robust, full-flavored sauce.

1 (12-ounce) box low-carb penne

6 ounces Gorgonzola cheese, crumbled (about 1½ cups)

⅔ cup toasted walnut pieces

½ cup chopped fresh parsley

¼ cup extra virgin olive oil

1½ teaspoons chopped fresh rosemary

1 garlic clove, minced (½ teaspoon)

½ teaspoon pepper

1 Cook penne according to package directions.

2 Meanwhile, combine cheese, walnuts, parsley, oil, rosemary, and garlic in a large serving bowl. Stir gently and season with pepper to taste.

3 Drain pasta thoroughly and toss with sauce. Serve hot.

nuts about nuts

Nuts are one of nature's most nutrient-rich foods. Walnuts are high in omega-3 fatty acids; almonds pack vitamin E and fiber; pine nuts and cashews boast iron; and macadamia nuts are rich in monounsaturated fats, which can lower blood cholesterol levels.

Toasting nuts heightens their flavor. Here are three ways to toast them; watch them carefully as they can burn easily.

Stovetop: Put nuts in a dry skillet over medium-low heat. Cook, shaking the pan almost constantly, for 2 to 3 minutes.

Oven: Spread nuts on a baking sheet. Toast in a 300°F oven until fragrant, 8 to 10 minutes.

Microwave: Set on a paper towel and microwave at full power until fragrant, 1 to 1½ minutes.

Pasta Carbonara

2 3 4 Per serving: **NET CARBS: 5.5 GRAMS** ▪ Carbohydrates: 6.5 grams ▪ Fiber: 1 gram ▪ Protein: 25.5 grams ▪ Fat: 38.5 grams ▪ Calories: 474 ▪ **PREP TIME: 10 MINUTES** ▪ **COOK TIME: 15 MINUTES** ▪ **SERVINGS: 4**

Cook the egg mixture in the hot saucepan (after the pasta has been cooked), but away from direct heat so that the eggs do not curdle. You'll still reduce the risk of foodborne illness without having pieces of scrambled egg in your pasta.

12 ounces low-carb fettuccine

4 ounces pancetta, coarsely chopped

2 large eggs

¾ cup freshly grated Parmesan cheese

¼ cup heavy cream

¼ teaspoon pepper

2 tablespoons unsalted butter

1 Cook fettuccine according to package directions.

2 Cook pancetta in microwave on paper towels until crisp, 3 to 4 minutes. Drain on clean paper towels.

3 Meanwhile, whisk eggs, cheese, cream, and pepper in a bowl until combined.

4 Drain fettuccine and return to hot saucepan. Turn off the heat, pour cream mixture over pasta and toss; add butter and toss until butter is melted and sauce is evenly coated. Transfer to serving bowl and crumble reserved pancetta on top. Serve hot.

Swordfish with Savory Balsamic Sauce

1 2 3 4

Per serving: **NET CARBS: 2.5 GRAMS** ■ Carbohydrates: 2.5 grams ■ Fiber: 0 grams ■ Protein: 31 grams ■ Fat: 14 grams ■ Calories: 269 ■ **PREP TIME: 5 MINUTES** ■ **COOK TIME: 12 MINUTES** ■ **SERVINGS: 4**

Choose steaks that are ¾ to 1 inch thick—increase the cooking time slightly if yours are thicker; decrease it if they're thinner. To properly cook fish, the rule of thumb is 8 to 10 minutes of cooking time for every 1 inch of thickness.

1½ tablespoons canola oil

4 (8-ounce) swordfish steaks, about ¾ inch thick, rinsed and patted dry

½ teaspoon salt

¼ teaspoon pepper

¼ cup balsamic vinegar

1 tablespoon unsalted butter

2 tablespoons capers, lightly crushed

1 Heat oil in a large nonstick skillet over high heat until it shimmers. Season fish with salt and pepper. Cook fish until browned, about 5 minutes; turn and cook until just barely opaque, 3 to 4 minutes longer. Transfer to a platter and cover loosely with foil to keep warm.

2 Add vinegar to pan and boil until reduced by about half, about 1 minute. Whisk in butter until melted; add capers. Pour over fish and serve.

time-saving techniques and pantry staples

No matter how hectic your schedule is, you're almost always better off carving out the time to prepare foods at home than relying on takeout, fast food, or eating out. But when you're running late, what can you do to speed things along? Here are tried-and-true short-cuts that can make short work of dinner preparation.

Plan the week. You'll spend less time at the supermarket if you have made a written schedule of dinners.

Fresh garlic and ginger are incomparable, but sticking a spoon in a jar of the prepared products can shave a few minutes off a recipe's prep time.

Alphabetize your spice rack. Knowing that paprika is between oregano and parsley means you won't have to empty a cabinet to find it (and then put everything back).

Save scraps. Don't toss the crumbs from the bottom of that bag of low-carb bread crusts.

Pasta with Spicy Tomato-Shrimp Sauce

2 **3** **4** Per serving: **NET CARBS: 7.5 GRAMS** ▪ Carbohydrates: 20 grams ▪ Fiber: 12.5 grams ▪ Protein: 55 grams ▪ Fat: 9 grams ▪ Calories: 336 ▪ **PREP TIME: 10 MINUTES** ▪ **COOK TIME: 15 MINUTES** ▪ **SERVINGS: 4**

Don't let the word "spicy" throw you—this versatile sauce can be adapted to suit any palate. Leave out the pepper flakes entirely if you're serving those who prefer mild foods.

8 ounces low-carb rotini

1 pound large shrimp, peeled and deveined

¼ teaspoon salt

2 teaspoons olive oil

½ teaspoon red pepper flakes, or to taste

1 cup low-carb marinara or tomato sauce

1 Cook pasta according to package directions. Drain, reserving ½ cup pasta cooking water.

2 Meanwhile, season shrimp with salt. Heat oil in a large nonstick skillet over medium-high heat. Stir in red pepper flakes and immediately add shrimp, arranging in a single layer. Cook until pink, 1 to 2 minutes; turn and cook until just opaque, 1 to 2 minutes longer. Transfer to a plate.

3 Add marinara sauce to pan and cook until heated through. Add pasta and shrimp; toss to combine. Use reserved cooking water if needed to thin the sauce to your preferred texture.

Cheesy Chicken Cutlets with Arugula

1 2 3 4 Per serving: **NET CARBS: 3 GRAMS** ▪ Carbohydrates: 4 grams ▪ Fiber: 1 gram ▪ Protein: 63.5 grams ▪ Fat: 21.5 grams ▪ Calories: 481 ▪ **PREP TIME: 10 MINUTES** ▪ **COOK TIME: 12 MINUTES** ▪ **SERVINGS: 4**

Arugula adds a peppery bite to this dish. Spinach is a fine substitute, especially if you are feeding more delicate palates.

4 ounces arugula, cleaned and dried

1 medium tomato, cut into 8 thin slices

½ pound fresh mozzarella, cut into 8 thin slices

3 teaspoons canola oil, divided

5 teaspoons unsalted butter, divided

8 (4-ounce) chicken cutlets

½ teaspoon salt

¼ teaspoon pepper

1 Place the tomato slices on a cutting board or large platter. Top each with one-eighth of the arugula and a slice of mozzarella.

2 Heat 1½ teaspoons of the oil and 1½ teaspoons of the butter in a large nonstick skillet over medium-high heat until it shimmers. Season chicken with salt and pepper. Add 4 cutlets and cook until lightly browned on one side, about 2 minutes. Turn and top each with a tomato, arugula, and cheese pile. Cover and cook until chicken is just opaque inside and cheese is melted, about 3 minutes. Transfer to serving plate and cover loosely with foil to keep warm.

3 Wipe out skillet; repeat with remaining oil, butter, chicken, and tomato piles. Serve hot.

Spicy Chicken Soup with Black Beans

Per serving: **NET CARBS: 8.5 GRAMS** ■ Carbohydrates: 13.5 grams ■ Fiber: 5 grams ■ Protein: 31.5 grams ■
3 4 Fat: 12.5 grams ■ Calories: 298 ■ **PREP TIME: 10 MINUTES** ■ **COOK TIME: 22 MINUTES** ■ **SERVINGS: 4** (1 cup each)

Tender and rich in flavor, dark chicken meat is the better choice for most chicken dishes. When cooked for longer periods of time, it's less likely to dry out than is white meat.

1 tablespoon olive oil

1 pound boneless, skinless chicken thighs, cut into 1-inch pieces

2 medium celery stalks, chopped (1 cup)

2 garlic cloves, minced (1 teaspoon)

4 cups lower sodium chicken broth

1 cup canned black beans, rinsed and drained

½ cup canned diced tomatoes with chilies

4 tablespoons sour cream

1 tablespoon finely chopped fresh cilantro

1 Heat oil in a large saucepan over high heat. Add chicken and cook, stirring as needed, until browned, about 5 minutes. Add celery; reduce heat to medium and cook until celery is bright green and crisp-tender, about 3 minutes longer. Add garlic and cook until fragrant, about 1 minute.

2 Stir in broth, scraping up any browned bits from the bottom of the pan. Add beans and tomatoes and bring to a boil. Reduce heat to low and simmer until chicken is cooked through, 10 to 13 minutes. Serve, topped with sour cream and cilantro.

Minestrone

Per serving: **NET CARBS: 11 GRAMS** ▪ Carbohydrates: 19.5 grams ▪ Fiber: 8.5 grams ▪ Protein: 7 grams ▪
Fat: 7.5 grams ▪ Calories: 164 ▪ **PREP TIME: 10 MINUTES** ▪ **COOK TIME: 30 MINUTES** ▪ **SERVINGS: 4** (2 cups each)

3 4

Hearty and full of greens, this vegetable soup takes a little bit longer to get on the table than other recipes in this chapter, but most of that time is unattended. You can return phone calls, do the laundry, or just take a deep breath while the soup simmers.

2 tablespoons olive oil

2 cups sliced mushrooms

1 **medium onion,** diced (¾ cup)

1 **small carrot,** halved and sliced (½ cup)

1 **pound escarole,** trimmed and coarsely chopped (7 cups)

1 (3- to 4-inch) Parmesan rind

1 (14½-ounce) can lower sodium vegetable broth, plus 1¼ cups water

⅓ cup dried lentils (2 ounces), rinsed and picked over

½ teaspoon salt

¼ teaspoon pepper

1 Heat oil in a large saucepan over medium heat; add mushrooms, onion, and carrot. Cover and cook until crisp-tender, about 5 minutes. Add escarole, broth, Parmesan rind, and water; increase heat to high, cover, and bring to a boil.

2 Stir in lentils. Reduce heat to medium-low; cover and simmer until lentils are tender, 20 to 25 minutes. Remove rind, season with salt and pepper, and serve.

tip

When you use Parmesan in cooking, it pays to use freshly grated cheese—it really is superior in flavor to pre-grated cheese. Buy a block that weighs about six ounces, and save the rinds for a soup like this one. They soften and add an incomparable depth of flavor to the broth. If you don't have an immediate need for the rinds, they will keep for up to 3 months tightly wrapped in the freezer.

Sesame Chicken with Gingery Greens

2
3 **4**
Per serving: **NET CARBS: 3.5 GRAMS** ■ Carbohydrates: 8 grams ■ Fiber: 4.5 grams ■ Protein: 62 grams ■ Fat: 36 grams ■ Calories: 655 ■ **PREP TIME: 15 MINUTES** ■ **COOK TIME: 20 MINUTES** ■ **SERVINGS: 4**

If your skillet isn't large enough to hold the chicken breasts without crowding, transfer them to a baking sheet before you put them in the oven.

Chicken:

⅔ cup sesame seeds

1 large egg

1 tablespoon water

1 teaspoon salt

4 (8-ounce) boneless, skinless chicken breasts

1½ tablespoons canola oil

Greens:

⅓ cup mayonnaise

¼ cup coarsely chopped red onion

2 tablespoons unseasoned rice wine vinegar

1½ tablespoons lower sodium chicken broth

2½ teaspoons tamari sauce

½ teaspoon grated fresh ginger

1 garlic clove

½ teaspoon salt

8 cups mesclun greens or other tender lettuce

tip

Cut the prep time for the dish by washing and drying the greens on the weekend, and then storing them in the fridge. You can also make the dressing in advance—keep it in an airtight container in the fridge for up to a week.

1 For the chicken: Heat oven to 350°F. Put sesame seeds on a plate.

2 Lightly beat egg, water, and salt in a shallow bowl. Dip chicken into egg mixture, shaking off excess; press each side into sesame seeds to coat.

3 Heat oil in a large ovenproof skillet over medium-high heat. Add chicken; cook until golden, 3 to 4 minutes per side. Turn chicken over and place in oven. Bake until cooked through or until an instant-read thermometer inserted into the thickest part of the breast registers 165°F, 6 to 8 minutes. Let stand 5 minutes, then cut into slices.

4 For the greens: Purée mayonnaise, onion, vinegar, broth, tamari, ginger, garlic, and salt in a blender until smooth. Toss greens with dressing and divide among plates. Top with chicken.

Snow Peas with Chili Oil

`1` `2` `3` `4` Per serving: **NET CARBS: 3.5 GRAMS** ▪ Carbohydrates: 6 grams ▪ Fiber: 2.5 grams ▪ Protein: 2.5 grams ▪ Fat: 1 gram ▪ Calories: 42 ▪ **PREP TIME: 10 MINUTES** ▪ **COOK TIME: 3 MINUTES** ▪ **SERVINGS: 4**

Look for chili oil in the Asian foods aisle of your market. If you can't find it, use ½ teaspoon vegetable oil and a pinch of red pepper flakes.

¾ **pound snow peas,** trimmed and strings discarded (4 cups)

½ **teaspoon chili oil**

1 **garlic clove,** minced (½ teaspoon)

¼ **teaspoon salt**

1 Bring a medium saucepan of salted water to a boil. Add peas and cook until bright and crisp-tender, 1½ to 2 minutes. Drain; wipe out saucepan.

2 Add oil, garlic, and salt to saucepan and set over medium heat. Return snow peas to pan. Cook, stirring, until coated, about 30 seconds; serve hot.

Buttermilk Sweet Potato Purée

`3` `4` Per serving: **NET CARBS: 13 GRAMS** ▪ Carbohydrates: 14.5 grams ▪ Fiber: 1.5 grams ▪ Protein: 1.5 grams ▪ Fat: 2 grams ▪ Calories: 82 ▪ **PREP TIME: 10 MINUTES** ▪ **COOK TIME: 7 MINUTES** ▪ **SERVINGS: 6** (⅓ cup each)

Be sure to vent the plastic wrap, either by folding part of the plastic back and leaving an inch or so open or by poking several holes in it with a fork.

1¼ **pounds sweet potatoes,** peeled and cut into 1-inch chunks

1 **tablespoon water**

⅓ **cup buttermilk**

1 **tablespoon unsalted butter**

½ **teaspoon salt**

¼ **teaspoon ground cardamom or ground cinnamon**

Put potatoes in a microwavable bowl with water and partially cover with plastic wrap. Microwave until fork-tender, 5 to 7 minutes. Transfer potatoes to a food processor. Add buttermilk, butter, salt, and cardamom. Process until smooth. Serve hot.

Tofu Italiano

1 2 3 4 Per serving: **NET CARBS: 7.5 GRAMS** ■ Carbohydrates: 10.5 grams ■ Fiber: 3 grams ■ Protein: 21 grams ■ Fat: 20.5 grams ■ Calories: 290 ■ **PREP TIME: 15 MINUTES** ■ **COOK TIME: 15 MINUTES** ■ **SERVINGS: 4**

Tofu may not have originated in Italy, but it takes beautifully to this Italian-inspired vegetable sauté. Don't forget to press and blot the tofu dry—removing as much moisture as possible will ensure a crispy crust. Let the tofu stand while you assemble the remaining ingredients and prepare the other vegetables.

1½ pounds extra-firm tofu, cut crosswise into 8 slices

3 tablespoons canola oil, divided

2 medium red bell peppers, thinly sliced (2 cups)

1 (10-ounce) package sliced button or cremini mushrooms

4 garlic cloves, minced (2 teaspoons)

½ teaspoon salt

¼ teaspoon red pepper flakes

¼ cup thinly sliced fresh basil

1 Set tofu on a plate lined with a double layer of paper towels; top with more paper towels and another plate, then put a can on top of plate so sides of tofu bulge slightly. Let stand 5 to 10 minutes, then pour off and discard liquid. Pat dry with clean paper towels.

2 Heat 1 tablespoon of the oil in a large nonstick skillet over medium-high heat. Add tofu and cook until golden, 3 to 4 minutes per side. Transfer to plates and keep warm in a 200°F oven.

3 Heat remaining 2 tablespoons oil in skillet over medium heat. Add peppers; cook until softened, about 5 minutes. Add mushrooms, garlic, salt, and red pepper flakes. Cover and cook until mushrooms begin to release their liquid, about 3 minutes. Uncover, increase heat to high, and cook until almost all of the liquid has evaporated, about 3 minutes longer.

4 Stir in basil. Divide vegetables over tofu and serve.

Green Beans and Carrots al Pesto

2
3 **4**
Per serving: **NET CARBS: 4.5 GRAMS** ▪ Carbohydrates: 7 grams ▪ Fiber: 2.5 grams ▪ Protein: 2 grams ▪ Fat: 2 grams ▪ Calories: 48 • **PREP TIME: 2 MINUTES** • **COOK TIME: 10 MINUTES** • **SERVINGS: 4**

Either store-bought or homemade pesto can be used in this simple yet tasty recipe. Quarter four or five baby carrots lengthwise and you won't have to scrub or peel a carrot.

⅛ teaspoon salt

1 (9-ounce) package frozen Italian-style green beans

1 large carrot, peeled and cut into coins (1 cup)

1 tablespoon basil pesto

Pepper

1 Bring ¼ inch water to a boil in a medium saucepan over high heat. Add salt, green beans, and carrot. Cover and cook, stirring occasionally, until beans are heated through, 5 to 6 minutes. Drain and transfer vegetables to a warmed dish.

2 Mix with pesto and season with pepper to taste.

Sugar Snap Peas with Tomatoes

2
3 **4**
Per serving: **NET CARBS: 7 GRAMS** ▪ Carbohydrates: 9.5 grams ▪ Fiber: 2.5 grams ▪ Protein: 2.5 grams ▪ Fat: 3.5 grams ▪ Calories: 77 ▪ **PREP TIME: 5 MINUTES** ▪ **COOK TIME: 2 MINUTES** ▪ **SERVINGS: 4**

Tarragon is a mild anise-flavored herb. It adds a unique dimension when combined with sweet sugar snap peas and slightly tart tomatoes.

1 tablespoon unsalted butter

1 (9-ounce) package frozen sugar snap peas, thawed and drained (or 2 cups fresh)

12 cherry tomatoes, halved (¾ cup)

¾ teaspoon dried tarragon

¼ teaspoon salt

⅛ teaspoon pepper

Heat butter in a large nonstick skillet over medium-high heat. Add peas and cook, stirring constantly, 1 minute. Add tomatoes and tarragon. Cook, stirring, until peas are bright green and tomatoes are heated through, about 2 minutes longer. Season with salt and pepper and serve.

Spinach Sauté with Roasted Peppers

1 2 3 4 Per serving: **NET CARBS: 1 GRAM** ▪ Carbohydrates: 3.5 grams ▪ Fiber: 2.5 grams ▪ Protein: 2.5 grams ▪ Fat: 3.5 grams ▪ Calories: 51 ▪ **PREP TIME: 3 MINUTES** ▪ **COOK TIME: 7 MINUTES** ▪ **SERVINGS: 4**

Bagged baby spinach makes a quick and delicious vegetable dish. Although the spinach may be "prewashed," it should still be rinsed before using. Don't worry about drying the spinach, as the water clinging to the leaves will help it to steam.

1 tablespoon extra virgin olive oil

3 **large garlic cloves,** peeled and smashed with flat side of chef's knife

2 (6-ounce) bags baby spinach

¼ teaspoon salt

2 **roasted red peppers,** patted dry and coarsely chopped

1 Combine oil and garlic in a large nonstick skillet over medium heat. Cook, stirring often and pressing down on garlic, until golden, about 1 minute. Remove and discard garlic, if desired.

2 Add spinach in 2 or 3 batches, tossing with tongs. When all has been added, season with salt and cook, tossing, until wilted, about 2 minutes. Add peppers and cook, tossing, until heated through, about 1 minute longer. Transfer to a warm dish and serve

tip

Red bell peppers are an excellent source of cancer-fighting pigments called carotenoids, and roasted red peppers are even higher. As with lycopene in tomatoes, cooking concentrates these compounds.

Broccoli and Cauliflower with Orange Butter

1 2
3 4
Per serving: **NET CARBS: 3 GRAMS** ■ Carbohydrates: 6 grams ■ Fiber: 3 grams ■ Protein: 2.5 grams ■
Fat: 6 grams ■ Calories: 80 ■ **PREP TIME: 3 MINUTES** ■ **COOK TIME: 15 MINUTES** ■ **SERVINGS: 4**

If you prefer, you can use two eight-ounce bags of fresh broccoli and cauliflower florets (or pick them up at a salad bar); you'll need to increase the cooking time to six or seven minutes.

2 (10-ounce) boxes frozen
   broccoli and cauliflower florets
2 tablespoons unsalted butter
2 teaspoons grated orange zest

¼ teaspoon salt
⅛ teaspoon pepper

1 Bring ¼ inch water to a boil in a large saucepan over high heat. Add broccoli and cauliflower. Cover and cook, stirring occasionally, until vegetables are crisp-tender, about 5 minutes. Drain vegetables in a colander. Wipe out saucepan.

2 Melt butter in saucepan over medium-low heat. Stir in orange zest and cook 30 seconds. Add vegetables, salt, and pepper; toss until evenly coated and heated through, about 1 minute.

tip

Look for a rasp-style microplane grater to make quick work of grating citrus zest—if you don't see one in a kitchenware store, check out a hardware store.

Stir-Fried Ginger-Garlic Greens

1 2 3 4 Per serving: **NET CARBS: 3 GRAMS** ▪ Carbohydrates: 6 grams ▪ Fiber: 3 grams ▪ Protein: 3 grams ▪ Fat: 7.5 grams ▪ Calories: 98 ▪ **PREP TIME: 6 MINUTES** ▪ **COOK TIME: 9 MINUTES** ▪ **SERVINGS: 4**

Iceberg lettuce doesn't just belong in the salad bowl. Here it makes a transformation into a delicious cooked vegetable. For photo, see page 37.

2 tablespoons canola oil

3 garlic cloves, thinly sliced

1 tablespoon chopped fresh
   ginger

3 large scallions, sliced (½ cup)

1 (12-ounce) bag iceberg lettuce
   mix with radishes and carrots

1 (16-ounce) bag baby spinach

1 tablespoon soy sauce

½ teaspoon dark sesame oil

Heat canola oil in a heavy saucepan over medium-high heat. Add garlic and ginger; cook, stirring, until fragrant but not browned, about 30 seconds. Add scallions, lettuce mix, and spinach in batches, tossing with tongs. Stir-fry until wilted, 2 to 3 minutes longer. Add soy sauce and sesame oil, toss, and serve.

spotlight on ginger

At first glance, ginger wouldn't impress anyone as a nutritional powerhouse. One teaspoon of fresh ginger—about the amount in a serving of a stir-fry—supplies only 8 milligrams of potassium and just trace amounts of vitamins and other minerals. Yet this rhizome is full of health-boosting properties.

Ginger contains several potent phytochemicals. Most of its punch comes from phenols, the same group of compounds that imbue red wine with its healthful properties. It also contains cucurmin, an anticarcinogen, and cap-saicin, the antioxidant that gives peppers their heat.

Look for ginger with plump knobs and smooth, somewhat shiny skin. The skin can be tough, so recipes often recommend peeling it before use. Because navigating the knobs with a paring knife or vegetable peeler can be tricky, use a spoon to scrape off the skin. Fresh ginger is quite fibrous. Although some recipes say to chop or mince it, you may prefer to grate ginger to obtain its pulp, then discard the larger strings.

busy people have

rediscovered the slow cooker in the
past decade: Combine the ingredients
in the morning, plug in the machine,
and come home to a wonderfully
aromatic, delicious meal. If you
don't have a slow cooker, simply keep
your pot over a bare simmer on the
stove top or in a 350°F oven. We've
provided cooking times for both low
and high heat, so choose which best
fits your schedule and kitchen tools.
These dishes take time to cook, but
because you don't need to stir the pot
or check it at all, you'll save time in
the end.

Shrimp, Chicken, and Sausage
Jambalaya, page 40

take it
slow

the slow cooker was invented for the time-challenged—but it is also tailor-made for those watching their wallets and their carb intake. Combine a terrific protein source like lamb, beef, or chicken with vitamin-filled vegetables—keep potatoes and other high-carb varieties to a minimum or omit them altogether—leave the house for the day, and come back to a savory, simmering dinner. Toss a salad together and dinner can be on the table in no time. (For the greatest efficiency, clean and cut up vegetables the night before.) Unless you have a big family, chances are you'll have some leftovers handy for lunch the next day.

One of the myths about doing Atkins is that you'll have to spend your grocery dollars on foods like steak and lobster. Nothing could be further from the truth, and the recipes that follow are just the solution for cooking less costly cuts of meat and poultry to perfection. In fact, the tender, more costly cuts do not hold up as well during a long cooking process. One of Dr. Atkins' favorite slow-cooked dishes was osso buco, made with veal shanks that simmer in a rich tomato-based stock all day until the meat literally falls off the bone. Lamb shanks, chuck roasts, and hearty sausages like kielbasa also lend themselves to this cooking method, as do lentils and other legumes. A slow cooker is also ideal for the slow simmering that makes a delectable soup. Recipes for Shrimp, Chicken, and Sausage Jambalaya (page 40), Pork Stew with Hominy and Collards (page 46), and Thai-Spiced Short Ribs (page 36) that follow will prove my point—deliciously. (For more on ways to manage your food budget, see With Budget in Mind on page 48.)

Brisket with Cabbage and Onions

2 **3 4** Per serving: **NET CARBS: 6 GRAMS** ▪ Carbohydrates: 10 grams ▪ Fiber: 4 grams ▪ Protein: 45.5 grams ▪ Fat: 48.5 grams ▪ Calories: 665 ▪ **PREP TIME: 20 MINUTES** ▪ **COOK TIME** (low heat): **9 TO 11 HOURS** ▪ **COOK TIME** (high heat): **4½ TO 5 HOURS** ▪ **SERVINGS: 6**

Brisket and cabbage is a hearty, homey combination; hot mustard on the side lends a little kick that cuts through the unctuousness of the brisket.

2 teaspoons salt, divided

½ teaspoon hot paprika

¾ teaspoon pepper, divided

½ teaspoon chopped fresh thyme

¼ teaspoon dried oregano

2 garlic cloves, minced (1 teaspoon)

2 tablespoons olive oil

1 (3-pound) beef brisket, well trimmed

1 (1½-pound) head green cabbage, thinly sliced (8 cups)

1 large onion, sliced (1 cup)

1 medium carrot, sliced (1 cup)

¾ teaspoon caraway seeds

2 (14½-ounce) cans lower sodium beef broth

2 tablespoons ThickenThin not/Starch thickener

¼ cup chopped fresh parsley (optional)

tip

It's unlikely you'll find hot paprika with the round glass or plastic canisters of spices— typically it comes in a rectangular tin and may be on a lower shelf. It is hotter than sweet paprika and should never be substituted for it in equal measure.

1 Combine 1 teaspoon of the salt, paprika, ½ teaspoon of the pepper, thyme, oregano, garlic, and oil in a small bowl and mix well. Rub on brisket.

2 Put cabbage, onion, and carrot in 4½-quart or larger slow cooker. Season with remaining teaspoon salt and remaining ¼ teaspoon pepper and caraway seeds. Set brisket on top of vegetables and pour in broth. Cover and cook until brisket is tender but not falling apart, 9 to 11 hours on low or 4½ to 5 hours on high.

3 Transfer brisket and vegetables to a serving platter. Skim excess fat from broth and whisk in thickener until smooth.

4 Thinly slice brisket against the grain. Arrange brisket slices over vegetables and pour sauce over meat. Sprinkle with parsley, if using, and serve.

Thai-Spiced Short Ribs

1 2 3 4 Per serving: **NET CARBS: 3.5 GRAMS** ▪ Carbohydrates: 4.5 grams ▪ Fiber: 1 gram ▪ Protein: 52 grams ▪ Fat: 34.5 grams ▪ Calories: 551 ▪ **PREP TIME: 15 MINUTES** ▪ **COOK TIME** (low heat): **6 TO 7 HOURS** ▪ **COOK TIME** (high heat): **3½ TO 4 HOURS** ▪ **SERVINGS: 4**

If you prefer a glazelike sauce, remove the lid to the slow cooker when the ribs are done. Turn the heat to high (if it isn't already) and simmer until thickened. Serve with Stir-Fried Ginger-Garlic Greens (page 31).

1 tablespoon olive oil

2 garlic cloves, minced (1 teaspoon)

1 tablespoon minced fresh ginger

1 tablespoon Thai red curry paste

¼ teaspoon ground allspice

½ teaspoon salt

¼ teaspoon pepper

4 (1-pound) short ribs

1 cinnamon stick, about 2 inches long

1 large onion, finely chopped (1 cup)

1 (14½-ounce) can lower sodium beef broth

¼ cup chopped fresh cilantro

1 Combine oil, garlic, ginger, curry paste, allspice, salt, and pepper in a small bowl to make a paste. Rub on ribs.

2 Put ribs, cinnamon, onion, and broth in a 4½-quart or larger slow cooker. Cover and cook until beef is tender, 6 to 7 hours on low or 3½ to 4 hours on high. Skim excess fat from broth. Sprinkle with cilantro and serve.

tip

Short ribs can be purchased bone in or boneless. Aficionados will tell you that meat cooked on the bone is more flavorful, but with a sauce as savory as this, boneless ribs are fine.

Lamb Shanks with Garlic and Herbs

1 2 3 4 Per serving: **NET CARBS: 4 GRAMS** ■ Carbohydrates: 5.5 grams ■ Fiber: 1.5 grams ■ Protein: 46.5 grams ■ Fat: 9 grams ■ Calories: 307 ■ **PREP TIME: 20 MINUTES** ■ **COOK TIME** (low heat): **8 TO 9 HOURS** ■ **COOK TIME** (high heat): **5 HOURS** ■ **SERVINGS: 6**

Slow cookers and lamb shanks are a match made in heaven. The moist heat helps to tenderize the shanks and allows the flavor of the garlic and herbs to infuse the meat. Freeze any leftovers for another day. Serve with the mashed cauliflower-potato topping from Shepherd's Pie (page 200).

6 (1-pound) lamb shanks

1 teaspoon salt

½ teaspoon pepper

10 garlic cloves, peeled

1 sprig fresh rosemary or
   1 teaspoon dried

1 sprig fresh thyme (3 to 4 inches
   long) or 1 teaspoon dried

1 large onion, chopped (1 cup)

¼ cup dry vermouth or dry
   white wine

½ cup diced tomatoes in juice

1 (14½-ounce) can lower sodium
   beef broth

3 tablespoons ThickenThin
   not/Starch thickener

¼ cup chopped fresh parsley

1 Season lamb with salt and pepper; arrange in a 4½-quart or larger slow cooker with meaty ends down. Add garlic, rosemary, thyme, onion, vermouth, tomatoes, and broth; the bone end of the shanks should be exposed slightly above the liquid. Cover and cook until lamb is very tender, 8 to 9 hours on low or about 5 hours on high.

2 Transfer lamb to a serving platter and cover. Remove and discard herb sprigs; remove garlic and mash with a fork, then return to broth. Skim excess fat from broth and whisk in thickener until smooth. Pour over lamb. Serve, sprinkled with parsley.

tip

Ten cloves of garlic? Indeed! Really, it isn't that many. Long, slow cooking mutes garlic's pungency, and leaving the cloves whole imparts a far subtler flavor than chopping them does.

Shrimp, Chicken, and Sausage Jambalaya

Per serving: **NET CARBS: 13.5 GRAMS** ▪ Carbohydrates: 16 grams ▪ Fiber: 2.5 grams ▪ Protein: 34.5 grams ▪
Fat: 13.5 grams ▪ Calories: 332 ▪ **PREP TIME: 35 MINUTES** ▪ **COOK TIME** (low heat): **6 HOURS** ▪
COOK TIME (high heat): **3 HOURS** ▪ **SERVINGS: 8** (1½ cups each)

*Browning the chicken and vegetables before adding them to the pot isn't necessary
for the dish to work, but the caramelization sweetens the flavor and makes the
chicken appear darker and richer. For photo, see page 33.*

2 tablespoons olive oil, divided

1 large onion, chopped (1 cup)

2 celery stalks, chopped (1 cup)

1 large green bell pepper,
chopped (1 cup)

2 garlic cloves, minced
(1 teaspoon)

1½ pounds boneless, skinless
chicken thighs, cut into chunks

½ bay leaf

½ cup uncooked brown rice

1 teaspoon chopped fresh thyme
or ½ teaspoon dried

¼ cup chopped fresh parsley

1 (14½-ounce) can diced tomatoes
in juice

¾ pound andouille sausage, sliced

1 pound large shrimp, peeled and
deveined

2 large scallions, green parts only,
sliced (¼ cup)

Hot pepper sauce, such as Tabasco
(optional)

1 Heat 1 tablespoon of the oil in a large nonstick skillet. Add onion, celery,
and bell pepper; cook, stirring frequently, until softened, about 7 minutes.
Add garlic and cook until vegetables begin to brown and garlic is quite fragrant, 2 to 3 minutes longer. Transfer to a 4½-quart or larger slow cooker.

2 Heat remaining tablespoon oil in skillet. Add chicken and cook until
browned, about 3 minutes on each side. Transfer to slow cooker and add
bay leaf, rice, thyme, parsley, tomatoes, and sausage, in the order listed.

3 Cover and cook until flavors are blended and rice and chicken are tender,
6 hours on low or 3 hours on high. Thirty minutes before the end of cooking
time, gently stir in shrimp; cover and cook until shrimp are pink and opaque.
Sprinkle scallions on top just before serving and serve with plenty of hot
sauce, if using, on the side.

Flemish Beef Stew

2 3 4 Per serving: **NET CARBS: 4.5 GRAMS** ▪ Carbohydrates: 5.5 grams ▪ Fiber: 1 gram ▪ Protein: 44 grams ▪ Fat: 16 grams ▪ Calories: 365 ▪ **PREP TIME: 10 MINUTES** ▪ **COOK TIME** (low heat): **8 HOURS** ▪ **COOK TIME** (high heat): **4 HOURS** ▪ **SERVINGS: 6** (1½ cups each)

Inspired by the classic Belgian stew called carbonnade à la flammande, this sweet yet savory stew is a marvelous blend of beef, beer, and onions.

2 large onions, sliced (2 cups)

3 pounds lean beef stew meat, cut into ¾- to 1-inch cubes

½ teaspoon chopped fresh thyme or ¼ teaspoon dried

2 teaspoons salt

½ teaspoon pepper

1 bay leaf

2 garlic cloves, minced (1 teaspoon)

½ cup water

1 (12-ounce) bottle low-carb beer

2 teaspoons ThickenThin not/Starch thickener

1 Layer one-fourth of the onions, one-third of the meat, a bit of thyme, salt, and pepper in a 4½-quart or larger slow cooker. Add bay leaf and garlic and continue layering, finishing with onions. Add water and beer. Cover and cook until beef is tender, 8 hours on low or 4 hours on high.

2 Transfer meat to a serving bowl. Skim excess fat from the broth and whisk in thickener until smooth. Pour over meat and serve.

best bets for braises

Braising—cooking meat over low heat in a covered pot with a little liquid—is just about as easy as it sounds. The trickier part is choosing the proper cut of meat. Because braising is a slow-cooking technique, the best cuts are the toughest. Short ribs, lamb shank or shoulder, beef chuck, brisket, pork shoulder or butt, and even oxtails are full of collagen, a protein found in bones, cartilage, and connective tissue (or gristle). As the meat cooks, collagen softens and imparts a rich, smooth, meltingly tender texture to the meat.

If you're a fan of chicken, ask your butcher for a stewing hen. Rarely seen in supermarkets these days, stewing hens are tough old birds with rich flavor; long, slow cooking makes them tender. If you can't track one down, a whole chicken or chicken thighs are better than breast meat alone.

Southern Country-Style Pork Ribs

1 2 3 4

Per serving: **NET CARBS: 3.5 GRAMS** ▪ Carbohydrates: 6.5 grams ▪ Fiber: 3 grams ▪ Protein: 27.5 grams ▪ Fat: 14.5 grams ▪ Calories: 282 ▪ **PREP TIME: 10 MINUTES** ▪ **COOK TIME** (low heat): **8 HOURS** ▪ **COOK TIME** (high heat): **4 HOURS** ▪ **SERVINGS: 6**

Lean country-style ribs are ideal for this dish. If you try this with fattier ribs, chill the dish overnight and lift off the fat before reheating.

1 cup low-carb ketchup	1 teaspoon fresh lemon juice
2 teaspoons Worcestershire sauce	1 teaspoon paprika
2 tablespoons Dijon mustard	1 garlic clove, minced (½ teaspoon)
1 teaspoon sugar-free pancake syrup	1 (14½-ounce) can lower sodium beef broth
1 teaspoon granular sugar substitute	6 (8-ounce) country-style pork ribs

1 Combine ketchup, Worcestershire sauce, mustard, syrup, sugar substitute, lemon juice, paprika, garlic, and broth in a 4½-quart or larger slow cooker, whisking until blended. Add ribs and stir to coat thoroughly. Cover and cook until tender, about 8 hours on low or 4 hours on high.

2 Transfer ribs to a platter. Skim fat from the liquid and pour over ribs. (If sauce is thinner than you prefer, turn slow cooker to high and let sauce cook until thickened. Cover ribs loosely with foil to keep warm, if necessary.) Serve, or refrigerate the meat and sauce together; the flavors improve overnight.

tip

Country-style pork ribs are meatier than baby back ribs or spareribs, and because they're cut from the loin, they're considerably lower in fat. That makes them perfect for braising, because the sauce will be less greasy.

Chicken in a Pot

2 **3** **4** Per serving: **NET CARBS: 9 GRAMS** ■ Carbohydrates: 11 grams ■ Fiber: 2 grams ■ Protein: 55.5 grams ■ Fat: 27 grams ■ Calories: 523 ■ **PREP TIME: 30 MINUTES** ■ **COOK TIME** (low heat)**: 6 TO 7 HOURS** ■ **COOK TIME** (high heat)**: 3 TO 4 HOURS** ■ **SERVINGS: 4**

Choose thin leeks—about the diameter of a large thumb—rather than thick ones. They're more tender and have better flavor.

2 (6- to 8-ounce) leeks, trimmed, cut in half lengthwise, and washed

2 small carrots, cut in half lengthwise

2 celery stalks, cut in half

1 (3½- to 4-pound) chicken, rinsed and patted dry

1 teaspoon salt

½ teaspoon pepper

¼ small onion

1 large garlic clove, peeled

1 sprig fresh thyme

1 sprig fresh parsley

1 (14½-ounce) can lower sodium chicken broth

1 Put leeks, carrots, and celery in a 4½-quart or larger slow cooker.

2 Season chicken inside and out with salt and pepper. Put onion, garlic, thyme, and parsley in chicken cavity and truss with string. Set chicken on top of vegetables and pour in broth. Cover and cook until chicken moves freely at the thigh joint, 6 to 7 hours on low.

3 Transfer chicken and vegetables to a large platter and remove string.

4 Skim fat from liquid. Cut chicken into 8 pieces. Serve chicken and vegetables with broth ladled over.

Hearty Turkey and Vegetable Soup

Per serving: **NET CARBS: 12 GRAMS** ▪ Carbohydrates: 17 grams ▪ Fiber: 5 grams ▪ Protein: 30.5 grams ▪

3 4 Fat: 7.5 grams ▪ Calories: 260 ▪ **PREP TIME: 30 MINUTES** ▪ **COOK TIME** (low heat): **6 HOURS** ▪

COOK TIME (high heat): **3 HOURS** ▪ **SERVINGS: 6** (2 cups each)

The best time to prepare this main-dish soup is after Thanksgiving, or whenever you have turkey bones on hand, so you can make a rich broth. Choose kale, collard greens, or Swiss chard—any will work beautifully, so use whichever looks freshest at your market.

6 ounces cooking greens, cleaned and chopped (3 cups)

¾ cup bite-size cauliflower florets

1 medium red or green bell pepper, chopped (¾ cup)

1 medium onion, chopped (¾ cup)

3 celery stalks, chopped (1½ cups)

1 bay leaf

⅓ cup dried chickpeas, soaked overnight, or ¾ cup canned chickpeas, rinsed and drained

1 garlic clove, minced (½ teaspoon)

1½ pounds thinly sliced raw turkey (preferably from thighs)

1 (14½-ounce) can diced tomatoes in juice

2 (14½-ounce) cans lower sodium chicken broth

3 tablespoons chopped fresh basil

3 tablespoons chopped fresh parsley

Layer greens, cauliflower, pepper, onion, celery, bay leaf, chickpeas, garlic, and turkey in a 4½-quart or larger slow cooker in the order listed. Pour in tomatoes and broth. Cover and cook on low until chickpeas are tender and turkey is cooked through, about 6 hours. Stir in basil and parsley and serve.

tip

If you purchase a whole head of cauliflower, instead of just the florets, and have some left over, this is a great time to make mashed potatoes and cauliflower (see method in step 1 on page 200). Show off the fancy florets with dishes like this, and use the stalks when appearance is less important, as in a purée.

Vegetable Curry

3 4

Per serving: **NET CARBS: 16 GRAMS** ▪ Carbohydrates: 24.5 grams ▪ Fiber: 8.5 grams ▪ Protein: 8.5 grams ▪ Fat: 21.5 grams ▪ Calories: 296 ▪ **PREP TIME: 30 MINUTES** ▪ **COOK TIME** (low heat): **4 HOURS** ▪ **COOK TIME** (high heat): **2 HOURS** ▪ **SERVINGS: 4** (2 cups main course); **8** (1 cup side dish)

We provide nutrient information based on four main-dish servings, but this makes a tasty side dish for eight; simply halve the per-serving information. Garnish with a few teaspoons of chopped peanuts or, if your carb threshold allows, raisins.

½ **head cauliflower,** broken into florets (3 cups)

1 **medium sweet potato,** peeled and cut into ½-inch dice (about 1½ cups)

1 **large red bell pepper,** diced (1 cup)

½ **small onion,** cut into 8 wedges

1 **medium bunch broccoli,** cut into florets (3 cups)

1½ **cups small white mushrooms**

1 **(13½-ounce) can unsweetened coconut milk**

¼ **cup water**

2½ **teaspoons Madras curry powder**

1 **teaspoon minced fresh ginger**

2 **garlic cloves,** minced (1 teaspoon)

1½ **teaspoons salt**

¼ **teaspoon pepper**

1 **cup chopped bok choy stems and leaves**

2 **tablespoons chopped fresh cilantro** (optional)

tip

Bags of broccoli and cauliflower florets save time but precut vegetables have more surfaces exposed, and thus vitamin loss increases. Some vitamins, especially vitamin C, deteriorate rapidly when exposed to oxygen.

1 Arrange cauliflower, sweet potato, bell pepper, onion, broccoli, and mushrooms in a 4½-quart or larger slow cooker, in the order listed.

2 Whisk coconut milk, water, curry powder, ginger, garlic, salt, and pepper in a bowl, mixing well; pour over vegetables. Arrange bok choy on top. Cover and cook until the vegetables are crisp-tender, 2 hours on high. Serve, sprinkled with cilantro, if using.

Pork Stew with Hominy and Collards

Per serving: **NET CARBS: 21 GRAMS** ▪ Carbohydrates: 28 grams ▪ Fiber: 7 grams ▪ Protein: 46.5 grams ▪ Fat: 25.5 grams ▪ Calories: 536 ▪ **PREP TIME: 25 MINUTES** ▪ **COOK TIME** (low heat): **6 HOURS** ▪ **COOK TIME** (high heat): **3 HOURS** ▪ **SERVINGS: 6** (2 cups each)

Although collards are the greens of choice in the South, kale will work just as well. The real secret to this dish is a bottle of vinegar seasoned with garlic and hot peppers—just splash on a few drops to heighten the flavors.

1 teaspoon salt

¼ teaspoon pepper

½ teaspoon dried oregano

3 pounds lean pork shoulder, trimmed and cut into ¾-inch cubes

1 tablespoon vegetable oil

1½ pounds collard greens, trimmed of stems and chopped (9 cups)

1 large onion, diced (1 cup)

4 garlic cloves, coarsely chopped (2 teaspoons)

1 small bay leaf

1 (29-ounce) can hominy, drained, or 1 cup dried yellow hominy, quick-soaked per package instructions

1 (14½-ounce) can lower sodium chicken broth, plus 1 can water

Hot pepper vinegar (optional)

tip
Hot pepper vinegar makes a wonderful addition to salad dressings, too. To make, simply add about a teaspoon of red pepper flakes and a crushed garlic clove to a cup of white wine vinegar. Seal and let steep in the refrigerator for a week, then strain into a clean bottle.

1 Combine salt, pepper, and oregano in a large bowl. Add pork; toss to coat.

2 Heat oil in a large skillet over medium-high heat. Add pork and brown on all sides, 5 to 7 minutes.

3 Layer one-third of the greens, half of the onion, garlic, bay leaf, half of the hominy, and half of the meat in a 4½-quart or larger slow cooker. Repeat, ending with greens. Pour in broth and water. Cover and cook until pork is tender, about 6 hours on low. Serve with vinegar, if using.

skyrocketing

food prices don't mean you have to skimp on nutrition—the most wholesome foods are often the least expensive. Processing foods increases their cost, which is why a 10-ounce bag of cleaned spinach or salad kit can cost three times more than a bunch of spinach or head of lettuce. Skip the bags of salad greens; instead, examine each head of lettuce to choose the most pristine. If your schedule allows, stop by the market in the afternoon or evening to see which meats are specially priced. Enjoy the luxury of fresh foods, deliciously prepared.

Egg Roulade with Spinach-Feta Stuffing, page 58

with budget
in mind

once you stop buying highly refined, high-carb foods like breakfast pastries, cookies, chips, and other foods full of sugar and bleached white flour, you will find you have dollars to spend on more nutritious foods like fresh vegetables and meat and poultry. Do you have to buy the priciest cuts of meat to do Atkins? Absolutely not! In fact, the more inexpensive cuts, which typically have greater fat marbling, often have more flavor, too. Does that mean you have to have hamburgers every night? Quite the contrary. With budget in mind, you'll concentrate on buying cuts such as lamb shanks, beef stew meat, and ham steaks. It also means buying certain cuts in bulk or when they are on sale and freezing what you don't use at once. Most sausages are another easy-on-the-budget choice.

Save by purchasing vegetables and fruit when they are in season, too. That's what people did years ago, before strawberries from Mexico, tomatoes from Israel, and asparagus from Chile were flown into the United States year-round. Not surprisingly, this increased availability usually comes with a higher price tag. Avoid paying inflated prices by buying such foods when they are in season and parboiling and freezing them so they are there for you even during the coldest months of the year.

You needn't have meat, fish, or poultry every night, either. Just make sure you have sufficient protein in the meal. Eggs and tofu (bean curd) fill the bill. Egg Roulade with Spinach-Feta Stuffing (page 58) may be elegant, but it is also definitely a budget dish, as is Crustless Broccoli Quiche (page 65). Try Veggie-Tofu Stir-Fry (page 62) as well as Vegetable and Tofu Lasagne (page 204) and Tofu Italiano (page 26).

Beef and Bean Stew

Per serving: **NET CARBS: 17 GRAMS** ▪ Carbohydrates: 24 grams ▪ Fiber: 7 grams ▪ Protein: 38 grams ▪
Fat: 22 grams ▪ Calories: 444 ▪ **PREP TIME: 30 MINUTES** ▪ **COOK TIME: 2½ HOURS** ▪ **SERVINGS: 6** (1½ cups each)

3 4

Chuck is one of the less-expensive cuts of beef. It comes from the area between the neck and shoulder, so it gets considerable exercise and as a result is quite tough and requires long, slow simmering to become tender. A hint of cinnamon and orange zest adds subtle "what-is-that flavor" nuance.

2 pounds boneless beef chuck, cut into 1-inch chunks

1¼ teaspoons salt, divided

¾ teaspoon pepper, divided

½ teaspoon ground cinnamon

2 teaspoons olive oil

1 pound white mushrooms, sliced

2 celery stalks, thinly sliced (1 cup)

1 medium onion, chopped (¾ cup)

1 medium carrot, grated (¾ cup)

2 garlic cloves, minced (1 teaspoon)

1 (28-ounce) can diced tomatoes or 1 (26-ounce) box chopped tomatoes

4 cups water

1 (15-ounce) can pinto beans, drained and rinsed

1 teaspoon grated orange zest

2 tablespoons chopped fresh parsley

tip

Often, stew recipes call for coating meat with flour before browning it, or for potatoes; both methods help to thicken the stew but they can increase the carb count dramatically. Puréeing a few cups of stew is another way to add body to the broth; it makes for a satisfying, hearty dish.

1 Season beef with 1 teaspoon of the salt, ½ teaspoon of the pepper, and cinnamon. Heat oil in a large heavy saucepan over medium-high heat. Add half of the beef and cook until browned, about 7 minutes. Transfer to a plate and repeat with remaining beef.

2 Add mushrooms, celery, onion, carrot, and garlic to saucepan and cook until onion is translucent and mushrooms have started to release moisture, about 7 minutes. Add beef, tomatoes, and water (add more water, if necessary, to cover). Bring to a boil. Reduce heat to low and simmer until meat is fork-tender, about 2 hours.

3 Add beans and cook until heated through, about 10 minutes. Stir in zest, remaining ¼ teaspoon salt, and remaining ¼ teaspoon pepper.

4 Remove 5 cups of stew; return any beef chunks to pot. Purée stew in 2 batches in a blender; return to saucepan and stir to combine. Serve, sprinkled with parsley.

Ham Steak with Cajun Green Beans

1 2 3 4 Per serving: **NET CARBS: 7 GRAMS** ▪ Carbohydrates: 11 grams ▪ Fiber: 4 grams ▪ Protein: 36 grams ▪ Fat: 18 grams ▪ Calories: 346 ▪ **PREP TIME: 15 MINUTES** ▪ **COOK TIME: 15 MINUTES** ▪ **SERVINGS: 4**

Ham tends to be reserved for special occasions, and unless you've got a large household, the leftovers seem to last forever (if not actually multiply in the refrigerator). Ham steaks usually weigh a pound or two and are an ideal solution for smaller families.

1 teaspoon paprika

1 teaspoon fresh thyme leaves, plus sprigs for garnish

1 (1½-pound) thick-cut ham steak, patted dry

3 tablespoons olive oil, divided

1 pound green beans, trimmed and cut in half

1 garlic clove, minced (½ teaspoon)

1 cup canned diced tomatoes with chilies

¼ teaspoon salt

tip
For safety's sake, before adding oil to a pan that held another liquid, be sure to wipe it out. Water, whether in foods or on metal, can spatter—and sometimes flare up—when it comes into contact with hot oil.

1 Combine paprika and thyme; sprinkle evenly over both sides of ham. Heat 1 tablespoon of the oil in a large skillet over medium-high heat. Add ham and cook until browned, about 3 minutes per side.

2 Meanwhile, fill a large saucepan two-thirds full with water and bring to a boil. Add green beans and cook until just crisp-tender and bright green, about 8 minutes. Drain in a colander and rinse under lukewarm water to cool. Wipe out saucepan.

3 Heat remaining 2 tablespoons oil in saucepan over medium heat. Add garlic and cook, stirring, until just golden, 30 to 40 seconds. Add tomatoes with chilies and salt; cook until slightly reduced, about 3 minutes. Stir in green beans and cook until hot. Serve with ham; garnish with thyme springs.

Sausage, Lentil, and Escarole Stew

Per serving: **NET CARBS: 19.5 GRAMS** ▪ Carbohydrates: 29 grams ▪ Fiber: 9.5 grams ▪ Protein: 18 grams ▪

3 4 Fat: 5 grams ▪ Calories: 232 ▪ **PREP TIME: 20 MINUTES** ▪ **COOK TIME: 1¼ HOURS** ▪ **SERVINGS: 6** (1½ cups each)

This dish is not only great on its own but it can be stretched further as a sauce for low-carb pasta.

1 tablespoon olive oil

1 **pound kielbasa,** cut into ⅓-inch slices

1 **garlic clove,** minced (½ teaspoon)

1½ **teaspoons caraway seeds**

1 **teaspoon fennel seeds**

1 **small red onion,** diced (½ cup)

4 **cups water or lower sodium chicken broth**

1 **cup dried lentils (6 ounces),** rinsed and picked over

½ **teaspoon pepper**

1 **large head escarole,** trimmed and coarsely chopped (8 cups)

2 **tablespoons chopped fresh parsley**

1 Heat oil in a large saucepan over medium-high heat. Add kielbasa and cook, turning occasionally, until well browned, about 10 minutes.

2 Add garlic, caraway, and fennel to saucepan. Cook, stirring, until fragrant, about 30 seconds. Add onion and cook until tender, about 5 minutes. Add water, lentils, and pepper. Reduce heat to medium-low and simmer until lentils are tender, 40 to 45 minutes.

3 Add escarole, stirring until it wilts. Serve, sprinkled with parsley.

tip

Some supermarket brands of kielbasa can contain fillers like cornstarch, potato starch, and sugar, adding empty carbs. Read ingredient lists carefully.

Cabbage and Meatball Soup

2 Per serving: **NET CARBS: 9 GRAMS** ▪ Carbohydrates: 12.5 grams ▪ Fiber: 3.5 grams ▪ Protein: 15.5 grams ▪
3 4 Fat: 12.5 grams ▪ Calories: 217 ▪ **PREP TIME: 25 MINUTES** ▪ **COOK TIME: 50 MINUTES** ▪ **SERVINGS: 6** (1½ cups each)

Cabbage becomes meltingly tender with long simmering. If you prefer a bit of crunch, reserve one cup of the sliced raw cabbage. Chop and use as a garnish.

12 ounces ground beef

2 tablespoons grated onion

1 teaspoon salt, divided

½ teaspoon pepper, divided

2 teaspoons Dijon mustard

¼ teaspoon red pepper flakes

¼ teaspoon ground allspice

3 tablespoons cider vinegar

2 tablespoons granular sugar substitute

1 (1- to 1¼-pound) head green cabbage, thinly sliced (6 cups)

1 (28-ounce) can diced tomatoes or 1 (26-ounce) box chopped tomatoes

4 cups water

½ cup sour cream

1 Gently combine beef, onion, ½ teaspoon of the salt, ¼ teaspoon of the pepper, and mustard in a bowl. With wet hands, form into 12 small meatballs and set in a large nonstick saucepan.

2 Set saucepan over medium-high heat and cook meatballs, turning frequently, until browned on all sides, about 7 minutes. Transfer meatballs to a plate; cover loosely with foil to keep warm. Add red pepper flakes and allspice to pan drippings; cook, stirring, until fragrant, about 30 seconds. Add vinegar and sugar substitute and bring to a simmer. Stir in cabbage, remaining ½ teaspoon salt, and remaining ¼ teaspoon pepper. Add tomatoes and water; bring to a boil. Reduce heat to low and simmer until cabbage is very tender, about 35 minutes.

3 Add meatballs to soup and cook to warm through, about 5 minutes. Serve, topped with sour cream.

Tuna and Cauliflower Cakes

1 2
3 4   Per serving: **NET CARBS: 5.5 GRAMS** ▪ Carbohydrates: 10.5 grams ▪ Fiber: 5 grams ▪ Protein: 49.5 grams ▪ Fat: 30.5 grams ▪ Calories: 517 ▪ **PREP TIME: 20 MINUTES** ▪ **COOK TIME: 6 MINUTES** ▪ **SERVINGS: 4**

Canned tuna ranges in price from less than 50 cents a can to nearly three dollars. Chunk light is one of the less expensive varieties.

2 slices low-carb white bread, toasted

1 (10-ounce) box frozen cauliflower or 2 cups fresh cauliflower florets

2 large eggs

2 (6-ounce) cans oil-packed chunk light tuna, drained

2 large scallions, thinly sliced (¼ cup)

8 tablespoons mayonnaise, divided

2 teaspoons finely grated lemon zest

¼ cup chopped fresh parsley

½ teaspoon pepper, divided

1 tablespoon olive oil, divided

2 tablespoons Dijon mustard

tip

Cauliflower should be heavy, have no space between the florets, and be white to cream-colored, with no brown spots. It can be stored in a perforated plastic bag for a few days. The leaves can be eaten but have a more pronounced flavor than the florets.

1 Pulverize toast in a food processor to make fine crumbs; transfer to a medium bowl.

2 Cook cauliflower according to package directions, or steam until tender, about 10 minutes. Completely drain off any water. Cool slightly; transfer to food processor. Add eggs and purée.

3 Add cauliflower mixture, tuna, scallions, 2 tablespoons of the mayonnaise, zest, parsley, and ¼ teaspoon of the pepper to bread crumbs.

4 Heat a griddle or nonstick skillet over medium-high heat; brush lightly with about 1 teaspoon of the oil. Form cauliflower mixture into twelve ¼-cup cakes and cook, turning once, until golden on the outside and heated through, about 3 minutes per side. Brush skillet with remaining oil as needed.

5 Mix remaining 6 tablespoons mayonnaise, mustard, and remaining ¼ teaspoon pepper in a small bowl. Serve tuna cakes with sauce on the side.

Egg Roulade with Spinach-Feta Stuffing

1 2 3 4

Per serving: **NET CARBS: 4.5 GRAMS** ▪ Carbohydrates: 7.5 grams ▪ Fiber: 3 grams ▪ Protein: 18.5 grams ▪ Fat: 31.5 grams ▪ Calories: 377 ▪ **PREP TIME: 45 MINUTES,** plus chilling ▪ **COOK TIME: 35 MINUTES** ▪ **SERVINGS: 6**

Elegant and delicious, this dish is deceptively easy to prepare. It makes an impressive addition to a brunch buffet without requiring expensive or exotic ingredients. For photo, see page 49.

Egg layer:

3 tablespoons unsalted butter, melted, plus more for pan and parchment

¼ cup Atkins Quick Quisine Bake Mix

¾ cup heavy cream

6 large eggs, separated

½ cup grated Parmesan cheese

¼ teaspoon salt

¼ teaspoon pepper

Filling:

1 tablespoon unsalted butter

1 small onion, minced (⅓ cup)

1 tablespoon water

1 pound fresh spinach, cleaned well and coarsely chopped

¼ teaspoon pepper

4 ounces feta cheese, crumbled (1 cup)

¼ cup grated Parmesan cheese

tip

Prepare the egg layer the night before and chill it, if you have time, to help make it easier to handle; heat the roulade in a 350°F oven for 10 minutes before adding filling.

1 For the egg layer: Heat oven to 350°F. Butter a 15½- by 10½-inch jelly-roll pan. Line with 20-inch-long sheet of parchment paper, allowing 2 inches to hang over each end; butter parchment lightly.

2 Mix butter, bake mix, cream, egg yolk, Parmesan, salt, and pepper in blender until combined. Transfer to a medium bowl.

3 Beat egg whites until stiff with electric mixer. In 3 additions, fold into yolk mixture. Pour into prepared pan and spread evenly. Bake until puffed and golden, 25 minutes. (If preparing ahead, cool, cover, and refrigerate.) Invert pan onto a sheet of buttered waxed paper. Remove pan and parchment from egg layer.

4 For the filling: Melt butter in a large skillet over medium-high heat. Add onion and cook until softened, about 3 minutes. Add water, half of the spinach, and pepper; cook, stirring, until spinach is partly wilted, about 1 minute. Add remaining spinach and continue cooking until partly wilted, 1 to 2 minutes longer. Add feta and Parmesan; cook until cheese is melted and spinach is just wilted, about 2 minutes longer.

5 Remove filling with slotted spoon, leaving excess liquid in skillet. Spread filling over egg layer, leaving ½-inch border. Roll up from long side and cut into 12 slices.

spotlight on oils

Most supermarkets stock shelf after shelf of oils, from inexpensive jugs to costly vials. Why the discrepancy in cost, particularly among "pure" and "cold-pressed extra virgin" olive oil? Although both of these oils come from olives, they're quite different—especially in flavor—due to how the olives are pressed. The price depends on how labor-intensive it is to extract the oil from the source. Oils that are cold-pressed, such as most nut oils and some olive oils, require more time, and more hands-on labor. Other methods are automated, but the heat generated by these processes can destroy nutrients and mute the flavors of some oils.

Which pressing the oil comes from also affects price. Extra virgin olive oil is from the first pressing; its fruity flavor and aroma come from its low acid level. Virgin olive oil is pressed from the pulp that remains after the first pressing; it is slightly higher in acid. Refined and pure oils are processed further or blended with virgin olive oil.

From both a nutritional and budgetary viewpoint, it makes sense to keep a variety of oils on hand. Choose a flavorless or mildly flavored oil like peanut, canola, corn, or pure olive oil for stir-frying or sautéing. For drizzling onto a bowl of lentil soup, mixing into a salad dressing, or dipping, use a delicate, cold-pressed extra virgin olive oil or flavorful nut oil like walnut or hazelnut oil.

Moroccan Roasted Vegetables

Per serving: **NET CARBS: 22.5 GRAMS** ■ Carbohydrates: 31 grams ■ Fiber: 8.5 grams ■ Protein: 7.5 grams ■
3 4 Fat: 15 grams ■ Calories: 278 ■ **PREP TIME: 30 MINUTES** ■ **COOK TIME: 1 HOUR** ■ **SERVINGS: 4** (1½ cups each)

Chickpeas are common in Mediterranean cuisines and complement the warm spices used in Moroccan cooking. They're an excellent—and inexpensive—source of protein, as well as fiber and iron.

¼ **cup olive oil**

1½ **teaspoons salt**

¾ **teaspoon ground cinnamon**

¾ **teaspoon ground coriander**

½ **teaspoon ground cumin**

½ **teaspoon red pepper flakes**

½ **teaspoon ground ginger**

1 **head cauliflower,** broken into florets (6 cups)

1 **medium bunch broccoli,** broken into florets (4 cups)

1 **medium onion,** chopped (¾ cup)

1 **medium carrot,** cut into ⅓-inch slices (1 cup)

1 **(15-ounce) can chickpeas,** drained and rinsed

3 **tablespoons chopped fresh cilantro**

1   Heat oven to 450°F. Mix oil, salt, cinnamon, coriander, cumin, red pepper flakes, and ginger in a large roasting pan. Add cauliflower, broccoli, onion, and carrot; toss gently to coat.

2   Cover with foil and roast 20 minutes. Stir vegetables; roast, uncovered, until cauliflower is browned but not fork-tender, about 20 minutes longer. Stir in chickpeas; continue to roast until all vegetables are tender, 20 minutes longer. Serve, sprinkled with cilantro.

Veggie-Tofu Stir-Fry

2
3 **4**

Per serving: **NET CARBS: 12 GRAMS** ▪ Carbohydrates: 20.5 grams ▪ Fiber: 8.5 grams ▪ Protein: 35 grams ▪ Fat: 41 grams ▪ Calories: 583 ▪ **PREP TIME: 15 MINUTES** ▪ **COOK TIME: 20 MINUTES** ▪ **SERVINGS: 2**

Pick up a small package of tofu and a selection of vegetables from the salad bar on your way home and dinner's virtually done. If your daily carb threshold allows, enjoy this dish with some brown rice in later phases.

3 tablespoons canola oil, divided

1 (14-ounce) package firm tofu, sliced into ½-inch rectangles, divided

1 tablespoon chopped fresh ginger

1 teaspoon red pepper flakes (optional)

2 cups small broccoli florets

1 red bell pepper, cut into strips (1 cup)

3 cups sliced bok choy

6 tablespoons no-sugar-added teriyaki sauce

1 thin scallion, greens only, diagonally sliced (2 tablespoons)

2 tablespoons water

1   Heat 1 tablespoon of the oil in a large nonstick skillet over medium-high heat. Add half of the tofu and cook until it releases easily from pan, about 3 minutes per side. Transfer to a paper towel and let cool; cut into ½-inch cubes. Repeat with another tablespoon oil and remaining tofu.

2   Add remaining tablespoon oil to skillet; stir in ginger and red pepper flakes, if using. Cook, stirring, until fragrant, 30 seconds.

3   Add broccoli, red pepper, and bok choy; reduce heat to medium. Stir-fry until nearly crisp-tender, 3 to 4 minutes. Add tofu, teriyaki sauce, scallion, and water. Toss gently to mix. Cook, tossing gently, until tofu is hot and broccoli is tender but not mushy, 2 to 4 minutes.

Confetti Meatloaf

1 **2** **3** **4**   Per serving: **NET CARBS: 5 GRAMS** ▪ Carbohydrates: 8.5 grams ▪ Fiber: 3.5 grams ▪ Protein: 20 grams ▪ Fat: 11 grams ▪ Calories: 217 ▪ **PREP TIME: 15 MINUTES** ▪ **COOK TIME: 70 MINUTES** ▪ **SERVINGS: 8**

This makes for a very moist, tender meatloaf. If you prefer yours drier, drain some of the liquid after measuring the tomatoes.

3 slices low-carb white bread, toasted

1½ pounds ground meatloaf blend (veal, pork, and beef)

1 cup canned diced tomatoes

1 cup green beans, cut into ¼-inch pieces

1 large egg

1 medium carrot, grated (¾ cup)

2 tablespoons Worcestershire sauce

1½ teaspoons salt

¾ teaspoon pepper

¼ cup no-sugar-added ketchup

1 Heat oven to 375°F. Pulverize toast in a food processor to make fine crumbs; transfer to a large bowl. Add ground meat, tomatoes, beans, egg, carrot, Worcestershire sauce, salt, and pepper; mix gently until just blended.

2 Spoon into 5- by 9-inch loaf pan, pressing firmly. Spread ketchup over top. Bake 60 to 70 minutes, until cooked through. Transfer to a platter, discarding any fat left in pan. Let stand at least 10 minutes before slicing.

tip

If you don't have a loaf pan this size, bake a free-form meatloaf. Line a jelly-roll pan with foil. Put the meat mixture on the pan and shape it into a 5- by 9-inch rectangle.

Open-Faced Roasted Chicken Sandwich

1 2 3 4 Per serving: **NET CARBS: 4.5 GRAMS** ▪ Carbohydrates: 9.5 grams ▪ Fiber: 5 grams ▪ Protein: 37 grams ▪ Fat: 12.5 grams ▪ Calories: 305 ▪ **PREP TIME: 5 MINUTES** ▪ **COOK TIME: 35 MINUTES** ▪ **SERVINGS: 4**

Chicken cooked on the bone is more flavorful than boneless chicken, though it takes longer to cook. If you're in a hurry, use leftover roast chicken. Thighs have richer flavor, but it can be easier to get attractive slices off the breast.

1½ pounds bone-in chicken breasts or thighs

¼ teaspoon salt

¼ teaspoon black pepper

1 teaspoon canola oil

1 teaspoon paprika, divided

¼ cup finely chopped onion

⅓ cup lower sodium chicken broth or water

3 tablespoons sour cream

1½ teaspoons Dijon mustard

Pinch cayenne pepper

4 slices low-carb white bread, toasted and sliced in half diagonally

Chopped fresh parsley

1 Heat oven to 450°F. Season chicken with salt and black pepper.

2 Heat oil in an ovenproof skillet over medium-high heat. Add chicken, skin-side down, and cook until crisp and lightly browned, about 5 minutes.

3 Turn chicken skin-side up and sprinkle with ½ teaspoon of the paprika. Pour any excess fat from pan. Transfer to oven and roast until chicken is just cooked through, 25 to 30 minutes.

4 Transfer meat to cutting board. Set skillet over medium-high heat. Add onion and cook until softened, about 3 minutes. Add broth, sour cream, mustard, remaining ½ teaspoon paprika, and cayenne. Simmer, scraping up browned bits from bottom of skillet, until liquid is reduced by half, 3 to 5 minutes.

5 Remove meat from bones and slice thinly. Arrange on toast and spoon gravy over chicken and bread. Serve, sprinkled with parsley.

Crustless Broccoli Quiche

1 2 3 4

Per serving: **NET CARBS: 3 GRAMS** ▪ Carbohydrates: 4.5 grams ▪ Fiber: 1.5 grams ▪ Protein: 12.5 grams ▪ Fat: 12 grams ▪ Calories: 173 ▪ **PREP TIME: 15 MINUTES** ▪ **COOK TIME: 1 HOUR** ▪ **SERVINGS: 6**

If you routinely discard broccoli stems, you're missing out on potent nutritional benefits—broccoli stems are rich in vitamin C, folate, and fiber. Because the skin can be fairly tough, peel it off with a vegetable peeler or very sharp knife—take care to remove just a thin layer—then cut the tender stems into slices or chunks.

1 teaspoon olive oil, plus more for pie plate

½ cup finely chopped onion

4 large eggs

1 cup reduced-carb, whole-milk dairy beverage

4 ounces sharp or extra-sharp **cheddar cheese,** grated (1 cup), and divided

½ cup water

¼ teaspoon dried thyme

¼ teaspoon dried oregano

½ teaspoon salt

¼ teaspoon pepper

¼ teaspoon chopped dried rosemary

1 medium bunch **broccoli,** cut into florets, stems peeled and cut ⅓ inch thick (4 cups)

tip

Dried rosemary can be hard to deal with: its texture is like pine needles, and when you try to chop it, it can fly all over. Moisten it with a few drops of oil, which will soften the dried herb and help it stay on your cutting board.

1 Heat oven to 375°F. Brush a 9- or 10-inch pie plate with olive oil.

2 Heat oil in a small skillet over medium-high heat. Add onion and cook until softened, about 3 minutes. Transfer to a medium bowl; let cool.

3 Add eggs to onion and lightly beat. Whisk in dairy beverage, ½ cup of the cheese, water, thyme, oregano, salt, pepper, and rosemary to blend.

4 Cover bottom of pie plate with broccoli. Pour cream mixture into pie plate. Sprinkle with remaining ½ cup cheese. Bake until a knife inserted in middle comes out clean and quiche is golden brown, 50 to 60 minutes.

treat yourself to a meal for *just you* tonight. With the exception of two soups, the recipes in this chapter are specially created to provide one delectable meal. Forget about dividing recipes by four, or having to find creative leftover ideas for several extra portions. Because most of these dishes can be whipped up in a half hour or so, you'll still have time to go to the gym or see a movie with friends.

Smoked Turkey Salad with Dried Cranberries, page 70

cooking
for one

whether you live alone

or occasionally eat by yourself when your spouse is out of town or your children are spending the night with friends, it's still important to prepare and savor a healthful meal. While it may be tempting to succumb to pizza delivery or other take-out food, or a carb-laden prepared meal you can pop in the microwave, having the raw ingredients in your fridge or on your windowsill at all times can put a delicious, satisfying meal at your fingertips. There are some ingredients I would absolutely never be without: an array of wonderful cheeses, an avocado, a ripe tomato, and salad greens. There are also always a few hard-boiled eggs at the ready in my fridge. Cans of tuna, salmon, and sardines reside in my cupboard, along with tinned tomatoes, a tube of tomato paste, and a few jars of marinated artichoke hearts. Finally, you will always find a stash of peeled, cooked shrimp in my freezer. With this little larder, I can make a main dish salad at the drop of the proverbial hat.

Avoid the tendency to nibble at the stove or eat in front of the television. The former can leave you feeling like you haven't really consumed a meal, and therefore subject to further nibbling, and the latter can lead to overeating because you aren't focusing on the food until it is all gone. Setting the table nicely for yourself and perhaps having a glass of wine (depending on the phase of Atkins you're in) can make dining alone an occasion to treat yourself well as you enjoy dishes such as Smoked Turkey Salad with Dried Cranberries (page 70), or Bacon, Clam, and Corn Chowder (page 74), or indulge with the Caviar and Potato Omelet (page 72). Check out Brown-Bag Lunches (page 80) for more meals perfect for one.

Veal Chop with Exotic Mushrooms

1 2 3 4

Per serving: **NET CARBS: 4.5 GRAMS** ■ Carbohydrates: 5.5 grams ■ Fiber: 1 gram ■ Protein: 36 grams ■ Fat: 26.5 grams ■ Calories: 405 ■ **PREP TIME: 4 MINUTES** ■ **COOK TIME: 25 MINUTES** ■ **SERVINGS: 1**

Look for packages of sliced mixed mushrooms in the market. They'll often include portobello, shiitake, and oyster mushrooms. Because this dish is unrelentingly brown, serve it with sautéed greens like spinach or kale.

¼ **teaspoon salt,** divided

¼ **teaspoon pepper,** divided

1 **sprig rosemary,** stem discarded, leaves chopped (1½ teaspoons)

1 **(8-ounce) bone-in rib or loin veal chop**

3 **teaspoons olive oil,** divided

1 **garlic clove,** minced (½ teaspoon)

1 **(4-ounce) package sliced mixed mushrooms** (about 2 cups)

1 **teaspoon unsalted butter,** cut into small pieces

1 **lemon wedge** (optional)

1 Set an oven rack 4 to 6 inches from the broiler element. Heat broiler.

2 Combine ⅛ teaspoon each salt and pepper and 1 teaspoon of the rosemary in a small bowl. Rub into chop. Set on a small broiler-pan rack and drizzle with 1 teaspoon of the oil. Broil until done to taste, turning once, 4 to 5 minutes per side for medium. Transfer to a warm plate and cover loosely with foil to keep warm.

3 Meanwhile, heat remaining 2 teaspoons oil in a medium nonstick skillet over medium-high heat for about 30 seconds. Stir in garlic and remaining ½ teaspoon rosemary. Cook, stirring, until fragrant but not brown, about 1 minute. Add mushrooms and sprinkle with a remaining ⅛ teaspoon each of salt and pepper. Cook, stirring often, until tender and lightly browned, 4 to 6 minutes. Remove from heat.

4 Add butter and any veal juices that have collected on the plate to mushrooms, and stir to melt butter. Spoon mushrooms over chop. Serve with a lemon wedge, if desired.

Smoked Turkey Salad with Dried Cranberries

Per serving: **NET CARBS: 16.5 GRAMS** ▪ Carbohydrates: 20 grams ▪ Fiber: 3.5 grams ▪ Protein: 23 grams ▪

3 4   Fat: 28.5 grams ▪ Calories: 423 ▪ **PREP TIME: 12 MINUTES** ▪ **SERVINGS: 1**

A few toasted pecans would add a pleasant crunch, but be sure to count the extra carbs. If you'd rather use bottled dressing, choose a low-carb vinaigrette or mustard dressing. For photo, see page 67.

Dressing:

4 teaspoons extra virgin olive oil

1 tablespoon red wine vinegar

½ teaspoon Dijon mustard

⅛ teaspoon salt

⅛ teaspoon pepper

Salad:

2 cups loosely packed mesclun greens

3 ounces thickly sliced smoked turkey (about 4 slices), cut into ½- by 2-inch pieces

1 celery stalk, sliced (½ cup; use tender leaves if desired)

½ cucumber, thinly sliced

3 radishes, thinly sliced

1 ounce blue cheese, crumbled (3 tablespoons)

2 tablespoons no-sugar-added dried cranberries

1 For the dressing: Whisk oil, vinegar, mustard, salt, and pepper in a medium bowl or salad bowl until well blended.

2 For the salad: Add greens, turkey, celery, cucumber, radishes, cheese, and cranberries; toss to coat.

tip

Skip the dried cranberries at the supermarket—they're loaded with sugar. Look in natural foods stores, but read labels carefully. Raisins or currants are higher-carb substitutions, as are dried cherries; and again be sure they haven't been processed with sugar.

Sunny-Side Up Eggs with Asparagus and Parmesan

1 2
3 4
Per serving: **NET CARBS: 5 GRAMS** ▪ Carbohydrates: 6.5 grams ▪ Fiber: 1.5 grams ▪ Protein: 16.5 grams ▪
Fat: 25.5 grams ▪ Calories: 317 ▪ **PREP TIME: 4 MINUTES** ▪ **COOK TIME: 15 MINUTES** ▪ **SERVINGS: 1**

The steps in this recipe move quickly, so have the eggs cracked into a bowl and Parmesan grated before you start cooking.

Salt

6 thick asparagus spears,
  tough ends broken off

Pepper

1 tablespoon extra virgin olive oil

1 large garlic clove, thinly sliced

2 large eggs

2 teaspoons grated Parmesan
  cheese

1 Bring ½ inch salted water to a boil in a medium skillet with a lid over high heat. Add asparagus. Cover and cook until tender, 4 to 6 minutes. Transfer asparagus to a plate. Season with pepper to taste; cover loosely with foil to keep warm.

2 Meanwhile, combine oil, garlic, and a pinch of salt in a small nonstick skillet over medium heat. Cook, stirring, until the garlic just starts to turn golden at the edges, 2 to 3 minutes.

3 Remove from heat and gently slide in eggs. Reduce heat to low, cover, and fry eggs, spooning oil over yolks 2 to 3 times, until eggs are set, about 3 minutes.

4 Remove from heat; season with pepper and cheese. Cover and let stand for 30 seconds. Slide eggs over the asparagus and serve.

tip

Don't break the eggs directly into the skillet and risk having to pick bits of shell from a hot pan; instead crack them first into a small bowl or custard cup, or onto a plate.

Caviar and Potato Omelet

Per serving: **NET CARBS: 17.5 GRAMS** ■ Carbohydrates: 19.5 grams ■ Fiber: 2 grams ■ Protein: 17.5 grams ■

3 4 Fat: 27 grams ■ Calories: 390 ■ **PREP TIME: 3 MINUTES** ■ **COOK TIME: 18 MINUTES** ■ **SERVINGS: 1**

This makes an omelet with a soft texture. If you prefer eggs more well done, cover the omelet during cooking to set the top. Serve with steamed spinach and sliced tomatoes.

1 small (2-ounce) thin-skinned red or white potato, cut into ¼-inch chunks (⅓ cup)

¼ teaspoon salt, divided

1 tablespoon unsalted butter

2 large scallions, long tips reserved, thinly sliced (4 tablespoons), greens and whites divided

2 large eggs

2 tablespoons reduced-carb, whole-milk dairy beverage

⅛ teaspoon pepper

1 tablespoon sour cream

1 teaspoon red or black caviar

1 Put potato in a small nonstick skillet. Add water just to cover and ⅛ teaspoon of the salt. Cover and bring to a boil over high heat. Reduce heat to medium-low and simmer until potato is tender, 8 to 12 minutes. Drain; transfer potato to a plate.

2 Wipe out skillet. Melt butter in skillet over medium-low heat. Add 3 tablespoons of the scallions (all whites and some greens) and cook until wilted, about 2 minutes. Add potato and stir to coat with butter.

3 Meanwhile, beat eggs, dairy beverage, pepper, and ⅛ teaspoon salt in a small bowl. Pour into skillet. Cook, shaking pan and lifting up the edges of cooked egg to allow uncooked egg to flow underneath, until omelet is set, about 4 minutes.

4 Remove from heat, fold over omelet, and slide onto a warm plate. Top with sour cream and caviar. Sprinkle with remaining tablespoon scallion greens and tips and serve.

Bacon, Clam, and Corn Chowder

3 4

Per serving: **NET CARBS: 25 GRAMS** ▪ Carbohydrates: 27.5 grams ▪ Fiber: 2.5 grams ▪ Protein: 44 grams ▪ Fat: 31.5 grams ▪ Calories: 561 ▪ **PREP TIME: 2 MINUTES** ▪ **COOK TIME: 20 MINUTES** ▪ **SERVINGS: 2** (2 cups each)

If you like, dust the chowder with celery salt before serving. This makes one serving for now and one for another meal. Pack it in a thermos to tote for lunch later in the week.

½ **slice thick-sliced bacon,** cut into ¼-inch pieces

1 **(7-ounce) can corn niblets,** drained (scant 1 cup)

2 **scallions,** thinly sliced (¼ cup)

¼ **teaspoon dried thyme,** crumbled

¼ **teaspoon pepper**

1 **tablespoon ThickenThin not/Starch thickener**

1 **(14½-ounce) can lower sodium chicken broth**

2 **(6½-ounce) cans minced clams,** drained, with juice reserved

½ **cup heavy cream**

¼ **teaspoon paprika**

1 Put bacon in a heavy medium saucepan over medium-high heat. Cook, stirring frequently, until it starts to become crisp and some drippings have rendered, about 3 minutes. Spoon off 2 teaspoons of rendered fat, leaving about 1 teaspoon in the pan.

2 Add corn, scallions, thyme, and pepper; cook, stirring frequently, until scallions are wilted, about 2 minutes. Sprinkle in thickener, coating vegetables evenly. Add broth and reserved clam juice; bring to a boil, stirring often. Whisk if necessary to break up any lumps.

3 Reduce heat to low; cover and simmer for 5 minutes. Stir in cream and clams. Increase heat and cook, stirring frequently, until the soup begins to boil. Serve, sprinkled with paprika.

tip

Omit the corn and you'll reduce the Net Carbs in the chowder to 11.5 grams per serving, which means you can enjoy it in Ongoing Weight Loss.

Lamb Chops with Mango-Cucumber Salad

Per serving: **NET CARBS: 11 GRAMS** ▪ Carbohydrates: 13 grams ▪ Fiber: 2 grams ▪ Protein: 34 grams ▪
Fat: 16 grams ▪ Calories: 334 ▪ **PREP TIME: 17 MINUTES** ▪ **COOK TIME: 8 MINUTES** ▪ **SERVINGS: 5**

To crisp the lamb chops' edges and bones, arrange chops rounded-side down in the pan, leaning them against the pan's edges. Avoid pressing against the meat or you'll squeeze out the succulent juices and dry out the lamb. Make the salad a few minutes ahead of time, if possible; it helps to blend the flavors.

½ **cup finely diced seedless cucumber**

½ **small mango,** peeled and diced (about ⅓ cup)

2 **tablespoons chopped fresh mint,** divided

1 **tablespoon chopped sweet white onion,** like Vidalia

2 **teaspoons fresh lime juice**

2 **teaspoons extra virgin olive oil,** divided

¼ **teaspoon salt,** divided

¼ **teaspoon pepper,** divided

11 **ounces baby rib lamb chops,** trimmed (about 3 chops)

1 Mix cucumber, mango, 1 tablespoon of the mint, onion, lime juice, 1 teaspoon of the oil, and ⅛ teaspoon each of salt and pepper in a bowl. Cover and let stand while you prepare the lamb.

2 Sprinkle lamb chops with remaining ⅛ teaspoon each of salt and pepper.

3 Heat a medium skillet over medium-high heat and add remaining teaspoon oil, or lightly brush a grill pan with oil and heat 3 minutes over medium-high heat.

4 Add chops to pan and cook, turning once, until done to taste, 2 to 3 minutes per side for medium. Cook until browned, 1 to 2 minutes longer.

5 Transfer chops to a plate and sprinkle with remaining tablespoon mint. Serve with salad.

Tuna and White Bean Salad

Per serving: **NET CARBS: 29 GRAMS** ▪ Carbohydrates: 41 grams ▪ Fiber: 12 grams ▪ Protein: 59.5 grams ▪ Fat: 43.5 grams ▪ Calories: 782 ▪ **PREP TIME: 7 MINUTES** ▪ **SERVINGS: 1**

3 4

Although this recipe calls for cannellini beans, you can use any white bean. Read labels, though, as the carb counts can vary from brand to brand. Omit the beans, if you prefer; you'll reduce the Net Carbs to 6.5 grams, making the dish suitable for Induction and Ongoing Weight Loss.

Dressing:

1 tablespoon extra virgin olive oil

1 tablespoon fresh lemon juice

1 tablespoon chopped sweet white onion, like Vidalia

¼ teaspoon dried oregano, crumbled

⅛ teaspoon salt

Salad:

1 (6-ounce) can olive oil–packed solid light tuna, drained

½ Haas avocado, peeled and cut into ½-inch chunks

½ cup canned cannellini beans, drained and rinsed

1 roasted red pepper, drained and patted dry, cut into strips

⅛ teaspoon pepper

1 For the dressing: Mix oil, lemon juice, onion, oregano, and salt in a small bowl.

2 For the salad: Break tuna into large chunks in a salad bowl. Add avocado, beans, and roasted pepper. Pour dressing over; season with pepper, and toss gently.

tip

When you use dried herbs, rub them between your fingers (or put larger amounts in your palm and rub with your fingertips) before you add them to the dish. This helps to release their aromas and makes them more flavorful.

tuna truths

Tuna is the most commonly eaten fish in the United States, and nearly all of that is canned. Odds are high you've got a can or two in your cupboard, but did you take time to decipher the labels before making your purchase?

HERE'S A PRIMER:

Color: Canned tuna is "white" or "light," depending on the fish from which it comes. White tuna comes from albacore or blackfin. Yellowfin and skipjack are used to make light tuna. Like chicken, white tuna tends to be drier and blander than its darker counterpart.

Texture: Canned tuna comes "chunk" or "solid." Because solid is cut from one piece of meat it's more expensive; chunk tuna includes smaller pieces left over after solid is canned. If your recipe instructs you to break the tuna into chunks, opt for solid.

Packing liquid: Water-packed tuna has long been the weight-conscious consumer's choice, and that's too bad because water-packed tuna is practically tasteless. Now that you're doing Atkins, you can comfortably choose the tuna packed in oil. Vegetable oil tastes better, but if you want surprisingly delicious canned tuna, look for light tuna packed in olive oil. Sometimes it's imported from Italy, but some domestic companies are starting to pack their own versions.

IS TUNA SAFE?

Recent news articles have reported that large fish, including tuna, can contain high levels of mercury, and different government agencies and organizations offer conflicting advice about the safety of canned tuna.

As a general rule, the nutritional benefits of tuna—and all fish—outweigh the risks, *assuming you eat a variety of foods*, including fish. The amount of mercury a fish contains depends on its size, diet, and the waters it once swam in. Canned light tuna has one of the lowest levels of mercury. Women who are pregnant, or may become pregnant, nursing mothers, and children are advised to eat no more than one serving of canned albacore (white tuna) a week.

Spinach and Chickpea Soup

Per serving: **NET CARBS: 19.5 GRAMS** ■ Carbohydrates: 25.5 grams ■ Fiber: 6 grams ■ Protein: 9 grams ■
Fat: 5.5 grams ■ Calories: 180 ■ **PREP TIME: 10 MINUTES** ■ **COOK TIME: 15 MINUTES** ■ **SERVINGS: 2** (scant 2 cups each)

3 4

This soup comes together easily with pantry and salad-bar items. Because it makes enough for two servings, you'll want to use a saucepan with a volume of three to four quarts.

1 teaspoon olive oil

2 **scallions,** thinly sliced (¼ cup)

¼ cup grated carrot

1 **garlic clove,** minced (½ teaspoon)

½ teaspoon ground cumin

¼ teaspoon turmeric

1 (7¾-ounce) can chickpeas, drained and rinsed (¾ cup)

1 (14½-ounce) can lower sodium chicken broth

1 cup water

2 packed cups baby spinach

1 Heat oil in a heavy medium saucepan over medium heat. Add scallions, carrot, and garlic; cook, stirring frequently, until tender, about 2 minutes. Add cumin and turmeric, then chickpeas, stirring to coat with spices.

2 Stir in broth and water. Increase heat to high and bring to a boil. Reduce heat to low; cover and simmer 5 minutes to blend the flavors.

3 Stir in spinach and cook until just wilted, about 30 seconds; serve.

tip

Try garnishing this soup with a hard-boiled egg; simply peel and chop. More than just another pretty garnish, it adds a boost of protein (3 grams), and helps to thicken the soup, as well.

preparing your lunch before work or school has several advantages: It saves money, saves time, and lessens the likelihood of making less-than-nutritious food choices while you're standing at the deli counter. Whether you prefer salads, sandwiches, or soups—or a combination of any two—the 16 recipes in this chapter provide a tremendous variety of flavors with a minimum of effort.

Pear, Boursin, and Watercress on Pumpernickel, page 88

brown-bag
lunches

old standbys and new products combine to make it easier than ever to eat low carb away from home. Make sure you have a good supply of mainstays like sliced roast beef, turkey, ham, and salami (the kind without added sugar or high-carb fillers) in the fridge and cans of tuna fish, sardines, pâté, and some flavorful mustards in the cupboard. The inner sandwich fixings have never been a problem, but until recently, proper bread was a challenge. (Most people can eat one or two slices per day of 100 percent whole-grain bread made without sugar once they are at or close to their goal weight.) Fortunately, Atkins and some other companies are now making low-carb breads, bagels, and wraps. That means achieving weight-loss success by trimming carbs and brown bagging are no longer at odds.

Think outside the lunch box. How about Monterey Jack cheese with guacamole, lettuce, and tomato on whole-grain bread? Low-carb wraps have opened up an endless array of options: Smoked Turkey Reuben Wrap (page 94), Spinach Salad Wrap (page 96), Crunchy Salmon Salad Wrap with Dill (page 92). If you are not in the mood for a sandwich, but still want to picnic at your desk, opt for a soup or tote the ingredients with you, perhaps a few chunks of cheese, a couple of hard-boiled eggs, and a tin of pâté with some celery sticks for dipping. Remember that a meal should have a least 30 grams of protein. There is one classic kid food that is also model low-carb fare, once you're out of Induction: natural peanut butter. Spread it or other nut butters—almond and macadamia nut are both delectable—on endive leaves or apples, or enjoy it as a sandwich on low-carb bread with no-sugar-added jam. Now that's a treat you never grow out of!

Pork Salad with Tortilla "Croutons"

1 2 3 4

Per serving: **NET CARBS: 3 GRAMS** ▪ Carbohydrates: 5.5 grams ▪ Fiber: 2.5 grams ▪ Protein: 49.5 grams ▪ Fat: 14 grams ▪ Calories: 353 ▪ **PREP TIME: 10 MINUTES** ▪ **SERVINGS: 1**

No leftover pork tenderloin? No problem. It's easy and quick enough to make: Rub a small tenderloin with cumin, salt, and pepper. Sear it in a pan with 1 tablespoon of olive oil, then transfer it to a 400°F oven and roast 20 to 30 minutes, or until an instant-read thermometer registers 145°F.

¼ (8-inch) low-carb tortilla

1 teaspoon olive oil

6 ounces cooked pork tenderloin, sliced

3 leaves romaine lettuce, ripped into small pieces

2 tablespoons finely diced jicama

1 tablespoon grated carrot

2 tablespoons chopped red bell pepper

1 tablespoon low-carb Italian dressing

1 Preheat oven to 350°F.

2 Cut tortilla quarter into thin strips. Put on a small baking sheet and brush on both sides with oil. Bake until crisp, 5 to 7 minutes.

3 Combine pork, lettuce, jicama, carrot, and pepper in a bowl. Add dressing and toss to combine. Sprinkle with tortilla strips just before serving.

tip

Larger jicamas can be woody, so buy the smallest one you can find (it'll probably be about 4 inches in diameter, so you'll still have plenty left over). Peel before using—the skin is very tough.

Chicken Salad with Citrus Dressing

1 2
3 4 Per serving: **NET CARBS: 6 GRAMS** ■ Carbohydrates: 10 grams ■ Fiber: 4 grams ■ Protein: 53 grams ■ Fat: 36 grams ■ Calories: 574 ■ **PREP TIME: 10 MINUTES** ■ **SERVINGS: 1**

By using packaged cooked chicken strips, you can have a delicious salad ready in minutes. Although you can whisk the dressing in a bowl, try making it in a small jar so toting it along with your lunch is effortless.

2 cups loosely packed mesclun greens

4 cherry tomatoes, halved or quartered

¼ cup cooked broccoli florets

6 ounces cooked chicken

1 tablespoon dark sesame oil

2 teaspoons canola oil

2½ teaspoons unseasoned rice vinegar

1 teaspoon lemon or lime juice and 1 teaspoon water

⅛ teaspoon finely chopped fresh ginger

Salt

1 Combine greens, tomatoes, broccoli, and chicken in a bowl.

2 Pour sesame oil, canola oil, vinegar, orange juice, and ginger into a small jar and shake to combine. Add salt to taste. When ready to serve, shake dressing again and pour over salad.

tip

You'll find two types of sesame oil in supermarkets. One is light and virtually flavorless; it can be used interchangeably with most vegetable oils. The second is made from toasted sesame seeds. It's a deep amber color with a pronounced flavor and is common in Asian cooking.

Italian Pasta Salad

2
3 4

Per serving: **NET CARBS: 9.5 GRAMS** ■ Carbohydrates: 17 grams ■ Fiber: 7.5 grams ■ Protein: 44.5 grams ■ Fat: 37.5 grams ■ Calories: 587 ■ **PREP TIME: 10 MINUTES** ■ **SERVINGS: 1**

Make a little extra low-carb pasta tonight. Lightly coat it with oil and refrigerate it overnight. Tomorrow, use it in this delightful, savory salad.

¾ cup cooked low-carb penne

1 olive oil–marinated artichoke heart, diced

1 ounce Genoa salami, rolled into a cylinder and sliced

2 ounces fresh mozzarella, diced

1 tablespoon chopped roasted red pepper

2 tablespoons chopped frozen green beans, thawed

1 tablespoon extra virgin olive oil

1 teaspoon balsamic vinegar

½ teaspoon chopped fresh oregano

Salt and pepper

1 Combine pasta, artichoke heart, salami, mozzarella, red pepper, and green beans in a bowl.

2 Whisk together oil, vinegar, and oregano in a small bowl. Season with salt and pepper to taste. Pour over pasta mixture and toss to coat.

tip

No leftover pasta? Figure you'll need 1½ ounces uncooked pasta to yield ¾ cup cooked. Because dry pasta doesn't conform neatly to the shape of the measuring cup it's hard to give a precise measure, but ½ cup uncooked pasta is a safe amount.

Corned Beef and Cabbage Salad

1 2 3 4 Per serving: **NET CARBS: 4.5 GRAMS** ▪ Carbohydrates: 6.5 grams ▪ Fiber: 2 grams ▪ Protein: 17 grams ▪ Fat: 30.5 grams ▪ Calories: 364 ▪ **PREP TIME: 4 MINUTES** ▪ **SERVINGS: 1**

Corned beef and cabbage isn't just for St. Paddy's Day. Make this any day of the year to enjoy for lunch. A bag of low-carb chips and some fresh berries round out the meal.

1 cup shredded green cabbage	1 teaspoon Dijon mustard
3 ounces sliced corned beef, diced	1 tablespoon extra virgin olive oil
1 tablespoon grated carrot	⅛ teaspoon caraway seeds
1 teaspoon balsamic vinegar	Salt and pepper

1 Combine cabbage, corned beef, and carrot in a bowl.

2 Whisk together vinegar and mustard in a small bowl. Slowly whisk in oil; add caraway seeds. Season with salt and pepper to taste. Pour over cabbage mixture and toss to coat.

Pear, Boursin, and Watercress on Pumpernickel

3 4 Per serving: **NET CARBS: 22 GRAMS** ▪ Carbohydrates: 25.5 grams ▪ Fiber: 3.5 grams ▪ Protein: 5 grams ▪ Fat: 8.5 grams ▪ Calories: 193 ▪ **PREP TIME: 5 MINUTES** ▪ **SERVINGS: 1**

If you can't find pumpernickel bread made only with rye and whole-wheat flours, substitute with low-carb rye bread. The Net Carb count will be about 6 grams.
For photo, see page 81.

2 tablespoons Boursin cheese	¼ small pear, thinly sliced
2 slices real pumpernickel bread	½ cup watercress, stems removed

Spread 1 tablespoon Boursin on each slice of bread. Top one slice with pear and watercress. Top with remaining slice of bread. Cut in half, then wrap.

Grilled Veggie Melt

2 3 4 Per serving: **NET CARBS: 10.5 GRAMS** ▪ Carbohydrates: 21 grams ▪ Fiber: 11.5 grams ▪ Protein: 29.5 grams ▪ Fat: 30.5 grams ▪ Calories: 470 ▪ **PREP TIME: 5 MINUTES** ▪ **COOK TIME: 12 MINUTES** ▪ **SERVINGS: 1**

This cheese-rich sandwich works as an open-faced sandwich or a wrap. If you're on the go, make it as a wrap—but do try it open-faced so you can see how pretty it is.

1 small zucchini, thinly sliced (½ cup)

¼ medium red bell pepper, cut into thin slices

2 teaspoons olive oil

Salt and pepper

⅛ teaspoon dried oregano

2 slices low-carb rye bread, lightly toasted

1 teaspoon Dijon mustard

2 ounces cheddar cheese, grated (½ cup)

1 Heat broiler. Line a small roasting pan or jelly-roll pan with foil.

2 Combine zucchini and red pepper in pan. Add oil, salt, pepper, and oregano and toss to coat. Broil, tossing vegetables once or twice, until vegetables have softened and are lightly browned, 7 to 10 minutes. Remove from oven, leaving broiler on.

3 Spread toast with mustard. Divide vegetables evenly on top of toast; top with cheese. Remove foil from baking sheet and set sandwiches on pan. Return to broiler and cook until cheese has melted, 1 to 2 minutes; watch closely so cheese and toast do not burn.

tip

Prefer a wrap? Soften a low-carb (8-inch) tortilla in the microwave for 10 to 15 seconds, then spread with about ½ teaspoon mustard. Fill with the veggies and cheese and roll up. When ready to eat, heat the wrap in the microwave until the cheese melts, 10 to 15 seconds. The wrap will have 9.5 grams of Net Carbs instead of 10.5 grams.

Overstuffed Tuna and Tapenade Sandwich

Per serving: **NET CARBS: 7.5 GRAMS** ■ Carbohydrates: 18.5 grams ■ Fiber: 11 grams ■ Protein: 55 grams ■ Fat: 11 grams ■ Calories: 405 ■ **PREP TIME: 5 MINUTES** ■ **SERVINGS: 1**

Tapenade stands in for mayo in this Provençal-inspired sandwich. If you're packing this for the office, make the tuna the night before so the flavors can blend. In the morning, spread the bread with mustard and slip the radicchio leaves between bread and filling to keep the bread from getting soggy.

tip

To make this (and some of the other sandwiches) suitable for Induction, use only one piece of low-carb bread and serve open-faced.

1 (6-ounce) can oil-packed solid white tuna, drained

3 tablespoons prepared tapenade

Pepper

2 slices low-carb multigrain bread

1 teaspoon Dijon mustard

2 small radicchio leaves

1   Combine tuna and tapenade in a small bowl; season with pepper to taste.

2   Spread both slices of bread with mustard; layer one with a radicchio leaf, tuna, and the remaining radicchio leaf. Top with remaining bread slice, and cut in half and serve.

quicky condiment: tapenade

Most people will probably describe tapenade as a paste made of olives, but its name actually comes from the Provençal word *tapeno*, or caper; to be a tapenade, the paste must contain capers. If your market doesn't sell tapenade, you can use jarred olive paste, but it's simple enough to make your own. Whirl ½ cup pitted Kalamata or Niçoise olives, 2 tablespoons capers, 1 teaspoon Dijon mustard, 1 or 2 peeled garlic cloves, 2 anchovy fillets, and pep-per (don't use salt; the olives and anchovies are salty enough) in a food processor. Transfer to a clean jar and refrigerate it for up to a week.

Tapenade makes an excellent dip for crudités or low-carb chips and a top-notch pasta sauce. Spoon it over grilled tuna steaks, or rub it between the skin and meat of a chicken breast before cooking. Try it as a sandwich spread instead of mustard or mayonnaise.

Favorite PB and Apple Sandwich

3 4 Per serving: **NET CARBS: 17.5 GRAMS** ▪ Carbohydrates: 29.5 grams ▪ Fiber: 12 grams ▪ Protein: 21.5 grams ▪ Fat: 20 grams ▪ Calories: 357 ▪ **PREP TIME: 5 MINUTES** ▪ **SERVINGS: 1**

Skip the cloying purple jelly and top this twist on a classic PB & J with thinly sliced apple. Be sure to buy peanut butter made without added sugar or hydrogenated oils.

1½ tablespoons natural peanut butter

2 slices low-carb multigrain bread

1 tablespoon roasted sunflower seeds

½ medium Granny Smith apple, peeled, cored, and thinly sliced (8 to 10 slices)

Spread peanut butter on 1 slice of bread. Sprinkle with sunflower seeds and top with apple. Top with remaining slice of bread, then cut in half.

Italian Sandwich

2
3 4 Per serving: **NET CARBS: 8 GRAMS** ▪ Carbohydrates: 16.5 grams ▪ Fiber: 8.5 grams ▪ Protein: 42.5 grams ▪ Fat: 30.5 grams ▪ Calories: 503 ▪ **PREP TIME: 4 MINUTES** ▪ **SERVINGS: 1**

The mild flavor and creamy texture of fresh mozzarella are a perfect foil for salty prosciutto, peppery arugula, and garlicky pesto.

1 tablespoon prepared pesto

2 slices low-carb multigrain bread

½ cup arugula leaves

2 ounces sliced prosciutto

2 ounces fresh mozzarella, sliced

Spread pesto on both slices of bread. Top one slice with arugula, prosciutto, and mozzarella. Top with remaining slice of bread and cut in half.

Crunchy Salmon Salad Wrap with Dill

1 2 3 4 Per serving: **NET CARBS: 5 GRAMS** ▪ Carbohydrates: 11 grams ▪ Fiber: 6 grams ▪ Protein: 41 grams ▪ Fat: 34 grams ▪ Calories: 489 ▪ **PREP TIME: 7 MINUTES** ▪ **SERVINGS: 1**

When using canned salmon, leave in the bones. They're soft and you can (and should) mash them easily—they're what make canned salmon such a rich source of calcium.

1 (6-ounce) can red salmon, drained, skin removed, bones mashed

½ **small cucumber,** peeled, seeded, and diced (¼ cup)

1 tablespoon mayonnaise

2 teaspoons chopped fresh dill

1 teaspoon fresh lemon juice

Salt and pepper

1 (8-inch) low-carb tortilla, heated

1 large leaf green leaf lettuce

1 Combine salmon, cucumber, mayonnaise, dill, and lemon juice in a bowl. Season with salt and pepper to taste.

2 Place tortilla on a flat surface. Top with lettuce, leaving a ½-inch border; top with salmon mixture. Roll or fold tortilla and cut in half, if desired. Wrap tightly in plastic wrap.

it's a wrap

There's more than one way to roll a tortilla, but the method you choose should be dictated by the filling as much as aesthetics or personal preference. Always start with a warm low-carb tortilla .

HALF-MOON
BEST FOR: cooked fillings
HOW TO: Spread filling over one half of wrap. Fold over to make a half-moon. Cook (as with a quesadilla), then cut into three wedges.

BI-FOLD
BEST FOR: flat or leaky fillings
HOW TO: Spread filling over one half of wrap. Fold over to make a half-moon, then fold again to make a wedge. Hold by the corner to eat.

ENVELOPE
BEST FOR: flat or cheese fillings
HOW TO: Spoon filling into center of wrap. Fold in sides, then fold up bottom. Fold top down to cover all.

Smoked Turkey Reuben Wrap

2
3 4
Per serving: **NET CARBS: 8.5 GRAMS** ▪ Carbohydrates: 14.5 grams ▪ Fiber: 6 grams ▪ Protein: 34 grams ▪
Fat: 25 grams ▪ Calories: 409 ▪ **PREP TIME: 5 MINUTES** ▪ **COOK TIME: 30 SECONDS** ▪ **SERVINGS: 1**

If your workplace has a microwave, pop this in for 15 or so seconds to melt the cheese. Otherwise, heat it in a 350°F oven or toaster oven for about 7 minutes. Be sure to squeeze the sauerkraut thoroughly before measuring it—you want it to be dry or the wrap will get soggy.

1 tablespoon mayonnaise

1 teaspoon no-sugar-added ketchup

1 (8-inch) low-carb tortilla, heated

4 ounces smoked turkey breast, thinly sliced

¼ cup well-drained sauerkraut

1 ounce Swiss cheese, shredded (¼ cup)

1 Combine mayonnaise and ketchup in a bowl.

2 Place tortilla on a flat surface. Spread with mayonnaise mixture, leaving a ½-inch border. Add turkey, sauerkraut, and cheese. Roll or fold tortilla.

3 When ready to eat, heat in microwave until cheese melts, 15 to 30 seconds (the times will vary depending on wattage).

tip

Skip the canned sauerkraut—it's often mushy and super-salty. Look in the meat department (near sausages) or dairy aisle for kraut in bags. It has a crisper texture and comparatively sweet flavor.

Mexican Chicken Wrap

2
3 4
Per serving: **NET CARBS: 10 GRAMS** ▪ Carbohydrates: 12 grams ▪ Fiber: 2.5 grams ▪ Protein: 48.5 grams ▪ Fat: 28 grams ▪ Calories: 489 ▪ **PREP TIME: 7 MINUTES** ▪ **SERVINGS: 1**

Mayonnaise mutes some of the spiciness in salsa, so choose salsa with a fair amount of heat. Salsas that are less chunky are a little easier to spread, too.

1 tablespoon mayonnaise

1 tablespoon salsa

1 (8-inch) low-carb tortilla, heated

½ cup shredded lettuce

4 ounces cooked chicken breast, cut into pieces or shredded

1 ounce grated Monterey Jack cheese with jalapeños (¼ cup)

¼ cup chopped tomato

1 Combine mayonnaise and salsa in a bowl.

2 Place tortilla on flat surface. Spread mayonnaise mixture on tortilla, leaving a ½-inch border. Top with lettuce, chicken, cheese, and tomato. Roll or fold tortilla and cut in half, if desired. Wrap tightly in plastic wrap.

smart snacks and sides

Once you've decided which soup, salad, or sandwich to bring, a low-carb accompaniment can round out the menu. You can keep some of these in your desk, but others will only keep until lunchtime.

▪ **Want something crunchy?** Try some flavored soy chips or nuts. Be sure they don't include added sugars or other caloric sweeteners.

▪ **Gotta have heat?** Pumpkin seeds roasted with chili or wasabi peas (look for no-sugar-added varieties) can pack punch.

▪ **For something cool and creamy,** tote a Haas avocado. Halve it with a plastic knife, remove the pit, and scoop out the pulp with a plastic spoon. Pour a few drops of balsamic vinegar into the hole left by the pit.

▪ **Looking to boost protein?** Bring a hard-boiled egg. Keep salt and pepper packets on hand.

▪ **Need a sweet?** Trail mix, especially blends with unsweetened coconut and sugar-free chocolate chips or dried fruit, fits the bill.

Spinach Salad Wrap

1 2 3 4 Per serving: **NET CARBS: 5 GRAMS** ▪ Carbohydrates: 11.5 grams ▪ Fiber: 6.5 grams ▪ Protein: 21.5 grams ▪ Fat: 26 grams ▪ Calories: 357 ▪ **PREP TIME: 10 MINUTES** ▪ **SERVINGS: 1**

A real challenge to locate until recently, baby spinach can now be found in most produce sections. Though it harbors considerably less grit than larger leaves, it still needs to be rinsed and dried before using.

1 tablespoon extra virgin olive oil

2 teaspoons red wine vinegar

Salt and pepper

1½ cups washed baby spinach

¼ cup sliced mushrooms

2 (1-ounce) slices Canadian bacon, cooked and cut into ¼-inch strips

1 hard-boiled egg, sliced

1 (8-inch) low-carb tortilla, heated

1 Whisk oil and vinegar in a medium bowl. Add salt and pepper to taste.

2 Add spinach, mushrooms, Canadian bacon, and egg to dressing and toss to coat.

3 Place tortilla on a flat surface. Top with salad mixture, leaving a ½-inch border. Roll or fold tortilla and cut in half, if desired. Wrap tightly in plastic wrap.

tip

Heating tortillas makes them easier to wrap around fillings; they can split or break if they're straight from the fridge. Heat them in a microwave according to package directions, or put them in a dry skillet for a minute on each side.

Miso Soup with Tofu and Shrimp

1 2 3 4

Per serving: **NET CARBS: 3 GRAMS** ▪ Carbohydrates: 3.5 grams ▪ Fiber: 0.5 gram ▪ Protein: 8.5 grams ▪ Fat: 3 grams ▪ Calories: 73 ▪ **PREP TIME: 4 MINUTES** ▪ **COOK TIME: 4 MINUTES** ▪ **SERVINGS: 1**

Take a package of instant miso soup and add some life to it with greens, cooked shrimp, and tofu. If your soup has seaweed or scallions in it, feel free to omit the spinach.

1 package instant miso soup mix

1 medium spinach leaf, chopped (1 tablespoon)

3 cooked shrimp

2 tablespoons diced extra-firm tofu

Prepare soup mix according to package instructions. Once water is boiling and you've added soup mix, add spinach, shrimp, and tofu and continue to cook until shrimp is warmed through, about 1 minute. Pour into a thermos for later, or serve.

Spinach and Bacon Soup

1 2 3 4

Per serving: **NET CARBS: 1.5 GRAMS** ▪ Carbohydrates: 2 grams ▪ Fiber: 0.5 gram ▪ Protein: 9 grams ▪ Fat: 11 grams ▪ Calories: 146 ▪ **PREP TIME: 3 MINUTES** ▪ **COOK TIME: 8 MINUTES** ▪ **SERVINGS: 1**

High-flavor, low-carb, and ready in minutes, this soup is a perfect pick-me-up for a busy day. Cutting the bacon with a pair of kitchen shears directly into the saucepan makes the task easier.

1 slice bacon, finely chopped

1 tablespoon chopped shallot or onion

2 medium spinach leaves, chopped (2 tablespoons) or 2 tablespoons frozen chopped spinach, thawed

1 cup lower sodium chicken broth

Combine bacon and shallot or onion in a small saucepan. Cook until bacon is very crispy, 4 to 5 minutes. Add spinach and cook, stirring, for about 30 seconds. Add broth and bring to a boil. Reduce heat to medium-low and simmer to blend flavors, about 4 minutes.

15-Minute Chicken Soup

Per serving: **NET CARBS: 4 GRAMS** ▪ Carbohydrates: 4 grams ▪ Fiber: 0 grams ▪ Protein: 12.5 grams ▪ Fat: 7.5 grams ▪ Calories: 128 ▪ **PREP TIME: 5 MINUTES** ▪ **COOK TIME: 10 MINUTES** ▪ **SERVINGS: 1**

In just 15 minutes you can have a thermos of chicken soup to accompany you to work.

1 teaspoon extra virgin olive oil

1 tablespoon diced shallot

1 tablespoon grated carrot

3 ounces cooked chicken breast, shredded (¾ cup)

1½ cups lower sodium chicken broth

Heat oil in a small saucepan over medium heat. Add shallot and carrot; cook until shallot is softened, 2 to 3 minutes. Add chicken and cook, stirring, about 1 minute. Add broth and bring to a boil. Reduce heat to medium-low and simmer until chicken is heated through, 2 to 3 minutes.

cures for the lunchtime blues

Bringing your lunch is the best way to ensure your midday meal meets your nutritional needs—after all, who knows what lurks in the sauces, glazes, and condiments of most deli or restaurant food? But brown bagging isn't without its problems. Here are some simple solutions to common conundrums:

Problem: Soggy sandwiches
Solution: Packing bread and fillings separately is the easiest way to prevent soggy bread, but if that isn't possible, use a crisp lettuce leaf as a barrier between bread and filling; layer high-moisture veggies like tomatoes between the lettuce and the filling, not between the lettuce and the bread.

Problem: Leaky dressings
Solution: Tiny tubs are fine if you're able to keep them upright, but they may spill when opened. Put the dressing into a small zip-close plastic bag. When you're ready for lunch, snip off a bit of the corner, then squeeze the dressing through the slit.

Problem: Crushed chips
Solution: Create an air cushion. After you've put your low-carb chips into a small zip-close bag, press most of the bag closed, leaving about an inch open in the center. Gently blow in a little air, then seal.

feel like a short-order cook,

preparing one meal for the grownups and another for your children? This chapter contains family-friendly recipes for meals, snacks, and desserts that appeal to people of all ages. Because most of us clamor for sweets, we've provided a variety of low-carb alternatives to sugary treats. Even the vegetable choices were created to appeal to diverse palates. By laying a veggie-friendly foundation, you may find it easier to get your family to taste and enjoy vegetables with stronger flavors (broccoli, spinach, onions) and weird names (kohlrabi, anyone?).

BLT Turkey Burgers, page 118

Waldorf Salad in Apple Bowls, page 108

Double Chocolate Ice Cream Soda,
page 120

family-friendly fare

a growing child should not be losing weight by any method unless his or her doctor recommends such action, and no one is suggesting that you put your child on a low-carb weight-loss program. But that said, look no farther than any school yard to see that American children have joined the obesity epidemic. So why not start them off with some good eating habits so they can sidestep a potential weight problem—and the health problems that often accompany excess pounds? At the very least, this means cutting back on junk foods, often marketed to kids, which are loaded with sugar, bleached white flour, and hydrogenated oils.

If you are following the Atkins Nutritional Approach, that means that your children can eat the way you do, but simply include more vegetables, fruits, and whole grains in their meals. It also means getting rid of those junk foods and non-nutritious beverages. If they are not good enough for you, they certainly aren't good enough for your children. Offer them whole fruit instead of juice, whole milk or yogurt instead of sweetened dairy beverages or flavored yogurt filled with, yes, still more sugar.

Many children enjoy preparing food. If your youngsters are old enough, involve them in the meal planning and making process. Explain to them why you have changed your eating habits. Chances are they will enjoy eating whole foods such as Chicken Fingers (page 104) and Tex-Mex Quesadillas (page 116) right alongside you. And as this chapter shows, with delicious treats like Raspberry-Kiwi Ice Pops (page 120) and Whoopie Pies (page 123), there is no reason to feel that cutting out the foods devoid of nutrients but sky-high in carbs can be defined as deprivation.

Note that appropriate phases for each recipe are indicated for adults doing Atkins only; children can eat any of these dishes.

Strawberry French Toast Triangles

Per serving: **NET CARBS: 11 GRAMS** ▪ Carbohydrates: 19 grams ▪ Fiber: 8 grams ▪ Protein: 21 grams ▪
Fat: 16 grams ▪ Calories: 300 ▪ **PREP TIME: 10 MINUTES** ▪ **COOK TIME: 15 MINUTES** ▪ **SERVINGS: 4**

3 4

Kids love finger foods, and dipping strawberry-stuffed French toast in flavored syrup makes it possible to eat everyone's favorite sticky breakfast without silverware.

8 slices low-carb white bread

4 tablespoons cream cheese,
   at room temperature

6 medium strawberries, thinly
   sliced (½ cup)

3 large eggs

¼ cup reduced-carb, whole-milk
   dairy beverage

1 tablespoon unsalted butter,
   divided

½ cup sugar-free pancake syrup

¼ cup no-sugar-added
   strawberry jam

1 Spread 4 slices of bread with 1 tablespoon cream cheese each and divide strawberries among them. Top with remaining bread to make sandwiches.

2 Lightly whisk eggs and dairy beverage in a shallow bowl.

3 Heat half of the butter in a large nonstick skillet or griddle over medium heat. Dip sandwiches, one at a time, into egg mixture until saturated. Cook sandwiches, in batches if necessary, until golden brown, 3 to 5 minutes per side. Add remaining butter to skillet as needed.

4 Meanwhile, combine syrup and jam in a small bowl. Microwave until jam is melted and syrup is heated, 15 to 30 seconds. Stir well. To serve, cut sandwiches into triangles and dip into strawberry syrup.

tip

Unless specifically instructed to use a different-size egg, assume that most recipes use large eggs. If you have jumbo eggs on hand, use two in this recipe; if you have medium or extra-large, use three; if you have small eggs, use four.

Chicken Fingers

2 3 4

Per serving: **NET CARBS: 8 GRAMS** ▪ Carbohydrates: 17 grams ▪ Fiber: 9 grams ▪ Protein: 75 grams ▪
Fat: 13 grams ▪ Calories: 480 ▪ **PREP TIME: 10 MINUTES** ▪ **COOK TIME: 15 MINUTES** ▪ **SERVINGS: 4**

Chicken breast fillets, sometimes called tenderloins or tenders, are small and tapered in shape—perfect for chicken fingers—but they tend to be pricey. For a less expensive alternative, simply cut a pound of chicken breasts into thin strips.

Cooking spray

6 (1-ounce) bags low-carb soy
   chips

½ cup Atkins Quick Quisine Bake
   Mix

2 teaspoons dried basil

1 teaspoon dried oregano

½ teaspoon salt

½ teaspoon pepper

2 large eggs

2 garlic cloves, minced (1 teaspoon)

2 pounds chicken breast fillets or
   tenders

1   Heat oven to 425°F. Lightly coat a jelly-roll pan or baking sheet with cooking spray.

2   Put soy chips in a large food storage bag; crush into fine crumbs with a rolling pin. Transfer crumbs to a shallow bowl. Stir in bake mix, basil, oregano, salt, and pepper.

3   Beat egg and garlic in another shallow bowl. Dip chicken pieces into egg mixture, then dip into crumb mixture to coat. Set on pan. Bake until crisp, 8 to 10 minutes; turn and bake until cooked through, 5 to 7 minutes longer.

tip

A food processor makes short work of grinding the low-carb chips; for a low-tech alternative you could crumble them in your hands, but that might leave some pieces on the large side. Better to put them in a plastic freezer storage bag and crush with a rolling pin, mallet, or small skillet. Leave the bag open a bit so air can escape.

Strawberry-Banana Smoothies

3 4 Per serving: **NET CARBS: 8 GRAMS** ▪ Carbohydrates: 8.5 grams ▪ Fiber: 0.5 gram ▪ Protein: 4 grams ▪ Fat: 3.5 grams ▪ Calories: 86 ▪ **PREP TIME: 5 MINUTES** ▪ **SERVINGS: 4** (¾ cup each)

If you're a fan of bananas, look for banana extract in natural foods stores or in gourmet supermarkets. It adds a boost of carb-free banana flavor to smoothies, as well as to baked goods like quick breads, muffins, and even pancakes.

1¼ cups plain whole-milk yogurt

½ cup silken tofu

⅓ cup no-sugar-added strawberry jam

½ small ripe banana

⅓ cup cold water

6 ice cubes

½ teaspoon banana extract (optional)

1 Place yogurt, tofu, jam, banana, water, ice cubes, and banana extract, if using, in a blender. Blend at high speed until very smooth. Serve immediately.

incogni-tofu

Looking for ways to get protein, fiber, and a host of vitamins and disease-preventing compounds into your—or your kids'—meals? Sneak in some tofu—up to two servings a day are considered fine.

You might not be able to tempt your family with big chunks of tofu floating in broth, but odds are high they won't know it's in Vegetable and Tofu Lasagne (page 204) or Strawberry-Banana Smoothies (see above) unless you tell them.

Other ideas: Use ¼ cup silken tofu in place of one egg in your favorite low-carb brownie recipe. Replace some of the cream in a soup with silken tofu; or purée it and use in lieu of mayonnaise, sour cream, or cream cheese in a recipe.

Look for tofu packed in aseptic boxes (Mori-Nu is one brand); they may be labeled "silken," and have a creamier texture than the water-packed variety that comes in tubs.

Mini Blueberry-Banana Pancakes

Per serving: **NET CARBS: 7.5 GRAMS** ▪ Carbohydrates: 10 grams ▪ Fiber: 2.5 grams ▪ Protein: 10.5 grams ▪
3 4 Fat: 7.5 grams ▪ Calories: 145 ▪ **PREP TIME: 10 MINUTES** ▪ **COOK TIME: 10 MINUTES** ▪ **SERVINGS: 4**

Blueberry pancakes are every kid's favorite, and the addition of banana will please them all the more. The berries will sink, so stir the batter to redistribute them before scooping it onto the griddle. (Alternatively, don't add the blueberries to the batter but drop them onto the pancakes before you flip them.)

½ cup low-carb pancake and
waffle mix

⅓ cup whole milk

2 large eggs

2 tablespoons vegetable oil, divided

½ teaspoon vanilla extract

½ cup blueberries

½ small ripe banana, chopped

½ cup sugar-free pancake syrup

⅛ teaspoon ground cinnamon

1 Whisk pancake mix, milk, eggs, 1 tablespoon of the oil, and vanilla in a bowl. Stir in blueberries and banana.

2 Combine syrup and cinnamon in a small bowl or pitcher.

3 Heat a large nonstick skillet or seasoned griddle over medium heat; lightly coat with about 1 teaspoon of the remaining oil. Pour batter onto pan, using 2 tablespoons batter per pancake. Cook until small bubbles appear at edges, 2 to 3 minutes; flip and cook about 45 seconds longer. Add remaining oil to skillet as needed. Serve with cinnamon syrup.

tip

Pancakes are best hot off the griddle, but that can mean that diners eat in shifts. If you prefer to eat at the same time, keep the cooked cakes warm by heating the oven to 200°F before you make the batter. As the pancakes are done, transfer them to a baking sheet and pop them in the oven.

Buttery Acorn Squash and Apples

Per serving: **NET CARBS: 16 GRAMS** ▪ Carbohydrates: 21 grams ▪ Fiber: 5 grams ▪ Protein: 1.5 grams ▪

3 4 Fat: 9 grams ▪ Calories: 162 ▪ **PREP TIME: 10 MINUTES** ▪ **COOK TIME: 45 MINUTES** ▪ **SERVINGS: 4**

Jam and warm spices bring out the natural sweetness of squash and apples—this side dish tastes like dessert. Gala apples are ideal: Their skins are thin, and their flesh holds its shape while cooking.

3 tablespoons unsalted butter

3 tablespoons no-sugar-added apricot jam

⅛ teaspoon ground cinnamon

⅛ teaspoon ground allspice

⅛ teaspoon salt

1 medium acorn squash, seeded and cut into 1-inch chunks

1 medium apple, cored and cut into ¼-inch rings

1 Heat oven to 375°F. Line a jelly-roll pan with foil.

2 Combine butter and jam in a large bowl and microwave until melted, 15 to 20 seconds. Stir and cook 5 to 10 seconds longer, if necessary. Stir in cinnamon, allspice, and salt. Add squash; stir gently with a rubber spatula until well coated.

3 Transfer squash to pan and bake 30 minutes. Add apple rings to butter mixture and combine. Add to pan; stir to combine with squash. Bake until squash and apple rings are tender, 15 to 20 minutes longer.

raising nutrition-savvy kids

You can help kids develop healthful eating habits from an early age. Take them to the supermarket with you; talk to your ten-month-old as you select produce, explaining what you're looking for as you examine each item. By the time she's three or four, she'll be able to pick out produce.

Once you have the groceries home, get your kids to help. Ask your seven-year-old to separate the broccoli into florets, your ten-year-old to stir the soup.

Children are more open to trying dishes that they've helped prepare, and you've given them the knowledge to eat well when they're on their own.

Waldorf Salad in Apple Bowls

3 4

Per serving: **NET CARBS: 10 GRAMS** ▪ Carbohydrates: 12.5 grams ▪ Fiber: 2.5 grams ▪ Protein: 2 grams ▪ Fat: 16.5 grams ▪ Calories: 193 ▪ **PREP TIME: 10 MINUTES** ▪ **SERVINGS: 4**

If you won't be serving these right away, brush the cut sides of the apple with lemon juice (or rub with a lemon half) to prevent them from browning. To turn this healthy snack into a meal, add some cubed chicken. For photo, see page 101.

1 **celery stalk,** diced (½ cup)	3 to 4 **tablespoons mayonnaise**
2 **ounces chopped walnuts,** toasted (½ cup)	2 **medium apples,** halved crosswise

1 Combine celery, walnuts, and 3 tablespoons of the mayonnaise in a medium bowl.

2 Hollow out apple halves with a melon baller or a spoon, discarding cores. Dice removed apple flesh and add to celery mixture. If mixture looks dry, add remaining tablespoon mayonnaise.

3 Set each apple half on a plate. Fill apples with salad mixture.

facts about fruit

One of the biggest misconceptions about doing Atkins is that fruit is forbidden. Berries are among the first foods you add back to your meals after you move from Induction to Ongoing Weight Loss, and in time everything from apples to kiwi and even the occasional banana is acceptable.

Fresh or sugar-free frozen fruits are the best options; once you start processing fruits you reduce the beneficial nutrients and may add harmful ones. Dried fruits are concentrated sources of sugars and carbohydrate. Juice is significantly lower in fiber than fresh fruit (for a refreshing quencher, pour yourself a tall glass of fruit-flavored seltzer and add a splash of juice), and packaged applesauce and fruit packs can be particularly problematic.

Chunky Tuna Salad in Tortilla Bowls

2 3 4 Per serving: **NET CARBS: 9 GRAMS** ■ Carbohydrates: 20 grams ■ Fiber: 11 grams ■ Protein: 44 grams ■ Fat: 46 grams ■ Calories: 650 ■ **PREP TIME: 15 MINUTES** ■ **COOK TIME: 10 MINUTES,** plus cooling ■ **SERVINGS: 4**

Edible bowls are a festive touch and can be used with many other recipes in this book. If you're in a hurry, skip the baking and just use the tortillas as wraps.

4 (8-inch) low-carb tortillas

1 tablespoon olive oil

3 (6-ounce) cans oil-packed solid white tuna, drained

6 celery stalks, chopped (3 cups)

1 small cucumber, peeled and cubed (2 cups)

⅔ cup mayonnaise

16 cherry tomatoes, halved or quartered

Salt and pepper

4 lettuce leaves

1 Heat oven to 400°F. Set 4 heatproof bowls on a jelly-roll pan.

2 Brush tortillas on both sides with oil. Drape over bowls. Bake until tortillas are crisp and hold their shape, 5 to 10 minutes. Allow tortillas to cool completely before removing from cups.

3 Combine tuna, celery, cucumber, mayonnaise, and tomatoes in a bowl. Season with salt and pepper to taste. Place a lettuce leaf in each tortilla bowl. Top with tuna salad.

tip

Tortilla bowls make terrific condiment cups on a buffet: Use for grated cheese, thinly sliced scallions, and chopped tomatoes.

Anytime Apricot Parfaits

3 4 Per serving: **NET CARBS: 8.5 GRAMS** ▪ Carbohydrates: 12 grams ▪ Fiber: 3.5 grams ▪ Protein: 8 grams ▪ Fat: 3.5 grams ▪ Calories: 109 ▪ **PREP TIME: 5 MINUTES** ▪ **SERVINGS: 4**

This combination of yogurt, fruit, and cereal is a delicious and healthy snack, dessert, or breakfast. When fresh apricots aren't in season, replace them with six dried apricot halves, snipped with a pair of scissors into small pieces. You'll up the Net Carbs to 9 grams.

1 cup plain whole-milk yogurt	3 apricots, diced
⅓ cup no-sugar-added apricot jam	1¼ cups low-carb cereal flakes

tip
Whole-milk yogurt often has a layer of cream on the top. Simply stir it back into the yogurt before you use it. (The liquid that collects on top of yogurt is called whey; it often contains nutrients and it too should be stirred back into the yogurt.)

Combine yogurt and jam in a bowl. Spoon 2 tablespoons of the yogurt mixture into each of 4 parfait glasses. Top each with 1 tablespoon apricot and 2 tablespoons cereal. Repeat layers once. Top parfaits with remaining yogurt mixture and apricots.

Apricot-Glazed Pork with Carrots

2 **3 4** Per serving: **NET CARBS: 5.5 GRAMS** ▪ Carbohydrates: 6.5 grams ▪ Fiber: 1 gram ▪ Protein: 25.5 grams ▪ Fat: 19 grams ▪ Calories: 307 ▪ **PREP TIME: 7 MINUTES** ▪ **COOK TIME: 25 MINUTES** ▪ **SERVINGS: 4**

This delicious, slightly sweet glaze does double duty: It coats the chops and makes them irresistible, and it acts as a dipping sauce for baby carrots.

¾ teaspoon salt, divided

1 (8-ounce) bag baby carrots

4 (4- to 5-ounce) boneless center-cut pork chops

¼ teaspoon pepper

1 tablespoon vegetable oil

1 cup lower sodium chicken broth

2 teaspoons Dijon mustard

¼ cup no-sugar-added apricot jam

2 tablespoons unsalted butter

1 Bring ½ inch of water and ¼ teaspoon of the salt to a boil in a medium skillet or large saucepan with a lid over high heat. Fit it with a steamer basket. Add carrots. Bring water to a boil, then reduce heat to medium-low and cook until tender, 10 to 15 minutes. Set aside.

2 Meanwhile, season pork chops with remaining ½ teaspoon salt and pepper. Heat oil in a large nonstick skillet over high heat. Brown chops 1 to 2 minutes per side until golden brown. Reduce heat to low; cover, and cook until chops are cooked through, 5 to 7 minutes longer. Transfer to a plate.

3 Increase heat to high. Stir broth and mustard into pan drippings; cook until reduced by half, about 5 minutes. Stir in jam and cook until thickened, 1 to 2 minutes. Stir in butter. Add pork and any juices on the plate; cook until just heated through and coated, about 1 minute per side. Transfer chops and reserved carrots to plates. Divide remaining sauce among small cups and serve as a dipping sauce for carrots.

tip

Carrots are among the richest sources of beta carotene, a plant pigment used to make vitamin A. They also provide considerable amounts of fiber and some vitamin C, too.

Sweet Potato Fritters

Per serving: **NET CARBS: 8 GRAMS** ▪ Carbohydrates: 10 grams ▪ Fiber: 2 grams ▪ Protein: 7 grams ▪ Fat: 13 grams ▪ Calories: 180 ▪ **PREP TIME: 15 MINUTES** ▪ **COOK TIME: 12 MINUTES** ▪ **SERVINGS: 4**

3 4

Deep orange and flecked with green, these little pancakes are as pretty as they are delicious, and they're an excellent source of vitamin A, to boot. Serve them with a dollop of sour cream, if you like.

1 small **zucchini,** coarsely grated (1 cup)

½ **medium apple,** peeled, cored, and coarsely grated (½ cup)

1 small (4-ounce) **sweet potato,** peeled and coarsely grated (¾ cup)

1 tablespoon **grated onion**

2 large **eggs**

3 to 4 tablespoons **Atkins Quick Quisine Bake Mix**

½ **teaspoon salt**

3 tablespoons **vegetable oil,** divided

1 Place zucchini and apple on a triple layer of paper towels. Cover with more towels and press down to squeeze out all excess moisture. Transfer to a bowl and add sweet potato, onion, eggs, 3 tablespoons of the bake mix, and salt. If mixture seems runny, add more bake mix as needed.

2 Heat 1 tablespoon of the oil in a large nonstick skillet over medium heat. Spoon batter by rounded tablespoons into skillet, flattening each with back of spoon into a 3-inch patty. Cook until deep golden brown, about 3 minutes per side. Transfer to a plate and cover loosely with foil to keep warm. Repeat with remaining mixture and oil to make 16 fritters.

tip

Grating onions releases far more of the compounds that make them pungent than slicing or chopping them does. That's why 1 tablespoon of grated onion should be enough to add flavor to these fritters.

Mini Meatballs and Spaghetti

2 **3** **4** Per serving: **NET CARBS: 9 GRAMS** ▪ Carbohydrates: 26.5 grams ▪ Fiber: 17.5 grams ▪ Protein: 65 grams ▪ Fat: 27 grams ▪ Calories: 509 ▪ **PREP TIME: 20 MINUTES** ▪ **COOK TIME: 30 MINUTES** ▪ **SERVINGS: 4**

Look for marinara sauce without any added sugar or corn syrup. The meatballs can be made with ground turkey as well.

1 tablespoon olive oil	1 **scallion,** finely chopped (1 tablespoon)
1 slice **low-carb white bread,** crust removed, torn into small pieces	½ **teaspoon salt**
2 tablespoons water	¼ **teaspoon pepper**
1 pound ground beef	8 ounces low-carb spaghetti
1 large egg	2 cups low-carb marinara sauce

1 Heat oven to 375°F. Pour oil onto a jelly-roll pan.

2 Combine bread and water in a large bowl and soak until bread is soft. Mash bread with fingers to break up. Add beef, egg, scallion, salt, and pepper; mix well. With wet hands, form into ¾-inch meatballs. Put meatballs on pan and roll to coat lightly in oil. Bake until cooked through and browned, 15 to 18 minutes.

3 Cook spaghetti according to package directions; drain.

4 Meanwhile, bring sauce to a simmer in a medium saucepan over medium heat. Add meatballs. Reduce heat to low; cover and simmer 5 to 10 minutes. Serve over spaghetti.

Tex-Mex Quesadillas

1 2 3 4 Per serving: **NET CARBS: 5.5 GRAMS** ■ Carbohydrates: 11 grams ■ Fiber: 5.5 grams ■ Protein: 41.5 grams ■ Fat: 27 grams ■ Calories: 449 ■ **PREP TIME: 15 MINUTES** ■ **COOK TIME: 14 MINUTES** ■ **SERVINGS: 4**

Adding chicken to Mexican-style grilled cheese sandwiches turns a favorite snack into a meal. It's easier to make quesadillas by folding one tortilla over than it is to make one with two tortillas; the half-moon-shaped ones are much easier to turn.

Salsa:

3 ripe plum tomatoes, diced
(¾ cup)

1 scallion, greens reserved, whites
finely chopped

1 tablespoon chopped fresh
cilantro (optional)

1 tablespoon fresh lime juice

Salt and pepper

Quesadillas:

1 pound boneless, skinless
chicken breasts

¼ teaspoon salt

¼ teaspoon chili powder

¼ teaspoon ground cumin

1 tablespoon olive oil

4 (8-inch) low-carb tortillas

8 ounces Monterey Jack cheese,
grated (2 cups)

1 Heat oven to 200°F. Set a wire rack on a baking sheet.

2 **For the salsa:** Combine tomatoes, scallion, cilantro, if using, and lime juice in a bowl; mix well. Season with salt and pepper to taste.

3 **For the quesadillas:** Halve chicken breasts lengthwise. Mix salt, chili powder, and cumin in a bowl; sprinkle over chicken.

4 Heat oil in a large nonstick skillet over medium heat. Add chicken and cook until opaque inside, 3 to 4 minutes per side. Transfer to a cutting board and let cool slightly; slice thinly.

5 Wipe out skillet and set over medium heat. Put 1 tortilla in skillet. Sprinkle one half of tortilla with ¼ cup of the cheese; top with one-fourth of the sliced chicken. Cook until cheese begins to melt, about 1 minute. Sprinkle with another ¼ cup of the cheese and fold tortilla in half over the chicken. Continue to cook, turning once or twice, until crispy on both sides, 2 to 3 minutes. Transfer to prepared baking sheet and keep warm in oven while repeating with remaining tortillas, cheese, and chicken.

6 Cut quesadillas into wedges. Serve with salsa and garnish with scallion greens.

BLT Turkey Burgers

2 3 4 Per serving: **NET CARBS: 7 GRAMS** ▪ Carbohydrates: 15 grams ▪ Fiber: 8 grams ▪ Protein: 50 grams ▪ Fat: 49 grams ▪ Calories: 700 ▪ **PREP TIME: 10 MINUTES** ▪ **COOK TIME: 10 MINUTES** ▪ **SERVINGS: 4**

If you think "diet food" when you hear "turkey burgers," you're missing out. A turkey burger won't taste any more like a hamburger than a roast turkey tastes like a steak—it's entirely different and should be enjoyed for the delicious food it is. Skip the rolls if you are in Induction. For photo, see page 101.

6 slices bacon, cooked until crisp

1½ pounds ground turkey

½ cup plus 2 tablespoons mayonnaise, divided

½ teaspoon salt

¼ teaspoon pepper

1 tablespoon olive oil

4 low-carb sandwich rolls, lightly toasted

4 green leaf lettuce leaves

4 (¼-inch) tomato slices

1 Crumble bacon into a medium bowl. Add turkey, 2 tablespoons of the mayonnaise, salt, and pepper. With wet hands, shape into four patties about 1 inch thick.

2 Heat oil in a large skillet over medium-high heat. Add burgers and cook until browned and cooked through, about 6 minutes per side.

3 Spread remaining mayonnaise on rolls. Place burgers on rolls and top with lettuce and tomato.

tip

Be sure to purchase "ground turkey," not ground skinless turkey or turkey breast. They are very low in fat and, as a result, are quite bland.

Personal Pizzas

2 3 4 Per serving: **NET CARBS: 7 GRAMS** ▪ Carbohydrates: 19 grams ▪ Fiber: 12 grams ▪ Protein: 21 grams ▪ Fat: 17 grams ▪ Calories: 289 ▪ **PREP TIME: 5 MINUTES** ▪ **COOK TIME: 12 MINUTES** ▪ **SERVINGS: 4**

A drinking glass, large biscuit cutter, cookie cutter, or even a well-rinsed empty soup or tuna can makes short work of cutting the rounds out of the bread for the pizza crusts. Don't throw out the crusts; use them to make low-carb bread crumbs.

8 slices low-carb white bread

2 tablespoons olive oil

½ cup low-carb marinara sauce

2 tablespoons grated Parmesan cheese, divided

4 ounces mozzarella cheese, grated (1 cup)

¼ teaspoon dried oregano

1 Heat oven to 400°F. Set a rack on a baking sheet.

2 Cut a 3-inch circle out of each slice of bread. Set on rack; brush tops of circles with oil. Bake until crisp and golden, 5 to 7 minutes.

3 Combine sauce and 1 tablespoon of the Parmesan in a small bowl. Spread each crust with sauce; top with mozzarella. Sprinkle with oregano and remaining tablespoon Parmesan. Bake until cheese is melted, about 5 minutes longer. Cool slightly before serving.

is very high in moisture, which means that it spoils
...nless you know you'll be using it up quickly,
...g it at home—but because it can be a
...der cheeses like cheddar, don't assign

Raspberry-Kiwi Ice Pops

3 4 Per serving: **NET CARBS: 4 GRAMS** ▪ Carbohydrates: 5 grams ▪ Fiber: 1 gram ▪ Protein: 0 grams ▪ Fat: 0 grams ▪ Calories: 20 ▪ **PREP TIME: 5 MINUTES**, plus chilling ▪ **SERVINGS: 6**

Chockful of vitamin C and fiber, these refreshing treats are tastier and more healthful than any frozen novelty you can buy. Use chilled juice to cut the freezing time.

1 small kiwi fruit, peeled and diced

⅓ cup small raspberries

1¼ to 1½ cups light cranberry juice cocktail

Divide kiwi and raspberries among six 2-ounce plastic ice-pop molds. Pour in cranberry juice. Freeze until solid, 1 to 2 hours.

Double Chocolate Ice Cream Soda

2
3 4 Per serving: **NET CARBS: 8.5 GRAMS** ▪ Carbohydrates: 13.5 grams ▪ Fiber: 5 grams ▪ Protein: 2.5 grams ▪ Fat: 17.5 grams ▪ Calories: 192 ▪ **PREP TIME: 5 MINUTES** ▪ **SERVINGS: 1**

On a sultry summer afternoon, this super-chocolatey soda is sure to satisfy. If you prefer milk shakes or egg creams to floats, whirl all the ingredients in a blender before heading for the hammock. If you can't find chocolate soda, use cream soda instead. For photo, see page 101.

8 ounces sugar-free chocolate soda

1 tablespoon heavy cream

½ cup low-carb chocolate ice cream, divided

Pour soda into a tall glass. Add cream and half of the ice cream; stir gently. Top with remaining ice cream.

Whoopie Pies

2 | Per serving: **NET CARBS: 9 GRAMS** ▪ Carbohydrates: 17 grams ▪ Fiber: 8 grams ▪ Protein: 2 grams ▪
3 4 | Fat: 8.5 grams ▪ Calories: 138 ▪ **PREP TIME: 20 MINUTES** ▪ **COOK TIME: 8 MINUTES** ▪ **SERVINGS: 12**

These soft, cakelike sandwiches filled with whipped cream are a delicious low-carb take on a classic. Fill them just before serving.

1 (8.5-ounce) package Atkins Quick Quisine Deluxe Fudge Brownie Mix

4 tablespoons (½ stick) unsalted **butter,** at room temperature

⅓ **cup water**

2 large eggs

2 tablespoons no-sugar-added raspberry jam

½ **cup heavy cream,** whipped

1 Heat oven to 350°F.

2 Combine brownie mix, butter, water, and eggs in a medium bowl. Beat with an electric mixer until fluffy, 30 seconds.

3 Drop batter by slightly rounded tablespoonfuls 2 inches apart on un-greased baking sheets, flattening with the back of the spoon, to make 24 cookies. Bake until tops are puffed and springy when touched, 8 to 10 minutes. Transfer to a rack to cool.

4 Spread the bottoms of 12 cookies with jam, then spread with whipped cream. Top with remaining 12 cookies.

looking

for a savory nosh or a sweet nibble? These versatile recipes fit the bill, whether you want a midafternoon snack with a cup of tea, a post-workout pick-me-up, or an after-school snack for ravenous teens. Although some are better eaten right after you've prepared them, many of these snacks can be made ahead and stashed in a desk drawer or locker.

Scallion-Cheddar Mini Quiche, page 141

snacks
& nibbles

one of the joys of doing Atkins is that snacks are allowed. As a matter of fact, they are encouraged! Dr. Atkins always used to say that if you are hungry, eat; and if you are ravenous, you should have eaten an hour ago. By that he meant that by never allowing yourself to get too hungry, you will be better able to stay in control when mealtimes roll around. His snack of choice was macadamia nuts; he kept them in a drawer in his desk and had a handful every afternoon.

But don't make the mistake of considering "snacks" and "sweet" as inextricably linked. Think of sweets as suitable only as a treat, after you have had your fill of fat and protein. I feel very strongly that until we can deal with our collective sweet tooth, we will not solve the epidemic of obesity in our country.

It is also important that a snack never be composed primarily of carbohydrates. (You will be hungry again in an hour or two.) So a stick of celery is not a suitable snack, but celery filled with peanut butter is a fine snack. Likewise, an apricot alone won't make the grade, but an apricot with a slice of cheddar cheese goes to the head of the class. Atkins Nosh Popcorn Mix (page 130), Coconut Almond Granola (page 144), and Bagel Chips (opposite) all offer a good balance of fat and protein to go with the nutritious carbs.

Some people find the best way for them to do Atkins is to eat four or five small meals instead of three larger ones. Many of the recipes in this chapter, such as Smoky Caponata Pizzas (page 138), Scallion-Cheddar Mini Quiches (page 141), Cheese and Bean Burritos (page 140), and Portobello Stacks (page 142) could stand in as a marvelous mini meal. For variety's sake, give it a try. You might just find that this approach keeps your energy up and weight down.

Bagel Chips

2 3 4 Per serving: **NET CARBS: 9 GRAMS** ▪ Carbohydrates: 20.5 grams ▪ Fiber: 11.5 grams ▪ Protein: 20.5 grams ▪ Fat: 27.5 grams ▪ Calories: 333 ▪ **PREP TIME: 10 MINUTES** ▪ **COOK TIME: 20 MINUTES** ▪ **SERVINGS: 1**

For a delicious savory version, slice a low-carb onion bagel; brush with olive oil, then sprinkle with minced garlic, dried oregano, and salt.

1 low-carb plain bagel,
halved crosswise

2 tablespoons unsalted butter,
melted

2 packets sugar substitute

¼ teaspoon ground cinnamon

1 Heat oven to 300°F.

2 Carefully cut each bagel half into thin slices with a sharp knife.

3 Combine butter, sugar substitute, and cinnamon in a bowl. Brush on both sides of the bagel slices. Set on a large baking sheet. Bake 10 minutes; flip slices and bake until crisp and golden brown, 5 to 10 minutes longer.

Hawaiian Roll

2 3 4 Per serving: **NET CARBS: 6.5 GRAMS** ▪ Carbohydrates: 13.5 grams ▪ Fiber: 7 grams ▪ Protein: 7.5 grams ▪ Fat: 23.5 grams ▪ Calories: 277 ▪ **PREP TIME: 5 MINUTES** ▪ **SERVINGS: 1**

In addition to macadamia nut butter, most natural foods stores carry almond, cashew, and hazelnut butter. Unlike most commercial brands of peanut butter, they are also free of artery-clogging hydrogenated oils, or trans fats.

1 (8-inch) low-carb tortilla

1 tablespoon no-sugar-added
macadamia nut butter

1 teaspoon no-sugar-added
pineapple or apricot preserves

2 tablespoons unsweetened
shredded coconut

Spread tortilla with nut butter and preserves. Sprinkle with coconut. Roll up.

Piña Colada Smoothie

Per serving: **NET CARBS: 8 GRAMS** ▪ Carbohydrates: 9 grams ▪ Fiber: 1 gram ▪ Protein: 2.5 grams ▪

3 4 Fat: 13 grams ▪ Calories: 159 ▪ **PREP TIME: 5 MINUTES** ▪ **SERVINGS: 2** (¾ cup each)

As rich as the cocktail it's based on, this smoothie is best in small amounts. If your refrigerator dispenses crushed ice, use about one cup instead of the ice cubes.

½ cup unsweetened coconut milk

¼ cup plain whole-milk yogurt

½ cup fresh pineapple chunks

¾ teaspoon coconut extract

2 packets sugar substitute

1 teaspoon fresh lime juice

8 ice cubes

2 lime slices

Put coconut milk, yogurt, pineapple, coconut extract, sugar substitute, lime juice, and ice cubes in a blender. Blend at high speed until smooth. Serve, garnished with lime slices.

crazy for coconuts

Fresh, unsweetened coconut has as much in common with the sweet flaky stuff in the baking aisle as fresh tomatoes have with a jar of spaghetti sauce. Although obtaining fresh coconut meat is still labor-intensive, you can find unsweetened coconut, as well as coconut milk and coconut cream, in most supermarkets.

The simplest way to get the best-tasting coconut is to head for the freezer section. You'll find a variety of tropical fruits packed in flat pouches. Grated coconut is one of the more common ones, particularly in markets with a large Latino, Indian, or Thai clientele.

Unsweetened shredded coconut can be found in some supermarkets' natural foods sections and in most natural foods stores; look for it with the baking products.

In addition to flaked or shredded dried coconut, most markets carry coconut milk, which is made by steeping coconut meat in boiling water and pressing out the liquid. Some stores also carry coconut cream. Like dairy cream, coconut cream rises to the top of the milk and is skimmed off. It can also be extracted by pressing the meat. Coconut cream is fairly solid and is unsweetened. It should not be confused with cream of coconut, a thick, sweetened liquid used primarily in tropical cocktails that is sky high in carbs.

Atkins Nosh Popcorn Mix

Per serving: **NET CARBS: 6 GRAMS** ▪ Carbohydrates: 9 grams ▪ Fiber: 3 grams ▪ Protein: 9 grams ▪
Fat: 13 grams ▪ Calories: 181 ▪ **PREP TIME: 10 MINUTES** ▪ **COOK TIME: 23 MINUTES** ▪ **SERVINGS: 8**

3 4

Adding the popcorn last and tossing it briefly with the other ingredients helps to keep the kernels from breaking apart. If you don't have an air popper, use a bag of microwave popcorn and omit the salt. Store in an airtight container.

Cooking spray

4 tablespoons (½ stick) unsalted butter, melted

2 large egg whites, at room temperature

2 packets sugar substitute

½ teaspoon vanilla extract

½ teaspoon ground cinnamon

¼ teaspoon salt

1½ cups low-carb cereal flakes

3 ounces peanuts, pecans, or almonds (¾ cup)

4 cups air-popped popcorn

1 Heat oven to 300°F. Line a baking sheet with foil and lightly coat with cooking spray.

2 Whisk butter, egg whites, sugar substitute, vanilla, cinnamon, and salt in a bowl.

3 Put cereal and nuts in a large bowl. Add butter mixture; toss to blend. Add popcorn and toss very briefly, just to coat. Transfer mixture to baking sheet and spread in an even layer. Bake until crispy, 20 to 23 minutes. Let cool on baking sheet.

tip

Individual-serve bags of chips or cups of ice cream cost more than the family-size bags or half-gallon tubs, but there's no chance you'll eat more than what the Nutritional Facts label says is a serving.

Crispy Cream Cheese and Jelly Triangles

2 **3** **4** Per serving: **NET CARBS: 4.5 GRAMS** ▪ Carbohydrates: 9.5 grams ▪ Fiber: 5 grams ▪ Protein: 6 grams ▪ Fat: 2 grams ▪ Calories: 155 ▪ **PREP TIME: 7 MINUTES** ▪ **COOK TIME: 4 MINUTES** ▪ **SERVINGS: 2**

Soften the cream cheese briefly in the microwave—if it's cold, you'll have to press harder on the tortillas and they may break. For an almost-instant snack, use low-carb, trans fat–free crackers in lieu of the wraps.

1 teaspoon unsalted butter, melted

2 (8-inch) low-carb tortillas

¼ teaspoon ground cinnamon

½ teaspoon granular sugar substitute

2 tablespoons cream cheese, softened

4 teaspoons no-sugar-added red raspberry preserves

1 Heat oven to 350°F. Brush baking sheet lightly with a little of the melted butter. Brush tortillas with remaining butter; sprinkle with cinnamon and sugar substitute. Cut each tortilla into 8 triangles and set on baking sheet. Bake until triangles are crisp, 3 to 4 minutes.

2 Turn triangles over; spread 8 with cream cheese and 8 with preserves. Sandwich jam triangles with cheese triangles. Serve warm or at room temperature.

tip

If you have a pizza wheel, it makes short work of cutting the tortillas; kitchen shears are another good alternative.

Vegetable Fries

Per serving: **NET CARBS: 11 GRAMS** ▪ Carbohydrates: 13.5 grams ▪ Fiber: 2.5 grams ▪ Protein: 1.5 grams ▪ Fat: 7 grams ▪ Calories: 116 ▪ **PREP TIME: 25 MINUTES** ▪ **COOK TIME: 20 MINUTES** ▪ **SERVINGS: 4**

Because these vegetables are significantly lower in starch than potatoes, they don't fry up as crisp. Instead, they're very tender, almost like fast-food fries. Even if you are not a fan of turnips, you'll be amazed at how delicious they are. Serve them with BLT Turkey Burgers (page 118).

1 small (4-ounce) sweet potato, peeled and sliced into 3- by ½-inch strips

1 medium (4-ounce) turnip, peeled and sliced into 2- by ⅜-inch strips

1 medium (4-ounce) parsnip, peeled and sliced into 3- by ⅜-inch strips

Vegetable oil

Salt

1 Place vegetables in a bowl of cool water and let stand 10 minutes. Drain. Dry off thoroughly with paper towels.

2 Fill a large deep saucepan with 1½ inches of oil. Heat to 365°F. Add about one-third of the vegetables and fry until golden brown, 3 to 4 minutes. Drain on paper towels. Repeat with remaining vegetables. Season with salt to taste.

tip

It's important to pat vegetables dry before you add them to a pan with hot oil. The wetter they are, the more the oil will spatter when you add them.

Cheese Biscuits

1 2 3 4 Per serving: **NET CARBS: 1.5 GRAMS** ■ Carbohydrates: 3 grams ■ Fiber: 1.5 grams ■ Protein: 8 grams ■ Fat: 7 grams ■ Calories: 108 ■ **PREP TIME: 15 MINUTES** ■ **COOK TIME: 10 MINUTES** ■ **SERVINGS: 6**

Cayenne adds a bit of zest to these delicious biscuits. Replace the cheddar with other cheeses—Gouda is particularly tasty. Serve these with Spicy Chicken Soup with Black Beans (page 22) or Southern Country-Style Pork Ribs (page 42).

Cooking spray

½ cup Atkins Quick Quisine Bake Mix

½ teaspoon cayenne pepper

½ teaspoon baking powder

1 large egg

3 tablespoons heavy cream

2 ounces cheddar cheese, grated (½ cup)

1 tablespoon grated Parmesan cheese

Paprika

1 Heat oven to 400°F. Lightly coat a baking sheet with cooking spray.

2 Combine bake mix, cayenne, baking powder, egg, cream, cheddar, and Parmesan in a bowl until well blended.

3 Drop 12 heaping teaspoonfuls onto baking sheet. Season with paprika. Bake until puffed and golden, 8 to 10 minutes.

tip

If you only have a large bag of low-carb candy or chips, be smart about your snack. Check the Nutrition Facts label to see how many pieces are considered a serving. Count out the number, then put the bag away. You'll lessen the likelihood that you'll find an excuse for a second helping.

Pigs in Blankets

1 2 3 4 Per serving: **NET CARBS: 2.5 GRAMS** ▪ Carbohydrates: 6 grams ▪ Fiber: 3.5 grams ▪ Protein: 12.5 grams ▪ Fat: 17 grams ▪ Calories: 219 ▪ **PREP TIME: 20 MINUTES** ▪ **COOK TIME: 18 MINUTES** ▪ **SERVINGS: 6**

Kids of all ages love these. Serve them at a slumber party or for an after-school snack. Dip them in your favorite mustard or no-sugar-added ketchup, if you like.

Cooking spray

1 cup Atkins Quick Quisine Bake Mix

¼ cup water

4 tablespoons (½ stick) unsalted butter, melted

24 cocktail franks

1 Heat oven to 375°F. Lightly coat a baking sheet with cooking spray.

2 Combine bake mix, water, and butter in a medium bowl just until dough comes together and is blended. Gather dough into a ball.

3 Dust a board or counter with a bit of bake mix; roll dough into a 12- by 3-inch rectangle. Cut in half lengthwise, then cut crosswise into 12 strips to make 24 pieces of dough. Roll dough around the middle of each frank, pinching end to seal.

4 Set, seam-side down, on baking sheet. Bake until puffed and golden, 15 to 18 minutes.

tip

Be sure to read labels when you buy cocktail franks; as with full-sized hot dogs, the smaller ones can be loaded with high-carb fillers and additives.

Classic Hummus

2 3 4

Per serving: **NET CARBS: 5 GRAMS** ■ Carbohydrates: 6 grams ■ Fiber: 1 gram ■ Protein: 1.5 grams ■ Fat: 5 grams ■ Calories: 71 ■ **PREP TIME: 10 MINUTES** ■ **SERVINGS: 16** (2 tablespoons each)

Chickpeas are traditional in this Middle Eastern spread, but use different beans and different seasonings—try black or pinto beans with chili powder and salsa; pink or white beans with rosemary.

1 (15½-ounce) can chickpeas, drained

¼ cup tahini

¼ cup water

3 tablespoons extra virgin olive oil

2 tablespoons fresh lemon juice

2 garlic cloves, peeled

½ teaspoon salt

⅛ teaspoon cayenne pepper

Combine chickpeas, tahini, water, oil, lemon juice, garlic, salt, and cayenne in a food processor. Purée until smooth, 2 to 3 minutes. Serve with low-carb crackers or cut-up vegetables.

snack savvy

Numerous studies have shown that eating fat can *help* your weight-loss and weight-maintenance efforts (and sufficient amounts are imperative for good health).

Fat adds flavor to a food on its own, and it intensifies other flavors in a dish. Fat is satisfying and helps you to feel full faster, which can mean that you eat less. Fat also helps to slow down the rate at which carbohydrates are absorbed; carbs eaten with fat (and protein) have less impact on blood sugar levels than carbs eaten alone.

Make popcorn the old-fashioned way, in a saucepan with oil, and pour on some melted butter or grated Parmesan cheese.

Don't have an apple or pear by itself; add some fat to slow down the impact on your blood sugar. Cut your fruit into wedges and nibble them with a slice of extra-sharp cheddar, or spread them with natural peanut butter or cream cheese.

Choose dips that are high in protein, like Classic Hummus (see above), or those that are high in beneficial fats like Tapenade (page 90) or Pomegranate Guacamole (page 294).

Smoky Caponata Pizzas

2 3 4 Per serving: **NET CARBS: 5 GRAMS** ▪ Carbohydrates: 11 grams ▪ Fiber: 6 grams ▪ Protein: 12.5 grams ▪ Fat: 16 grams ▪ Calories: 235 ▪ **PREP TIME: 10 MINUTES** ▪ **COOK TIME: 12 MINUTES** ▪ **SERVINGS: 4**

Caponata, sometimes called eggplant appetizer, is an Italian side dish or relish made with eggplant, onions, tomatoes, anchovies, and olives. It is sold in jars or cans and is available in most supermarkets.

8 slices low-carb multigrain bread

2 tablespoons olive oil

½ cup caponata

4 ounces smoked mozzarella cheese, grated (1 cup)

2 tablespoons roasted red pepper, patted dry and chopped

1 Heat oven to 400°F. Set a rack on a baking sheet.

2 Cut a 3-inch circle out of each slice of bread. Set on rack; brush tops of circles with oil. Bake until crisp and golden, 5 to 7 minutes.

3 Spread each crust with the caponata; top with mozzarella and red pepper. Bake until cheese melts, about 5 minutes longer.

tip

A tuna fish can is about 3¼ inches in diameter; 14- to 15-ounce soup cans are about 3 inches, so both will make bread circles of about the right size. If you don't have an empty one in your recycle bin, use a drinking glass, or use a pair of scissors or a knife.

Tortilla Chips

1 **2** **3** **4** Per serving: **NET CARBS: 3 GRAMS** ■ Carbohydrates: 8 grams ■ Fiber: 5 grams ■ Protein: 5 grams ■ Fat: 6.5 grams ■ Calories: 100 ■ **PREP TIME: 5 MINUTES** ■ **COOK TIME: 8 MINUTES** ■ **SERVINGS: 4**

Make a double or triple batch of these and store them in an airtight tin. Serve them with Classic Hummus (page 137) or Garden Vegetable Dip (page 145), or alongside a sandwich.

4 (8-inch) low-carb tortillas	⅛ teaspoon salt
2 teaspoons olive oil	⅛ teaspoon ground cumin

Heat oven to 400°F. Brush tortillas on both sides with oil. Sprinkle with salt and cumin. Cut each tortilla into 6 wedges. Set on a jelly-roll pan and bake until browned, about 6 minutes. Flip and bake until crisp, about 2 minutes longer. Watch closely, as they can burn rapidly.

Cheese and Bean Burritos

3 **4** Per serving: **NET CARBS: 8 GRAMS** ■ Carbohydrates: 15 grams ■ Fiber: 7 grams ■ Protein: 14.5 grams ■ Fat: 17 grams ■ Calories: 259 ■ **PREP TIME: 5 MINUTES** ■ **COOK TIME: 30 SECONDS** ■ **SERVINGS: 2**

Keep the ingredients on hand for after-school snacks or post-workout pick-me-ups; use Monterey Jack with jalapeño cheese for more zing, or choose a spicy salsa.

2 (8-inch) low-carb tortillas	2 tablespoons shredded lettuce (optional)
¼ cup canned organic refried beans	2 tablespoons salsa
2 ounces cheddar cheese, grated (½ cup)	2 tablespoons sour cream

Spread tortillas with refried beans, then sprinkle with cheese and lettuce, if using. Fold envelope fashion (see page 92). Microwave until hot and cheese melts, about 30 seconds. Serve with salsa and sour cream.

Scallion-Cheddar Mini Quiches

Per serving: **NET CARBS: 2 GRAMS** ▪ Carbohydrates: 2.5 grams ▪ Fiber: 0.5 gram ▪ Protein: 11 grams ▪ Fat: 18.5 grams ▪ Calories: 218 ▪ **PREP TIME: 5 MINUTES** ▪ **COOK TIME: 25 MINUTES** ▪ **SERVINGS: 2**

These quiches make a tasty and satisfying snack. Or pop them into the oven before you shower for an easy and elegant breakfast. For photo, see page 125.

1 teaspoon Atkins Quick Quisine Bake Mix

1 ounce cheddar or Gruyère cheese, grated (¼ cup)

1 scallion, thinly sliced (1 tablespoon)

1 teaspoon dried onion flakes

2 large eggs

3 tablespoons heavy cream

⅛ teaspoon salt

1 Heat oven to 350°F. Butter two 6-ounce custard cups.

2 Put ½ teaspoon bake mix in each cup. Top with cheese, scallion, and onion flakes.

3 Whisk eggs, cream, and salt in a bowl. Gently pour over cheese mixture. Bake until a knife inserted in a quiche comes out clean, 20 to 25 minutes. Serve immediately, as the quiches fall quickly.

tip

If you're afraid you'll eat too many pieces of low-carb chocolate, stash your supply in the freezer. It takes longer to eat, so you'll savor the experience—and be less likely to return for more.

Portobello Stacks

1 2 3 4 Per serving: **NET CARBS: 4.5 GRAMS** ▪ Carbohydrates: 6 grams ▪ Fiber: 1.5 grams ▪ Protein: 7 grams ▪ Fat: 19.5 grams ▪ Calories: 246 ▪ **PREP TIME: 5 MINUTES** ▪ **COOK TIME: 10 MINUTES** ▪ **SERVINGS: 2**

Remember these pretty little stacks when you're looking for a light lunch or a first course for an Italian supper. They're tasty on their own, or serve them with Italian Pork Chops with Leeks (page 226). They also make delicious sandwiches served on low-carb buns.

2 portobello mushroom caps

2 tablespoons extra virgin olive oil, divided

Salt and pepper

2 ounces mozzarella cheese, cut into 2½-inch-thick slices

4 basil leaves

⅓ cup roasted red peppers

1 tablespoon red wine vinegar

1 Brush mushrooms with 1 tablespoon of oil. Season with salt and pepper.

2 Heat a nonstick skillet over medium-high heat. Add mushrooms, stem-side down, and cook until warm, about 4 minutes. Turn; top with cheese, basil, and peppers. Continue cooking until mushrooms are piping hot and cheese is warm but not melted, 3 to 5 minutes longer.

3 Transfer mushroom stacks to plates. Drizzle with vinegar and remaining tablespoon oil. Season with additional salt and pepper to taste.

Coconut Almond Granola

3 4 Per serving: **NET CARBS: 18.5 GRAMS** ▪ Carbohydrates: 25 grams ▪ Fiber: 6.5 grams ▪ Protein: 11 grams ▪ Fat: 21.5 grams ▪ Calories: 332 ▪ **PREP TIME: 5 MINUTES** ▪ **COOK TIME: 30 MINUTES,** plus cooling ▪ **SERVINGS: 6** (½-cup)

Look for kamut puffs and soy nuts in the natural foods stores, or in the natural foods section of your supermarket.

2¼ cups kamut puffs

¾ cup slivered almonds

¾ cup old-fashioned oats

½ cup unsweetened shredded coconut

¼ cup soy nuts

½ teaspoon salt

½ cup sugar-free vanilla syrup

2 tablespoons canola oil, plus more for baking sheet

2½ teaspoons coconut extract

1½ teaspoons almond extract

1 Preheat oven to 325°F. Lightly coat a baking sheet with oil.

2 Combine kamut, almonds, oats, coconut, soy nuts, and salt in a large mixing bowl. Set aside.

3 Combine syrup, oil, and extracts in a small measuring cup. Pour over dry ingredients and toss gently until ingredients are well-coated.

4 Spread granola onto baking sheet and bake for 30 minutes, stirring every 10 minutes, until crisp. Cool completely before serving.

Garden Vegetable Dip

1 2 3 4 Per serving: **NET CARBS: 3 GRAMS** ▪ Carbohydrates: 3.5 grams ▪ Fiber: 0.5 gram ▪ Protein: 1.5 grams ▪ Fat: 12 grams ▪ Calories: 139 ▪ **PREP TIME: 10 MINUTES** ▪ **SERVINGS: 6**

Zesty but not overpowering, and full of crunch, this dip is at home as a snack, or spread on a low-carb bagel and serve with chicken or tuna salad for lunch.

1 (8-ounce) tub chive and onion cream cheese

¼ medium red bell pepper, diced (¼ cup)

½ celery stalk, chopped (¼ cup)

2 radishes, sliced (¼ cup)

1 to 2 tablespoons prepared horseradish

1 teaspoon dried parsley

Combine cream cheese, pepper, celery, radishes, horseradish, and parsley in a bowl, stirring thoroughly. If mixture is stiff, microwave for 10 seconds to soften.

Rancho Deluxe Salad

1 2 3 4 Per serving: **NET CARBS: 3 GRAMS** ▪ Carbohydrates: 4.5 grams ▪ Fiber: 1.5 grams ▪ Protein: 17 grams ▪ Fat: 21.5 grams ▪ Calories: 282 ▪ **PREP TIME: 10 MINUTES** ▪ **SERVINGS: 2**

Look for packaged coleslaw salad mix in the produce section of your market. One with red cabbage and shredded carrots makes for a prettier salad.

1½ cups coleslaw mix or shredded cabbage

½ cup cubed Black Forest ham or smoked turkey

½ cup cubed Gruyère cheese

2 tablespoons low-carb ranch dressing

1 teaspoon cider vinegar

Combine coleslaw mix, ham, cheese, ranch dressing, and vinegar in a bowl. Toss to coat.

if you like to end a meal on a sweet note, look to the recipes in this chapter. These meal enders require minimal preparation—some don't even require you to turn on the oven. You'll find old favorites like Creamy Lemon Bars, Cinnamon Brown Rice Pudding, and Oatmeal Raisin Cookies, as well as those that might be new combinations of flavors, such as Figs with Sweet Mascarpone and Amaretti Semifreddo.

Creamy Lemon Bars, page 163

Oatmeal Raisin Cookies, page 155

sweet & simple

when it comes to desserts, I know from

personal experience that the key to successful weight control is moderation. This is not to say that you cannot occasionally enjoy a decadent-tasting dessert, even during the week, but appropriate quantities and smart choices are essential when you're trying to lose pounds or maintain your weight.

Like all of the recipes created in The Atkins Kitchen, the 15 that follow also emphasize fresh whole ingredients, in this case fruits and berries, nuts, butter, and real cream, steering your taste buds away from a taste for the syrupy sweet flavor of so many desserts that have helped contribute to our nation's collective sweet tooth—and weight woes. In fact, on Atkins, you will probably notice that many of the desserts you once found enjoyable are simply too sweet for your taste.

While none of these recipes is suitable for Induction, once you've reached Ongoing Weight Loss, you will be able to begin to add berries and nuts back to your meal plans, meaning that Blueberry Walnut Dessert Bread (opposite) and Chocolate-Dusted Strawberries with Orange Cream (page 150), among others, are fine for most people. Alternatively, a bowl of blueberries or other berries with whipped cream is one of the sweetest and simplest meal enders and a personal favorite of both mine and Dr. Atkins. When it comes to other fruits, focus on low-glycemic fruits—the ones that have a minimal impact on blood sugar. These include cherries, citrus fruits, apples, peaches, and plums. You may also want to explore the European tradition of having cheese after dinner instead of dessert as an alternative on certain nights. Fruit and cheese are a natural combination that is ideally suited to doing Atkins.

Blueberry Walnut Dessert Bread

Per serving: **NET CARBS: 4.5 GRAMS** ■ Carbohydrates: 9 grams ■ Fiber: 4.5 grams ■ Protein: 10 grams ■
Fat: 10.5 grams ■ Calories: 163 ■ **PREP TIME: 10 MINUTES** ■ **COOK TIME: 55 MINUTES**, plus cooling ■ **SERVINGS: 12**

Cut your prep time by using a packaged mix, but add nutritious homemade flavors with fresh blueberries and chopped walnuts.

Cooking spray

1 (8-ounce) package Atkins Quick Quisine Deluxe Blueberry Muffin & Bread Mix

¼ cup chopped walnuts

½ cup blueberries

1 teaspoon ground cinnamon

2 large eggs

⅔ cup water

⅓ cup vegetable oil

⅓ cup sour cream

1 Heat oven to 350°F. Lightly coat an 8- by 4-inch loaf pan with cooking spray.

2 Combine bake mix, walnuts, blueberries, and cinnamon in a bowl; make a well in the center.

3 Lightly beat eggs in a medium bowl; whisk in water, oil, and sour cream. Pour into well and stir until combined.

4 Pour into pan and bake until a toothpick inserted in the center comes out clean, 45 to 55 minutes. Cool in the pan about 10 minutes, then remove from pan and cool to room temperature on a rack. Cut into twelve ¾-inch slices.

tip

Buying berries is tricky—you see only a fraction of what you're buying. To help boost your odds of bringing home a pristine package, shake the container to be sure you can hear or feel berries moving around. If they don't, they may be stuck together, a sign they've been crushed or are going bad.

Chocolate-Dusted Strawberries with Orange Cream

2
3 4
Per serving: **NET CARBS: 7 GRAMS** ▪ Carbohydrates: 9 grams ▪ Fiber: 2 grams ▪ Protein: 1 gram ▪ Fat: 12.5 grams ▪ Calories: 115 ▪ **PREP TIME: 10 MINUTES** ▪ **SERVINGS: 4**

Make a tropical version of this by replacing the vanilla with coconut extract and the orange zest with toasted unsweetened coconut.

½ cup heavy cream

2 packets sugar substitute

½ teaspoon vanilla extract

½ teaspoon grated orange zest

½ (1-ounce) Atkins Endulge Chocolate Candy Bar, grated

2 cups whole strawberries

1 Combine cream, sugar substitute, vanilla, and orange zest in a medium bowl. Beat with an electric mixer until stiff peaks form.

2 Transfer cream to a serving bowl and top with chocolate. Serve strawberries on the side for dipping.

Figs with Sweet Mascarpone

3 4
Per serving: **NET CARBS: 11 GRAMS** ▪ Carbohydrates: 13 grams ▪ Fiber: 2 grams ▪ Protein: 1.5 grams ▪ Fat: 8 grams ▪ Calories: 119 ▪ **PREP TIME: 10 MINUTES** ▪ **SERVINGS: 4**

This fruit and cheese combo is an unexpectedly delicious treat. You can also make this with fresh apricots.

4 large fresh figs

4 tablespoons mascarpone

½ teaspoon granular sugar substitute

2 teaspoons chopped toasted walnuts

Slice figs in half. Stir mascarpone and sugar substitute in a small bowl. Divide among figs; dollop each half with mascarpone. Sprinkle with nuts and serve.

Grilled Plums with Butter Pecan Ice Cream

Per serving: **NET CARBS: 11 GRAMS** ■ Carbohydrates: 13.5 grams ■ Fiber: 2.5 grams ■ Protein: 3 grams ■
Fat: 21 grams ■ Calories: 261 ■ **PREP TIME: 5 MINUTES** ■ **COOK TIME: 10 MINUTES** ■ **SERVINGS: 6**

3 4

Grilling fruit brings a new dimension to its taste. Make sure your grill is clean and oiled to prevent sticking. Apricots can easily fill in for the plums, but be sure your fruit is sweet. Fruit that isn't as ripe may taste unpleasantly tart when paired with ice cream.

6 ripe plums, halved and pitted

1 tablespoon ground cinnamon

**6 scoops low-carb butter pecan
ice cream**

6 tablespoons chopped pecans,
lightly toasted

1 Prepare a medium-heat grill. Sprinkle cinnamon over fruit on the cut sides.

2 Grill fruit, cut-side down, 5 minutes (for crosshatch grill marks, rotate 90 degrees after 3 minutes). Turn over and cook until fruit is slightly soft but still holds its shape, about 5 minutes longer.

3 Place 2 fruit halves into each of six bowls. Top with ice cream and nuts. Serve immediately.

mascarpone

Pronounced *mas-car-po-nay*, this is Italy's version of cream cheese. It ranges in color from ivory to pale yellow, but it's treasured among cooks for its creamy, silky-rich texture—its consistency is not unlike butter on a hot day, or thick whipped cream. Although some like it savory and mix it with anchovies or mustard or garlic to use as a spread or sauce, mascarpone shines as a dessert or an ingredient in desserts. Spoon it over broiled peaches and drizzle with sugar-free caramel syrup. Or try it with Grilled Plums (see above) instead of butter pecan ice cream.

Almond Pancakes with Chocolate Sauce

Per serving: **NET CARBS: 12.5 GRAMS** ■ Carbohydrates: 19 grams ■ Fiber: 6.5 grams ■ Protein: 29 grams ■
Fat: 34.5 grams ■ Calories: 514 ■ **PREP TIME: 10 MINUTES** ■ **COOK TIME: 25 MINUTES** ■ **SERVINGS: 4**

3 4

Try pancakes for dessert! They are also a great breakfast for a birthday or special occasion, with puréed fruit or sugar-free pancake syrup instead of the chocolate sauce.

1 cup Atkins Quick Quisine Bake Mix

1 teaspoon baking powder

½ teaspoon salt

2½ tablespoons granular sugar substitute

½ cup toasted sliced almonds, divided

4 large eggs

1 teaspoon vanilla extract

1 teaspoon almond extract

1½ cups unsweetened soymilk

2 tablespoons unsalted butter, melted

Cooking spray

½ cup heavy cream

2 (1-ounce) Atkins Endulge Chocolate Candy Bars, broken in small pieces

1 Combine bake mix, baking powder, salt, sugar substitute, and ¼ cup of the almonds in a bowl; make a well in the center.

2 Lightly beat eggs in a medium bowl; whisk in vanilla and almond extract, soymilk, and butter. Pour into well and mix until smooth. Let batter stand 5 minutes.

3 Heat oven to 200°F. Heat a nonstick skillet or seasoned griddle over medium-high heat; lightly coat with cooking spray. Pour on ¼ cup batter for each pancake. Cook until edges are dry and the top is bubbling, 1½ to 2 minutes. Flip pancakes and cook until browned, 1 minute longer. Transfer pancakes to a baking sheet and keep warm in the oven. Repeat until all batter is used.

4 Put ¼ cup of the cream in a 1-cup microwavable glass bowl and microwave on high 40 seconds. Add the candy bar pieces. Let stand for 30 seconds, then stir until melted. If pieces do not melt completely, microwave on low 20 seconds longer.

5 Whip remaining ¼ cup cream. To serve, top pancakes with whipped cream; drizzle with chocolate sauce and sprinkle with remaining ¼ cup almonds.

Oatmeal Raisin Cookies

3 4 Per serving: **NET CARBS: 17 GRAMS** ▪ Carbohydrates: 20 grams ▪ Fiber: 3 grams ▪ Protein: 7 grams ▪ Fat: 13.5 grams ▪ Calories: 224 ▪ **PREP TIME: 15 MINUTES** ▪ **COOK TIME: 10 MINUTES**, plus cooling ▪ **SERVINGS: 8** (2 cookies each)

Old-fashioned oats will give the chewiest texture to these cookies, but quick-cooking oats are also acceptable; just be sure to avoid using instant oats. The cookies freeze beautifully, so save time by making a double batch. For photo, see page 147.

½ cup (1 stick) unsalted butter, at room temperature

¾ cup granular sugar substitute

1 large egg

½ teaspoon vanilla extract

½ teaspoon baking soda

½ teaspoon salt

6 tablespoons Atkins Quick Quisine Bake Mix

1 cup old-fashioned or quick-cooking oats

¼ cup raisins

1 Preheat oven to 350°F.

2 Combine butter and sugar substitute in a large bowl. Beat with an electric mixer until pale and creamy; beat in egg and vanilla. Add baking soda, salt, and bake mix; beat until well blended. Add oats and raisins and beat until just combined.

3 Drop 16 heaping tablespoons on an ungreased baking sheet. Bake until bottoms of cookies are browned and tops are lightly browned, 8 to 10 minutes. Cool on a rack.

tip

Instant oats have been cooked and then dehydrated. Their texture is quite different from old-fashioned, or even quick-cooking, oats. They can become mushy in baked goods rather than chewy.

Cinnamon Brown Rice Pudding

3 4 Per serving: **NET CARBS: 10 GRAMS** ■ Carbohydrates: 11 grams ■ Fiber: 1 gram ■ Protein: 8.5 grams ■ Fat: 6 grams ■ Calories: 137 ■ **PREP TIME: 10 MINUTES** ■ **COOK TIME: 20 MINUTES** ■ **SERVINGS: 4**

This is the perfect way to use up leftover rice—if you have to cook rice, you'll add about 45 minutes to the prep time.

¾ cup cooked medium-grain brown rice

1½ cups reduced-carb, whole-milk dairy beverage

2 teaspoons granular sugar substitute

2 large eggs

2 teaspoons vanilla extract

1 teaspoon ground cinnamon

2 tablespoons sugar-free pancake syrup

¼ cup sliced strawberries (optional)

1 Combine rice, dairy beverage, sugar substitute, eggs, vanilla, and cinnamon in a medium saucepan. Cook, stirring constantly, over medium heat until mixture comes to a low boil.

2 Continue to cook, stirring often, until pudding thickens, about 8 minutes. Remove from heat and stir in syrup. Serve hot or cold topped with strawberries, if desired.

tip
Reduced-carb dairy beverages are a fine substitute for milk. If you don't have any on hand, use unsweetened soymilk or half-and-half in its place.

Almond-Orange Macaroons

2 3 4 Per serving: **NET CARBS: 3 GRAMS** ▪ Carbohydrates: 5.5 grams ▪ Fiber: 2.5 grams ▪ Protein: 5.5 grams ▪ Fat: 12.5 grams ▪ Calories: 154 ▪ **PREP TIME: 15 MINUTES** ▪ **COOK TIME: 10 MINUTES,** plus cooling ▪ **SERVINGS: 4** (4 cookies each)

Coconut and almond are both naturally sweet; they combine with chocolate and a hint of orange to make a slightly chewy nibble that's sure to satisfy a sweet tooth. Serve with a cup of steaming-hot Earl Grey tea.

Cooking spray

½ cup blanched slivered almonds, plus 16 slivers for topping cookies

3 tablespoons unsweetened shredded coconut

1 tablespoon granular sugar substitute

½ teaspoon grated orange zest

1 large egg white

¼ (1-ounce) Atkins Endulge Chocolate Candy Bar, chopped (1 tablespoon)

1 Preheat oven to 350°F. Lightly coat a baking sheet with cooking spray.

2 Combine ½ cup of the almonds, coconut, and sugar substitute in a food processor and pulse until almonds are finely ground. Add orange zest and egg white and pulse until combined.

3 Roll mixture into 16 balls; set 1 to 2 inches apart on baking sheet. Slightly flatten balls and top each with 1 of the remaining 16 almond slivers, pressing gently. Bake until bottoms of macaroons are lightly browned, about 10 minutes. Transfer cookies to a rack to cool completely.

4 Microwave chocolate in a bowl until melted, about 1 minute. Dip knife in chocolate and drizzle chocolate on macaroons. Refrigerate until chocolate hardens.

Nutty Chocolate Ice-Cream Cups

Per serving: **NET CARBS: 8 GRAMS** ▪ Carbohydrates: 10 grams ▪ Fiber: 2 grams ▪ Protein: 5.5 grams ▪

3 4 Fat: 25 grams ▪ Calories: 278 ▪ **PREP TIME: 10 MINUTES** ▪ **COOK TIME: 20 MINUTES**, plus cooling ▪ **SERVINGS: 4**

If you prefer, press the crust mixture into ramekins or custard cups, rather than cupcake liners.

½ cup walnuts

3 tablespoons old-fashioned or quick-cooking oats

⅛ teaspoon ground cinnamon

½ teaspoon granular sugar substitute

1 tablespoon unsalted butter, melted

1 cup low-carb chocolate ice cream

4¼ cup heavy cream, whipped

2 teaspoons chopped walnuts

1 Heat oven to 350°F. Combine walnuts, oats, cinnamon, and sugar substitute in a food processor and pulse until finely ground. Add butter and pulse until blended.

2 Place 4 foil cupcake liners (or doubled paper liners) in a muffin tin. Divide nut mixture evenly among liners and press into bottom to form a crust. Bake until firm, about 20 minutes. Remove from oven and cool completely.

3 Scoop ¼ cup ice cream into each cup. Top with whipped cream and walnuts. Serve immediately.

compatible toppings for low-carb ice cream

Is it possible to build a low-carb sundae? Pick and choose carefully among toppings and it is indeed:

Sugar-free syrup, particularly caramel, chocolate, and fruit flavors, are an obvious choice.

You'll also find several recipes for chocolate and fruit sauces as part of a dessert recipe in this book that can be spooned atop a scoop. Check out

Chocolate Sauce (page 154), Caramelized Pear Topping (page 257), Black Forest Cherry Sauce (page 291), Puréed Raspberries (page 313), Raspberry Sauce (page 336), and Berry Sauce (page 352).

Toast a handful of chopped macadamia or other nuts to sprinkle on ice cream.

Finally, tally up the carbs to be sure your carb threshold can handle it.

Mixed Fruit with Indulgent Sauce

2
3 4

Per serving: **NET CARBS: 7 GRAMS** ▪ Carbohydrates: 11 grams ▪ Fiber: 4 grams ▪ Protein: 3 grams ▪ Fat: 6.5 grams ▪ Calories: 119 ▪ **PREP TIME: 15 MINUTES** ▪ **SERVINGS: 8**

Kiwis are ripe and ready to use when they feel soft but not mushy when gently squeezed. The skins are edible (try rubbing off the fuzz first), but this dish is prettier when the fruit is peeled. The sauce can be made ahead and refrigerated. Reheat it in the microwave.

¼ cup heavy cream

3 (1-ounce) Atkins Endulge Chocolate Candy Bars, broken into pieces

¼ teaspoon almond extract

1 pound strawberries, hulled and quartered (3 cups)

1½ cups fresh raspberries

2 kiwis, peeled, halved, and sliced

1 Pour cream into a 2-cup glass measure. Add chocolate. Cover with vented plastic wrap and microwave on full power for 30 seconds. Stir. If necessary, continue to microwave in 5- to 10-second increments, stirring after each one, until chocolate is melted and smooth. Add almond extract.

2 Combine strawberries, raspberries, and kiwis in a bowl; divide among 8 dessert dishes. Top each with a scant tablespoon of sauce and serve.

chocolate: secret health food

Chocolate boasts remarkable health benefits:

Dark chocolate contains compounds called catechins, which are thought to protect against heart disease and some forms of cancer. These are the same substances that make tea and red wine healthful.

Stearic acid is a saturated fat found in significant amounts in dark chocolate, which acts like a monounsaturated fat in the body and doesn't raise cholesterol levels. In fact, chocolate's antioxidants may actually help to decrease the risk of stroke and heart attack.

Adding milk to chocolate lowers the amount of catechins in each serving, but can supply respectable amounts of calcium. Look for unsweetened cocoa powder to use in recipes.

Mixed Fruit Crisp-Tart

Per serving: **NET CARBS: 8.5 GRAMS** ▪ Carbohydrates: 10.5 grams ▪ Fiber: 2 grams ▪ Protein: 1.5 grams ▪
Fat: 13 grams ▪ Calories: 155 ▪ **PREP TIME: 10 MINUTES** ▪ **COOK TIME: 30 MINUTES**, plus cooling ▪ **SERVINGS: 6**

Crisps don't usually have a crust, and tarts don't usually have a topping. This homey, rustic dessert combines the best of both.

1 (13- by 18-inch) sheet frozen whole-wheat phyllo dough, thawed

3 tablespoons unsalted butter, melted, divided

1 Granny Smith apple, cored and sliced

1 medium pear, cored and sliced

½ teaspoon ground cinnamon, divided

¼ cup old-fashioned or quick-cooking oats

¼ cup chopped walnuts

¼ cup chopped pecans

1 teaspoon granular sugar substitute

tip
Look for whole-wheat phyllo dough in the freezer case of some supermarkets and in natural foods stores. It has the same delicate flake as regular phyllo, but has a heartier flavor.

1 Heat oven to 350°F. Line an 8-inch square baking pan with foil, letting ends of foil hang over side of pan. Lay phyllo on a flat surface and brush with about 2 teaspoons of the butter. Fold phyllo in half, buttered side in, and place in pan. Fold sides of phyllo down to fit tightly into the bottom of the pan.

2 Combine apple, pear, and ¼ teaspoon of the cinnamon in a bowl. Transfer to pan, spreading evenly over phyllo.

3 Mix oats, walnuts, pecans, sugar substitute, and remaining ¼ teaspoon cinnamon in a bowl. Add remaining butter and stir to combine. Crumble over fruit. Bake until topping is crunchy and fruit has softened, 25 to 30 minutes. Cool slightly; use foil to lift tart out of pan to make cutting easier.

Creamy Lemon Bars

2 **3** **4** Per serving: **NET CARBS: 5 GRAMS** ▪ Carbohydrates: 7 grams ▪ Fiber: 2 grams ▪ Protein: 8.5 grams ▪ Fat: 17 grams ▪ Calories: 211 ▪ **PREP TIME: 20 MINUTES** ▪ **COOK TIME: 25 MINUTES,** plus cooling ▪ **SERVINGS: 8**

Cream cheese is the secret ingredient in these luscious snack bars. Use an 8-ounce block of cream cheese, and don't throw away the packaging while the cheese comes to room temperature. Similar to butter wrappers with tablespoon markings, cream cheese boxes have lines marking the ounces to make it easier to divide accurately. Be sure to use full-fat cream cheese. For photo, see page 147.

Crust:

4 tablespoons unsalted butter, at room temperature, plus more for buttering dish

¾ cup Atkins Quick Quisine Bake Mix

5 packets sugar substitute

3 ounces cream cheese, at room temperature

Filling:

5 ounces cream cheese, at room temperature

12 packets sugar substitute

2 large eggs, at room temperature

1½ teaspoons grated lemon zest

⅓ cup fresh lemon juice

1 Heat oven to 350°F. Butter an 8-inch square baking dish.

2 **For the crust:** Combine bake mix, butter, sugar substitute, and cream cheese in a bowl. Beat with an electric mixer until mixture comes together, about 2 minutes. (Mixture will be crumbly at first.) Pat dough onto bottom and ½ inch up sides of pan. Bake until just golden, 5 to 7 minutes.

3 **For the filling:** Beat cream cheese until smooth. Add sugar substitute, eggs, zest, and lemon juice and beat until smooth, scraping down sides of bowl as needed. Pour onto crust. Bake until set, 16 to 18 minutes. Cool to room temperature in pan. Chill before serving.

tip

To get the maximum juice out of a lemon or lime, use an electric or mechanical juicer. Or roll the lemons on a counter, which breaks up the lemon pulp, and then microwave them for 20 seconds to make the juice flow more easily before squeezing them.

Applesauce Pumpkin Muffins

2 **3 4** Per serving: **NET CARBS: 6.5 GRAMS** ▪ Carbohydrates: 10 grams ▪ Fiber: 3.5 grams ▪ Protein: 9.5 grams ▪ Fat: 12.5 grams ▪ Calories: 179 ▪ **PREP TIME: 10 MINUTES** ▪ **COOK TIME: 30 MINUTES,** plus cooling ▪ **SERVINGS: 12**

Applesauce and pumpkin add incomparable flavor and plenty of moisture to these muffins—wrap them individually in waxed paper and freeze to maintain freshness. Be sure to use canned pumpkin purée, not canned pumpkin pie filling, as the latter includes sweeteners.

Cooking spray

1½ cups Atkins Quick Quisine Bake Mix

1¼ cups granular sugar substitute

¾ cup chopped walnuts

1 teaspoon baking soda

2 teaspoons ground cinnamon

1 teaspoon ground ginger

½ teaspoon ground cloves

½ teaspoon salt

3 large eggs

6 tablespoons unsalted butter, at room temperature

½ cup canned pumpkin purée

½ cup no-sugar-added applesauce

⅓ cup water

1 Heat oven to 350°F. Lightly coat a 12-cup muffin tin with cooking spray, or line with paper or foil liners.

2 Combine bake mix, sugar substitute, walnuts, baking soda, cinnamon, ginger, cloves, and salt in a food processor; pulse until nuts are finely chopped. Add eggs, butter, pumpkin, applesauce, and water. Process until combined, scraping down sides as needed, about 10 seconds.

3 Scoop batter into muffin cups. Bake until a toothpick inserted in one of the center muffins comes out clean, 20 to 30 minutes. Cool completely in pan.

Amaretti Semifreddo

2 **3** **4** Per serving: **NET CARBS: 7.5 GRAMS** ▪ Carbohydrates: 11.5 grams ▪ Fiber: 4 grams ▪ Protein: 9.5 grams ▪ Fat: 29 grams ▪ Calories: 332 ▪ **PREP TIME: 10 MINUTES,** plus chilling ▪ **SERVINGS: 4**

This dessert's name means "half frozen" in Italian.

½ cup heavy cream

1 packet sugar substitute

½ teaspoon almond extract

12 low-carb amaretti cookies,
  finely crushed

Ground cinnamon

Combine cream, sugar substitute, and almond extract in a medium bowl. Beat with an electric mixer until stiff peaks form. Fold in crushed cookies. Spoon into 4 small bowls or custard cups. Freeze until partially frozen, about 20 minutes. Sprinkle with cinnamon before serving.

Chocolate Chocolate Chunk Meringues

2 **3** **4** Per serving: **NET CARBS: 4 GRAMS** ▪ Carbohydrates: 4.5 grams ▪ Fiber: 0.5 gram ▪ Protein: 1 gram ▪ Fat: 1.5 grams ▪ Calories: 31 ▪ **PREP TIME: 5 MINUTES** ▪ **COOK TIME: 2½ HOURS** ▪ **SERVINGS: 16** (1 cookie each)

These cookies have to dry in the oven for 2½ hours before they are ready to eat.

3 large egg whites

⅓ cup granular sugar substitute

¼ teaspoon cream of tartar

2 tablespoons unsweetened cocoa powder

3 ounces sugar-free chocolate, chopped into small pieces

1　Heat oven to 450°F. Line a large baking sheet with parchment.

2　Put egg whites in large bowl and beat with an electric mixer until foamy. Add sugar substitute, cream of tartar, and cocoa and beat until soft peaks form. Fold in chopped chocolate.

3　Drop 16 spoonfuls on baking sheet, leaving a small space between cookies (they do not spread). Put in oven and turn oven off. Leave cookies in the oven at least 2½ hours.

on the weekend

invite friends for brunch or plan a special meal for your family. Several of these 18 recipes, from make-ahead dishes that are at home on a buffet table to family favorites sure to entice sleepyheads from their beds, can double as dinner, too—either one of the waffle recipes or frittatas would make a fine supper.

Salmon-Asparagus Crêpes with Swiss Cheese Sauce, page 186

Chai, page 194

breakfasts
& brunches

Dr. Atkins was big on eggs for breakfast. He never became bored with them, probably because I was always looking for new ways to cook them! I often made him a frittata, using whatever vegetables were left over from the night before. The following recipes—with and without eggs—will help you keep your taste buds interested by looking beyond scrambled, sunny-side up, and hard-boiled, introducing you to creations you'll want to savor on lazy Sunday mornings: Caramelized Onions, Lox, and Egg Sandwich (page 192); Turkey Hash with Paprika Cabbage and Poached Eggs (page 176); and Mushroom and Vegetable Strata (page 180).

There are also plenty of options when you're in the mood for something sweeter or fruitier. All manner of waffles, muffins, pancakes, and morning cakes—even blintzes—banish the myth that a low-carb breakfast is synonymous with eggs. The good news is that many of these items can be prepared on the weekend, then frozen so you can enjoy a warm muffin with no-sugar-added jam or a homey waffle, even when you're short on time during the week.

You'll also find lovely beverages that are a welcome change from pricey coffee-bar drinks. Chai (page 194), Hot Mocha (page 195), and Hot Coco Cocoa (page 194) are ideal morning eye-openers. Or feel free to use decaffeinated coffee and tea in the recipes. If you're a juice drinker, consider adding just a splash of juice to a glass of ice-cold sparkling water in the A.M. instead of drinking pure juice, which is loaded with sugar and can send your blood sugar on a roller-coaster ride.

Always take the time to eat this most important meal of the day—the dishes in the following chapter can also help make it one of the most special!

Very Berry Bran Coffee Cake

Per serving: **NET CARBS: 10.5 GRAMS** ■ Carbohydrates: 16.5 grams ■ Fiber: 6 grams ■ Protein: 7.5 grams ■
Fat: 13 grams ■ Calories: 198 ■ **PREP TIME: 20 MINUTES** ■ **COOK TIME: 35 MINUTES** ■ **SERVINGS: 9**

3 4

This cake manages to be both delicate and hearty; chopped nuts and wheat bran give it a toothsome texture, but it is moist and tender.

¼ cup vegetable oil, plus more for pan

½ cup Atkins Quick Quisine Bake Mix

½ cup whole-wheat flour

1 cup unprocessed wheat bran

½ cup granular sugar substitute

1 tablespoon baking powder

½ teaspoon ground cinnamon

¼ teaspoon salt

½ cup toasted chopped pecans

2 large eggs

⅓ cup no-sugar-added strawberry jam

½ cup unsweetened soymilk

½ cup blueberries

½ cup raspberries

tip

For best results, make this coffee cake in the early summer when berries are at their best—and feel free to use all blueberries, all raspberries, or even add cut-up strawberries to the mix. Just use a total of about 1 cup.

1 Move a rack to the middle of the oven and heat to 350°F. Lightly coat a 9-inch square baking pan with vegetable oil.

2 Whisk together bake mix, flour, bran, sugar substitute, baking powder, cinnamon, salt, and pecans in a medium bowl; make a well in the center. Lightly beat eggs in another bowl, then whisk in jam, soymilk, and ¼ cup oil. Pour into well in dry ingredients and mix until combined; fold in berries.

3 Pour into pan and bake until a toothpick inserted in center of cake comes out clean, 30 to 35 minutes. Transfer cake to a rack and cool to room temperature. Cut cake into nine 3-inch square pieces and serve.

Just Peachy Bread Pudding

Per serving: **NET CARBS: 6 GRAMS** ▪ Carbohydrates: 10 grams ▪ Fiber: 4 grams ▪ Protein: 8.5 grams ▪
Fat: 13.5 grams ▪ Calories: 196 ▪ **PREP TIME: 20 MINUTES** ▪ **COOK TIME: 1 HOUR** ▪ **SERVINGS: 12**

*When fresh peaches are in season, use two of the juiciest, most aromatic ones you
can find in this pudding. If you use white peaches, toss them with a bit of lemon
juice—they're sweeter than their yellow counterparts. White peaches are more likely
to be clingstone, and the flesh can indeed cling to the stone. Look for freestone
peaches, which are easier to pit.*

1 teaspoon butter, at room
temperature

6 slices low-carb white bread, cut
into cubes

1¼ cups coarsely chopped
no-sugar-added frozen peaches
(6 ounces)

4 large eggs

1 cup heavy cream

⅓ cup granular sugar substitute

⅛ teaspoon ground nutmeg

1½ teaspoons vanilla extract

2 tablespoons sliced almonds

Boiling water, for pan

1 Heat oven to 350°F. Butter an 8-inch square baking dish; toss bread cubes
and peaches in baking dish.

2 Lightly beat eggs in a medium bowl, then whisk in cream, sugar substitute, nutmeg, and vanilla. Pour over bread and peaches and let soak for 10
minutes. Scatter almonds on top.

3 Set baking dish in a pan large enough to hold it. Put in oven and pour boiling water into outer pan to come halfway up the sides of baking dish. Bake
until a knife inserted in the center of the egg mixture comes out clean, 45 to
60 minutes. Serve hot.

tip

Unlike cakes, which can be tested with a toothpick or wooden skewer,
custards, flans, and puddings should be tested with a knife. It's acceptable
for a couple of small pieces of egg to cling to the knife, but if the knife is
coated with a thin layer of egg the pudding needs to cook longer.

Carrot Muffins with Currants

Per serving: **NET CARBS: 12.5 GRAMS** ▪ Carbohydrates: 16 grams ▪ Fiber: 3.5 grams ▪ Protein: 8 grams ▪
Fat: 13 grams ▪ Calories: 208 ▪ **PREP TIME: 15 MINUTES** ▪ **COOK TIME: 22 MINUTES** ▪ **SERVINGS: 12**

The grated carrot adds moisture as well as flavor to these muffins; they make a fine addition to a brunch buffet, or serve them with tea as an afternoon snack. For portion control, wrap them individually and freeze for up to a month; thaw them in the wrapping at room temperature.

Cooking spray

1 cup Atkins Quick Quisine Bake Mix

1 cup whole-wheat flour

1¼ teaspoons baking powder

1 teaspoon baking soda

½ teaspoon ground cinnamon

⅛ teaspoon ground nutmeg

⅛ teaspoon ground cloves

½ teaspoon salt

1½ cups granular sugar substitute

4 large eggs

½ cup sour cream

½ cup vegetable oil

1 medium carrot, peeled and grated (¾ cup)

3 tablespoons dried currants

1 Move a rack to the middle of the oven and heat to 350°F. Spray a 12-cup muffin tin with cooking spray.

2 Whisk together bake mix, flour, baking powder, baking soda, cinnamon, nutmeg, cloves, salt, and sugar substitute in a medium bowl; make a well in the center. Lightly beat eggs in another bowl, then whisk in sour cream and oil until combined; stir in carrot and currants. Pour into well in dry ingredients, mixing until just blended.

3 Scoop ⅓ cup batter into each muffin cup, filling it approximately two-thirds full. Bake until a toothpick inserted in one of the center muffins comes out clean, 20 to 22 minutes. Cool in pan for a few minutes so they will be easier to remove. Serve hot.

tip Dried currants are completely unrelated to the fresh currants you may see at farm stands and markets in the summer. Dried currants come from the champagne, or Corinth, grape (*currant* is a corruption of *Corinth*); these are sometimes called Zante grapes.

French Toast Bagels with Ginger Syrup

Per serving: **NET CARBS: 10.5 GRAMS** ■ Carbohydrates: 21.5 grams ■ Fiber: 11 grams ■ Protein: 29.5 grams ■ Fat: 19 grams ■ Calories: 304 ■ **PREP TIME: 15 MINUTES** ■ **COOK TIME: 15 MINUTES** ■ SERVINGS: 4

3 4

Bagels are firmer than bread, so they're an ideal texture for French toast. However, they have so much outer crust that it can be somewhat like eating the heels from a loaf of bread. If you like, cut a very thin slice off the top and bottom of the bagel before you cut it in half.

½ cup sugar-free pancake syrup

1 teaspoon grated peeled fresh ginger

4 large eggs

1 cup reduced-carb, whole-milk dairy beverage or ½ cup water mixed with ½ cup heavy cream

¼ cup granular sugar substitute

½ teaspoon ground cardamom

⅛ teaspoon ground nutmeg

4 low-carb plain bagels, cut in half

2 tablespoons unsalted butter, divided

2 tablespoons sour cream

1 Combine syrup and ginger in a small saucepan; bring to a boil over medium heat. Remove from the heat and keep warm.

2 Lightly beat eggs in a shallow bowl; whisk in dairy beverage, sugar substitute, cardamom, and nutmeg until combined.

3 Pierce bagel crusts in several places with a knife or fork to help absorb the egg mixture. Soak 4 bagel halves in egg mixture for 1 to 2 minutes.

4 Heat a large nonstick skillet or well-seasoned griddle over medium-low heat. Melt 1 tablespoon butter. Add bagels and cook until golden brown, about 3 minutes per side. Repeat with remaining butter and bagel halves.

5 Serve with sour cream and ginger syrup.

tip

Ginger will keep for a few weeks in the vegetable crisper of your refrigerator. You can also freeze it for up to a year; slice it thinly or grate it (measure into ½-teaspoon and 1-teaspoon portions) before freezing. Or peel and chop ginger, put it in a clean jar, and add white wine or dry sherry to cover. Refrigerate, taking out the ginger as you need it; then use the liquid in salad dressings.

Turkey Hash with Paprika Cabbage and Poached Eggs

2 3 4 Per serving: **NET CARBS: 8.5 GRAMS** ▪ Carbohydrates: 15 grams ▪ Fiber: 6.5 grams ▪ Protein: 49.5 grams ▪ Fat: 34 grams ▪ Calories: 567 ▪ **PREP TIME: 15 MINUTES** ▪ **COOK TIME: 20 MINUTES** ▪ **SERVINGS: 4**

Hash was originally devised as a meal to use up leftover roasts, so substitute whatever meat or poultry you have on hand for the turkey. Be sure the egg yolks remain somewhat soft—they add moisture to the hash.

4 slices low-carb white bread, cubed

4 teaspoons olive oil, divided

½ teaspoon salt, divided

½ teaspoon pepper, divided

¼ teaspoon Hungarian paprika

1 medium onion, chopped (¾ cup)

¼ small head green cabbage, shredded (2 cups)

1 pound chopped cooked turkey breast (3 cups)

½ teaspoon Worcestershire sauce

1 cup heavy cream

1 teaspoon vinegar

4 large eggs

2 tablespoons chopped fresh parsley

tip

Paprika comes from several countries, but aficionados say the best is Hungarian—and indeed, in Hungary paprika is used as a flavoring, not as a light dusting for color. Most paprika is sweet (though it is rarely labeled as such); there is also hot paprika and smoked paprika, which is a Spanish specialty.

1 Heat oven to 350°F. Put the bread cubes on a baking sheet, drizzle with 2 teaspoons of the olive oil, season with ¼ teaspoon of the salt and ¼ teaspoon of the pepper, and toss lightly. Bake until golden brown, about 7 minutes.

2 Meanwhile, heat remaining 2 teaspoons oil in a large nonstick skillet over medium-low heat. Add paprika and onion; cover and cook until onion is softened, about 3 minutes. Stir in cabbage, cover again, and continue cooking until vegetables are tender, about 7 minutes. Stir in turkey, Worcestershire sauce, cream, remaining ¼ teaspoon salt, and remaining ¼ teaspoon pepper. Cook, uncovered, stirring often, until heated through, about 5 minutes.

3 Meanwhile, fill a saucepan with about 2 inches of water. Set over medium heat and bring almost to a boil. Add vinegar and reduce heat so water is barely simmering. Crack eggs onto a plate, then slide into water one at a time. Cook until whites are set and yolks are still soft, 4 to 5 minutes.

4 To serve, spoon hash onto plates and top with eggs. Surround with croutons and sprinkle with parsley.

Chili Waffles with Salsa

1 2 3 4

Per serving: **NET CARBS: 7 GRAMS** ▪ Carbohydrates: 15.5 grams ▪ Fiber: 8.5 grams ▪ Protein: 25.5 grams ▪ Fat: 19.5 grams ▪ Calories: 323 ▪ **PREP TIME: 10 MINUTES** ▪ **COOK TIME: 16 MINUTES** ▪ **SERVINGS: 4**

This savory variation on the traditional breakfast entrée is versatile enough to double as dinner. Serve it with a slaw made of grated jicama, raw broccoli stems, and carrot.

1½ cups Atkins Quick Quisine Bake Mix

1 teaspoon chili powder

1 tablespoon baking powder

1 teaspoon salt

2 cups water

4 tablespoons unsalted butter, melted and cooled

3 large eggs, beaten

¼ cup chopped fresh cilantro

Cooking spray

¼ cup sour cream

½ cup salsa

1 Heat a waffle iron.

2 Combine bake mix, chili powder, baking powder, and salt in a bowl. Stir in water, butter, eggs, and cilantro to combine.

3 When waffle iron is hot, spray lightly with cooking spray. For each waffle, pour ½ cup batter into center of iron. Cook until iron stops steaming and waffle is crisp. Serve, topped with sour cream and salsa.

tip

Customize the heat level of your chili powder by making your own. Start with ¼ cup of ancho chili powder (mild), jalapeño (medium), or habanero (hot!) and mix with ½ to 1 teaspoon each of ground cumin, garlic powder, and oregano, and the tiniest pinch of cinnamon. Store in a dry container.

Bacon Waffles with Cheddar Sauce

1 2 3 4 Per serving: **NET CARBS: 6.5 GRAMS** ▪ Carbohydrates: 14 grams ▪ Fiber: 7.5 grams ▪ Protein: 36.5 grams ▪ Fat: 28 grams ▪ Calories: 440 ▪ **PREP TIME: 25 MINUTES** ▪ **COOK TIME: 25 MINUTES** ▪ **SERVINGS: 4**

In England and Wales, melted cheese is served over toast and called rarebit. In this version, bacon-studded waffles boost the flavor of the classic dish considerably.

1½ cups Atkins Quick Quisine Bake Mix

1 tablespoon baking powder

½ teaspoon salt

¼ teaspoon pepper

1½ cups water

3 tablespoons unsalted butter, melted and cooled

3 large eggs, beaten

4 slices bacon, cooked crisp, drained well, and crumbled

Cooking spray

1¼ cups Cheddar Sauce (Recipe follows)

2 scallions, thinly sliced (2 tablespoons)

1 Heat a waffle iron.

2 Combine bake mix, baking powder, salt, and pepper in a bowl. Stir in water, butter, eggs, and bacon to combine.

3 When waffle iron is hot, spray lightly with cooking spray. For each waffle, pour ½ cup batter into center of iron. Cook until iron stops steaming and waffle is crisp.

4 To serve, top with cheese sauce and scallions.

tip

Waffles freeze beautifully. Make a double batch for a "do ahead" party dish—just reheat in a 350°F oven or toaster.

Cheddar Sauce

1 2 3 4

Per serving: **NET CARBS: 1.5 GRAMS** ■ Carbohydrates: 1.5 grams ■ Fiber: 0 grams ■ Protein: 10 grams ■ Fat: 11.5 grams ■ Calories: 148 ■ **PREP TIME: 4 MINUTES** ■ **COOK TIME: 5 MINUTES** ■ **SERVINGS: 4**

Use this sauce for more than just our Bacon Waffles—try spooning it over steamed vegetables or steak. You can use white cheddar, but yellow makes for a prettier sauce.

1 cup reduced-carb, whole-milk dairy beverage or ½ cup water mixed with ½ cup heavy cream

¼ teaspoon salt

Pinch cayenne pepper

½ teaspoon Worcestershire sauce

1 teaspoon ThickenThin not/Starch thickener

1 cup grated extra-sharp cheddar cheese (4 ounces)

1 Mix dairy beverage, salt, pepper, Worcestershire sauce, and thickener in a small saucepan; let stand until thickened, about 3 minutes.

2 Heat over medium-high heat until liquid boils. Remove from heat and gradually stir in cheese until it melts and sauce is smooth. Keep warm over low heat or serve immediately.

eggs: eat the real thing

Eggs are an important part of doing Atkins. Research shows that high-cholesterol foods such as egg yolks are rarely responsible for elevated levels of blood cholesterol. One study, conducted by researchers at Michigan State University, showed that people who ate four or more eggs per week actually had lower levels of blood cholesterol than those who didn't eat eggs. The egg eaters obtained more of all nutrients except vitamin B6 and fiber than those who didn't eat eggs on a regular basis.

Egg yolks are an excellent source of nutrients. One large egg provides 70 calories, 6 grams of protein, about half a gram of carbohydrate, 4.5 grams of fat, and generous amounts of many vitamins and minerals, which is why it is often called the perfect food. It is one of the few foods that provides vitamin D, and the egg boasts respectable amounts of riboflavin, folate, vitamin A, and selenium.

Remember, as long as you are keeping your carbohydrate intake under control, you can eat healthy fats while lowering your total cholesterol.

Mushroom and Vegetable Strata

1 2 3 4 Per serving: **NET CARBS: 7 GRAMS** ▪ Carbohydrates: 12.5 grams ▪ Fiber: 5.5 grams ▪ Protein: 18 grams ▪ Fat: 31 grams ▪ Calories: 400 ▪ **PREP TIME: 45 MINUTES,** plus chilling ▪ **COOK TIME: 1 HOUR** ▪ **SERVINGS: 6**

Stratas are like savory bread puddings and are perfect for entertaining. They often must be prepared in advance, so you get the dirty work out of the way before guests arrive. They're adaptable and can work with a variety of ingredients; this one in particular is both pretty and delicious.

2 tablespoons unsalted butter, divided

2½ ounces sliced shiitake mushrooms (1 cup)

2½ ounces sliced cremini mushrooms (1 cup)

1 scallion, sliced (1 tablespoon)

2 cups chopped fresh spinach

¼ cup chopped roasted red pepper

6 slices low-carb white bread, cut into ¼-inch strips

1 (5.2-ounce) package Boursin cheese, crumbled

8 large eggs

1½ cups reduced-carb, whole-milk dairy beverage

½ teaspoon salt

¼ teaspoon pepper

Dash grated nutmeg

tip
About half of a 10-ounce bag of fresh spinach yields two cups; you can also use frozen spinach in this recipe. You'll need about half of a 10-ounce box of frozen spinach. Thaw it, and then squeeze out as much moisture as possible.

1   Melt 1 tablespoon of the butter in a large nonstick skillet over medium heat. When the foam subsides, add mushrooms and cook, stirring occasionally, until the liquid they release evaporates, 8 to 10 minutes. Add scallion and spinach and cook until spinach wilts, 2 to 3 minutes. Stir in roasted pepper, remove from the heat, and let cool.

2   Grease an 8-inch square baking dish with remaining tablespoon butter. Cover bottom of baking dish with one-third of the bread strips, then one-third of the mushroom mixture, then one-third of the cheese. Repeat layers twice.

3   Lightly beat eggs in a bowl, then whisk in dairy beverage. Season with salt, pepper, and nutmeg. Carefully pour over bread and vegetables, taking care that vegetables stay evenly distributed. Cover with plastic wrap, then set a similar-size dish on top of plastic to keep bread submerged. Refrigerate overnight.

4   Heat oven to 350°F. Remove dish that is weighting bread and plastic wrap. Bake until a knife inserted in the center comes out clean and strata is golden brown and puffed, about 1 hour. Serve immediately.

Asparagus, Pepper, and Goat Cheese Frittata

1 2 3 4 Per serving: **NET CARBS: 4.5 GRAMS** ▪ Carbohydrates: 6 grams ▪ Fiber: 1.5 grams ▪ Protein: 17 grams ▪ Fat: 27.5 grams ▪ Calories: 336 ▪ **PREP TIME: 20 MINUTES** ▪ **COOK TIME: 15 MINUTES** ▪ **SERVINGS: 4**

Let the water evaporate completely after the asparagus is cooked—if the asparagus is wet it will make the frittata watery.

4 tablespoons olive oil, divided

1 pound asparagus, trimmed and cut into ½-inch pieces (2½ cups)

8 large eggs

¾ cup roasted red peppers, patted dry and diced

1 (2-ounce) log goat cheese, crumbled

1 scallion, thinly sliced (1 tablespoon)

1 tablespoon chopped fresh parsley

½ teaspoon salt

¼ teaspoon pepper

¼ cup chopped fresh basil

tip

Scrambled eggs, whether in an omelet, frittata, or just plain, can become watery if cooked over too high a flame or cooked for too long, so keep tabs on the stove's temperature; remove the eggs from the heat when they are just set.

1 Heat a large ovenproof nonstick skillet over medium heat. Add 2 table-spoons of the olive oil and asparagus. Cover and cook, stirring occasionally, until asparagus is tender, 7 to 8 minutes. Uncover to let moisture evaporate, then remove from heat and let asparagus cool.

2 Lightly beat eggs in a medium bowl. Add asparagus, red peppers, cheese, scallion, parsley, salt, and pepper. Mix gently.

3 Heat skillet over medium heat for 1 to 2 minutes. Add remaining 2 table-spoons oil and heat for 30 seconds, then pour in egg mixture and cook, stirring gently from the outside edge to the center until eggs are set on the sides and soft in the center, 6 to 7 minutes.

4 Heat broiler. Place skillet under broiler and cook until eggs are set, 1 to 2 minutes. Loosen frittata from pan. Place a large plate upside down over pan and, using both hands with pot holders, invert the frittata. Sprinkle with basil and serve.

Sweet Potato, Sausage, and Feta Frittata

3 4

Per serving: **NET CARBS: 10 GRAMS** ■ Carbohydrates: 11.5 grams ■ Fiber: 1.5 grams ■ Protein: 23.5 grams ■ Fat: 31.5 grams ■ Calories: 424 ■ **PREP TIME: 20 MINUTES** ■ **COOK TIME: 20 MINUTES** ■ **SERVINGS: 4**

Use your favorite sausage in this dish—besides breakfast links cut into thin slices, try crumbled bulk sausage or even Italian-style sausage.

4 no-sugar-added breakfast
   sausage links (4 ounces)

3 tablespoons olive oil, divided

½ small (4-ounce) sweet potato,
   peeled and diced (½ cup)

1 small onion, diced (½ cup)

½ cup drained canned diced
   tomatoes

8 large eggs

2 tablespoons chopped fresh
   parsley

4 ounces feta cheese, crumbled
   (1 cup)

¼ teaspoon salt

¼ teaspoon pepper

tip

To measure canned diced tomatoes accurately, pour off the liquid (you may wish to save it to use in another recipe), then spoon the tomatoes into a measuring cup.

1 Cook sausage in a large ovenproof nonstick skillet over medium heat until lightly browned and cooked through, 5 to 6 minutes. Cut into ¼-inch slices. Transfer to a medium bowl.

2 Heat 1 tablespoon of the oil in skillet. Add sweet potato and cook, stirring occasionally, until it begins to brown, about 5 minutes. Add onion and continue to cook, stirring occasionally, until onion is soft, about 5 minutes longer. Add tomatoes and cook 2 minutes longer. Remove mixture from heat, add to the sausage, and let cool to room temperature.

3 Lightly beat eggs in a medium bowl. Add sausage, vegetables, parsley, cheese, salt, and pepper, mixing gently.

4 Heat skillet over medium heat for 1 to 2 minutes. Add remaining 2 tablespoons oil and heat for 30 seconds. Pour in egg mixture and cook, stirring gently from the outside edge to the center, until the eggs are set on the sides and soft in the center, 6 to 7 minutes.

5 Heat broiler. Place skillet under broiler and cook until eggs are set, 1 to 2 minutes. Loosen frittata from sides of pan. Place a large plate upside down over the pan and, using two hands with pot holders, invert the frittata. Serve immediately.

Apple-Cinnamon Oatmeal Pancakes

Per serving: **NET CARBS: 11.5 GRAMS** ▪ Carbohydrates: 17.5 grams ▪ Fiber: 6 grams ▪ Protein: 25.5 grams ▪
Fat: 17 grams ▪ Calories: 309 ▪ **PREP TIME: 10 MINUTES** ▪ **COOK TIME: 15 MINUTES** ▪ **SERVINGS: 4**

Sweet-tart apple and chewy oatmeal add texture and flavor to these hot cakes. For crispier cakes, use butter on the griddle rather than oil.

1½ cups low-carb pancake and waffle mix

¼ teaspoon ground cinnamon

3 tablespoons vegetable oil, plus more for griddle

3 large eggs, beaten

1¼ cups water

⅓ cup unflavored instant oatmeal (see Tip)

½ large apple, peeled, cored, and finely chopped (¾ cup)

½ cup sugar-free pancake syrup

1 Whisk together pancake mix, cinnamon, oil, eggs, water, oatmeal, and apple in a bowl until blended. Allow batter to stand for 2 to 3 minutes.

2 Heat a nonstick skillet or griddle over low heat. Coat lightly with oil and pour in ¼ cup batter per pancake. Cook until edges are dry and top is covered with bubbles, 1½ to 2 minutes; flip and cook until done, about 1 minute longer.

3 Serve pancakes as they are done, topped with syrup, or keep warm in a 200°F oven.

tip

Be sure your instant oatmeal is the kind that comes in a cylinder-shaped canister, not a packet. The former is simply precooked oats, but the latter contains sugar and other additives.

Salmon-Asparagus Crêpes with Swiss Cheese Sauce

2 3 4 Per serving: **NET CARBS: 8 GRAMS** ▪ Carbohydrates: 11 grams ▪ Fiber: 3 grams ▪ Protein: 36 grams ▪ Fat: 29 grams ▪ Calories: 544 ▪ **PREP TIME: 1 HOUR** ▪ **COOK TIME: 30 MINUTES** ▪ **SERVINGS: 6**

When you buy salmon, ask for it to be cut from the belly, not from the tail. The fillets are thicker and meatier and will cook more uniformly. Cuts from the tail taper and cook more rapidly as a result. For photo, see page 169.

1 lemon

6 cups water

1½ teaspoons salt

1 teaspoon peppercorns

1 to 1¼ pounds salmon fillet

4 teaspoons unsalted butter, divided

1 pound **asparagus,** trimmed and cut into ¾-inch pieces (2½ cups)

¼ teaspoon salt

⅛ teaspoon pepper

2 cups Swiss Cheese Sauce (Recipe follows)

12 Herbed Crêpes (see Tip, page 188)

tip

Blintzes and crêpes are both thin pancakes, rolled with sweet or savory fillings. A crêpe is served just after filling, while a blintz is sautéed before serving.

1 Cut lemon in half; squeeze juice into a large, straight-sided skillet or shallow saucepan. Add water, salt, and peppercorns and bring to a boil. Reduce heat to medium-low. Add salmon and simmer until cooked through, about 10 minutes. Transfer salmon to a plate; flake with a fork.

2 Heat oven to 375°F. Butter a 9- by 13-inch baking dish with 2 teaspoons of the butter.

3 Melt remaining 2 teaspoons butter in a nonstick skillet over medium heat. Add asparagus and season with salt and pepper; cover and cook, stirring occasionally, until tender, 6 to 8 minutes. Uncover and continue cooking until liquid evaporates, 1 to 2 minutes longer.

4 Add 1 cup of the cheese sauce to asparagus and bring to a boil. Remove from heat and gently stir in the salmon. Let cool for 5 minutes.

5 Set crêpes on a flat surface. Spoon ⅓ cup salmon mixture on each crêpe and roll up; set, seam-side down, in baking dish. Cover top of crêpes with remaining sauce and bake until sauce is bubbling and edges are lightly browned, 25 to 30 minutes.

Swiss Cheese Sauce

1 2 3 4 Per serving: **NET CARBS: 1.5 GRAMS** ▪ Carbohydrates: 1.5 grams ▪ Fiber: 0 grams ▪ Protein: 4 grams ▪ Fat: 14 grams ▪ Calories: 148.5 ▪ **PREP TIME: 5 MINUTES** ▪ **COOK TIME: 5 MINUTES** ▪ **SERVINGS: 6** (⅓ cup each)

Based loosely on the classic Mornay sauce, Swiss Cheese Sauce is versatile; serve it with eggs, fish and shellfish, or chicken.

1 tablespoon ThickenThin not/Starch thickener	3 ounces Swiss cheese, shredded (1 cup)
1 cup heavy cream	¼ teaspoon salt
¼ cup dry white wine	Pinch cayenne pepper
1 (8-ounce) bottle clam juice	Pinch grated nutmeg

1 Combine thickener and cream in a bowl; let stand for 3 minutes.

2 Meanwhile, bring wine to a boil in a small saucepan and let boil until almost completely evaporated, about 3 minutes. Add broth and thickened cream and return to a boil.

3 Remove from heat and stir in cheese until melted. Season with salt, cayenne, and nutmeg. Use right away or cover and refrigerate for up to three days.

tip

If you'll be making this sauce to serve with chicken, replace the clam juice with lower sodium chicken broth.

Basic Crêpes

1 **2** **3** **4** Per serving: **NET CARBS: 5 GRAMS** ▪ Carbohydrates: 7.5 grams ▪ Fiber: 2.5 grams ▪ Protein: 13 grams ▪ Fat: 8.5 grams ▪ Calories: 158 ▪ **PREP TIME: 10 MINUTES** ▪ **COOK TIME: 15 MINUTES** ▪ **SERVINGS: 6**

A seven-inch skillet is the perfect size to use when making these crêpes. If yours is six inches in diameter, use a little less batter; if it's eight inches, use a bit more. To freeze, layer crêpes between sheets of waxed paper. Wrap in plastic wrap, then in a freezer bag. Thaw at room temperature before using.

¾ cup Atkins Quick Quisine Bake Mix

½ teaspoon salt

1½ cups unsweetened soymilk

4 large eggs

2 tablespoons unsalted butter, melted and cooled

Cooking spray

1 Combine bake mix and salt in a medium bowl and make a well. Pour in soymilk, eggs, and butter, whisk until combined. Strain through a sieve, pressing any lumps through strainer with a rubber spatula. Let stand 5 minutes.

2 Heat a small nonstick skillet over medium heat, then remove from the heat and spray with cooking spray. Pour ¼ cup batter in the center of the pan, immediately tilting pan to evenly coat the bottom. Cook until light brown, about 45 to 60 seconds. Depending on the recipe you are using, either flip crêpe and cook 15 seconds longer or transfer to a plate and cover with a piece of waxed paper. Continue, spraying the skillet as needed, until all batter is used.

tip

For Sweet Crêpes, add 1 to 2 tablespoons granulated sugar substitute and 1 teaspoon vanilla extract with the soymilk.

For Herbed Crêpes, add 2 tablespoons chopped fresh parsley, 2 tablespoons chopped fresh chives, and ¼ teaspoon pepper after straining batter.

Cheese Blintzes

3 4 Per serving: **NET CARBS: 12.5 GRAMS** ▪ Carbohydrates: 15.5 grams ▪ Fiber: 3 grams ▪ Protein: 27.5 grams ▪
Fat: 23 grams ▪ Calories: 383 ▪ **PREP TIME: 15 MINUTES** ▪ **COOK TIME: 10 MINUTES** ▪ **SERVINGS: 6**

Blintzes are thin pancakes traditionally made with buckwheat flour; they're usually filled with creamy cottage or ricotta cheese and are briefly sautéed after they're filled and rolled.

2½ cups creamed cottage cheese

1 (4-ounce) package cream cheese
 or ½ (8-ounce) package

5 tablespoons granular sugar
 substitute

½ teaspoon almond extract

⅛ teaspoon ground cinnamon

2 large egg yolks

12 Sweet Crêpes, cooked on one
 side only (see Tip, page 188)

Cooking spray

¾ cup no-sugar-added jam or fruit
 purée (such as applesauce)

¼ cup sour cream

1 Combine cottage cheese, cream cheese, sugar substitute, almond extract, cinnamon, and egg yolks in a medium bowl, whisking until well blended.

2 Lay crêpes, cooked side up, on flat surface. Spoon ¼ cup cheese mixture near the top of the crêpe, then fold envelope fashion (see page 92). Place blintz, seam-side down, on wax paper and continue until all blintzes are folded.

3 Heat a nonstick skillet or griddle over medium-low heat. Spray with cooking spray and add blintzes, seam-side down. Cook until golden brown, about 2 minutes per side. Serve with jam or fruit purée and sour cream.

Egg, Cheese, and Canadian Bacon Sandwiches

2 3 4 Per serving: **NET CARBS: 10 GRAMS** ▪ Carbohydrates: 21.5 grams ▪ Fiber: 11.5 grams ▪ Protein: 35 grams ▪ Fat: 18 grams ▪ Calories: 321 ▪ **PREP TIME: 15 MINUTES** ▪ **COOK TIME: 15 MINUTES** ▪ **SERVINGS: 4**

These are as far from fast-food egg-and-bacon sandwiches as filet mignon is from a burger. Basting the eggs with butter while they cook adds incomparable flavor.

1 (6-ounce) package Canadian bacon (8 thin slices)

¼ cup grated cheddar cheese (1 ounce)

4 teaspoons fresh chopped chives, divided

1 large tomato, cut into 8 thin slices

Salt and pepper

4 teaspoons unsalted butter, divided

4 low-carb plain bagels, split and toasted

4 large eggs

¼ teaspoon salt

¼ teaspoon pepper

1 teaspoon Hungarian paprika

1 Lay 4 Canadian bacon slices on a plate and top each with ½ tablespoon cheese and ½ teaspoon chives. Arrange 2 tomato slices over cheese for each. Season tomato with salt and pepper, another ½ teaspoon chives, and another ½ tablespoon cheese. Top with remaining 4 slices Canadian bacon.

2 Melt 2 teaspoons of the butter in a large nonstick skillet over medium heat. When butter begins to foam, add Canadian bacon stacks and cook until cheese is melted and bacon begins to brown, 1 to 2 minutes per side. Transfer to bagel bottoms and keep warm.

3 Melt remaining 2 teaspoons butter in skillet. Crack eggs on a plate and slide them in; sprinkle with salt, pepper, paprika, and remaining 2 teaspoons chives. Reduce heat to low, cover, and fry eggs, spooning butter over yolks 2 or 3 times, until eggs are set, about 4 minutes. Set 1 egg on top of each Canadian bacon stack, top with the remaining bagel halves, and serve.

Caramelized Onions, Lox, and Egg Sandwich

2
3 **4**
Per serving: **NET CARBS: 11 GRAMS** ▪ Carbohydrates: 22.5 grams ▪ Fiber: 11.5 grams ▪ Protein: 38.5 grams ▪
Fat: 23 grams ▪ Calories: 382 ▪ **PREP TIME: 10 MINUTES** ▪ **COOK TIME: 15 MINUTES** ▪ **SERVINGS: 4**

Lox is a type of smoked salmon that is brine-cured before smoking. It's quite salty and pairs with sweet caramelized onions to make an elegant egg sandwich.

4 teaspoons unsalted butter, divided

1 large onion, sliced

8 large eggs

2 tablespoons heavy cream

Salt and pepper

4 ounces lox, cut into bite-size pieces

4 low-carb plain bagels, toasted

2 tablespoons chopped chives (optional)

1 Melt 2 teaspoons of the butter in a large nonstick skillet over medium heat. Add onion and cook, stirring frequently, until golden brown, 8 to 10 minutes. Transfer to a plate.

2 Meanwhile, lightly beat eggs and cream in a bowl until just combined. Reduce heat to medium-low and add remaining 2 teaspoons butter to skillet. When foam subsides, pour in egg mixture. Season with a pinch of salt and a bigger pinch of pepper (the lox will add saltiness) and cook, stirring constantly, until eggs are almost set, 4 to 5 minutes.

3 Add onion and lox to eggs and continue cooking until eggs are set and lox is heated through. Set bagel halves on plates and top with eggs; sprinkle with chives, if desired.

improving on mother nature?

Here is a quick tour through the dairy case to look at some of the "designer" eggs, to help you decide if you are willing to pay the extra freight.

Brown eggs come from hens with red feathers and earlobes. Red breeds tend to be larger than white chickens, which lay white eggs, so they require more food, hence their higher price. Brown and white eggs are identical nutritionally.

Organic eggs come from hens that eat a diet free from pesticides, herbicides, and commercial fertilizers. Organic eggs cost more to produce; this cost is passed along to you. Organic eggs contain the same amount of nutrients as generic eggs, but they contain fewer chemicals. Don't be too impressed if carton makes the claim "hormone-free." Virtually all eggs sold in the U.S. meet this claim.

"Free-range" conjures images of chickens scratching for feed in front of the chicken coop—which may or may not be how the birds actually live. It's legal to sell eggs from caged hens as "free-range" if the chickens have access to open areas, even if these areas are indoors. Free-range eggs are nutritionally identical to generic eggs.

Fertile eggs will hatch if they are incubated, but they are not any more nutritious. Fertile eggs do not keep as well as unfertilized eggs, and they require special handling, which increases their cost.

Nutritionally enhanced eggs. The nutrient makeup of an egg can be changed by manipulating a hen's diet to make it higher in omega-3 fatty acids, for example, or another nutrient. Depending on the brand, enhanced eggs can provide 100 to 200 milligrams of omega-3s per eggs; a 3-ounce serving of Atlantic salmon contains 165 milligrams of omega-3s. If you're not fond of fish, omega-3-enhanced eggs can be an important source of this essential fatty acid.

Chai

1	2
3	4

Per serving: **NET CARBS: 2 GRAMS** ▪ Carbohydrates: 2 grams ▪ Fiber: 0 grams ▪ Protein: 1.5 grams ▪ Fat: 1 gram ▪ Calories: 22 ▪ **PREP TIME: 5 MINUTES** ▪ **COOK TIME: 15 MINUTES** ▪ **SERVINGS: 4**

Chai is original to India. It's easy to make and so delicious. For photo, see page 169.

1 (⅛-inch-thick) slice fresh ginger

1 (1-inch) piece cinnamon stick

3 whole green cardamom pods

2 whole cloves

6 black peppercorns

2½ cups water

½ cup reduced-carb, whole-milk dairy beverage

2 tablespoons granular sugar substitute

4 teaspoons loose black tea

Combine all ingredients except tea in a saucepan; bring to a boil. Turn off heat, cover, and steep for 10 minutes. Uncover; return to a boil. Stir in tea; remove from heat, cover, and steep for 5 minutes. Strain into heated cups.

Hot Coco Cocoa

2
3	4

Per serving: **NET CARBS: 7.5 GRAMS** ▪ Carbohydrates: 11 grams ▪ Fiber: 3.5 grams ▪ Protein: 4.5 grams ▪ Fat: 38.5 grams ▪ Calories: 386 ▪ **PREP TIME: 5 MINUTES** ▪ **COOK TIME: 5 MINUTES** ▪ **SERVINGS: 2**

Coconut milk adds a subtle flavor but distinctively rich consistency to cocoa.

3 tablespoons unsweetened cocoa powder

¼ cup granular sugar substitute

½ cup unsweetened coconut milk

½ cup heavy cream

1 cup water

½ teaspoon vanilla extract

2 tablespoons whipped cream

1 teaspoon finely grated Atkins Endulge Chocolate Candy Bar

Put cocoa powder and sugar substitute in a saucepan. Whisk together coconut milk, cream, and water in a bowl. Stir a bit of liquid into cocoa mixture, then gradually stir in remaining liquid. Cook over medium heat, stirring constantly, until hot. Add vanilla extract. Pour into cups.

Hot Mocha

1 2 3 4 Per serving: **NET CARBS: 3 GRAMS** ▪ Carbohydrates: 4 grams ▪ Fiber: 1 gram ▪ Protein: 1 gram ▪ Fat: 4.5 grams ▪ Calories: 56 ▪ **PREP TIME: 5 MINUTES** ▪ **COOK TIME: 8 MINUTES** ▪ **SERVINGS: 4**

Forget the overpriced mocha concoctions at the local coffee bar. This special treat is a snap to prepare, especially if you brewed extra coffee in the morning. Use unflavored coffee; those with nut or other flavors can interfere with the seasonings in this blend. Choose decaf if you or your guests are sensitive to the effects of caffeine.

4 cups brewed coffee or decaf (24 ounces)

2 (3-inch) cinnamon sticks

3 tablespoons granular sugar substitute

3 teaspoons orange zest, divided

2 tablespoons unsweetened cocoa powder

3 tablespoons heavy cream, whipped

1 Heat coffee, cinnamon, sugar substitute, and 2 teaspoons of the orange zest in an enameled or stainless steel saucepan until hot but not boiling. Reduce heat to keep at a simmer and steep for 8 minutes. Strain through a mesh strainer into a coffeepot and keep hot.

2 In a heatproof glass measuring cup, make a paste of the cocoa powder and a little of the coffee. Gradually stir in 1 cup coffee until blended, and pour this back into coffeepot. Pour coffee into 4 heated mugs. Top with whipped cream, then sprinkle with remaining teaspoon orange zest.

tip

Don't rely on the markings on your coffeemaker to get four cups of coffee—most coffeemakers and coffee brewing instructions figure that a "cup" of coffee is five to six ounces. For this recipe, you'll want to use a standard 8-ounce cup measure.

smart shoppers stock up on meat and poultry when the price is marked down, then use them to prepare make-ahead meals. If you're tempted to buy enough chicken or ground beef to feed an army but aren't sure what to do with it, remember Chicken Tortilla Pie and Bolognese Sauce or Pork and Beef Chili. Spend an hour or so cooking on the weekend in between chores and freeze—we provide instructions. On a night you come home and realize you've nothing in the pantry or fridge, take out one of your prepared dishes. Many can be heated straight from the freezer to the oven (although they will need a bit more time in the oven).

Vegetable and Tofu Lasagne, page 204

make-ahead *meals*

remember being in your mother's—or grandmother's—kitchen as a child? If it was like my mother's kitchen, it was often filled with the tantalizing aromas of savory stews, homemade soups, and soul-satisfying casseroles. But all these comfort foods are full of carbohydrates, right? Wrong. Then they're too time-consuming to make these days, right? Wrong again. Of course, I must admit that I am not necessarily up for making Bolognese Sauce every night. But when the weekend comes, that's a whole different kettle of fish. In fact, one of my favorite weekend activities is to spend a day cooking up a storm, creating dishes to enjoy in the week to come—or to pop in the freezer for those nights when I come home too tired to cook.

Satisfying casseroles can be adapted easily to the Atkins lifestyle, particularly now that there are low-carb breads, pastas, and tortillas on the shelves of virtually every supermarket. If you had despaired of ever eating lasagne again, our Vegetable and Tofu Lasagne (page 204) will be a pleasant surprise: Strips of thin-sliced zucchini team up with low-carb noodles to bring the carb count under control. Another modified classic, our Shepherd's Pie (page 200), is made with mashed cauliflower instead of just potatoes. You'll also find old standards like chili and stuffed peppers, Atkins-style.

Stews are perfect make-ahead meals. In fact, the flavors improve after "marrying" for a few days. That stew you made on Saturday afternoon will be better than ever by Tuesday night. But don't assume that make-aheads have to be time-consuming. Our Quick Beef Stew (page 211) takes less than an hour to prepare and cook.

Here's another weekend cooking perk: Cooking with a friend or relative is a special way to spend quality time together.

Bolognese Sauce

1 2 3 4 Per serving: **NET CARBS: 5 GRAMS** ■ Carbohydrates: 7 grams ■ Fiber: 2 grams ■ Protein: 17.5 grams ■ Fat: 37.5 grams ■ Calories: 457 ■ **PREP TIME: 10 MINUTES** ■ **COOK TIME: 2¼ HOURS** ■ **SERVINGS: 6** (⅓ cup each)

Although this version of Bolognese is made with beef, it can also be made with ground pork or ground veal. The preparation time is minimal, but this sauce benefits from a long, slow simmering; it's quite rich, which is why the serving size seems small. The recipe can be doubled easily and frozen in batches to be used for several easy dinners.

2 tablespoons olive oil	1¼ pounds lean ground beef
2 tablespoons unsalted butter	1 cup dry white wine
½ cup finely chopped onion	1 (14½-ounce) can diced tomatoes
1 small carrot, finely chopped (½ cup)	½ teaspoon salt
1 small celery stalk, finely chopped (⅓ cup)	¼ teaspoon pepper
	1 cup heavy cream

tip

The wine you use for cooking should be one you'd serve with the meal, so pass by the stuff in the vinegar aisle of your supermarket. Not only is it inferior wine to begin with, but it often contains salt or other additives.

1 Heat oil and butter over medium-low heat in a large saucepan. Add onion, carrot, and celery and cook, stirring occasionally, until vegetables are tender, 10 minutes. Add beef and cook, stirring to break up clumps, until no longer pink, about 5 minutes. Drain off fat.

2 Add wine. Increase heat to high and simmer until almost evaporated, 7 to 10 minutes. Stir in tomatoes. When mixture starts to bubble, reduce heat to low. Partially cover and simmer, stirring occasionally, until liquid evaporates, about 1½ hours. Stir in salt, pepper, and cream and simmer 15 minutes longer.

To freeze: Cool completely. Place in airtight plastic container, allowing some space at the top for expansion.

To reheat: Defrost overnight in refrigerator. Place in saucepan and reheat, stirring occasionally, over medium heat until hot, about 15 minutes. Serve with low-carb pasta.

Shepherd's Pie

Per serving: **NET CARBS: 10.5 GRAMS** ▪ Carbohydrates: 13 grams ▪ Fiber: 2.5 grams ▪ Protein: 23 grams ▪
Fat: 29 grams ▪ Calories: 407 ▪ **PREP TIME: 20 MINUTES** ▪ **COOK TIME: 1 HOUR** ▪ **SERVINGS: 8**

*Traditionally made with leftover roast lamb, shepherd's pie can be made with
ground lamb, too; just brown it well. If you use beef, it's no longer shepherd's pie but
cottage pie.*

Topping:

**3 small (¼-pound) baking
potatoes,** peeled and quartered

1 small (1½-pound) cauliflower,
trimmed and cut into small florets
(3 cups)

⅓ cup heavy cream

4 tablespoons unsalted butter

½ teaspoon salt

¼ teaspoon pepper

Meat Layer:

1 tablespoon vegetable oil

1 small onion, coarsely chopped
(½ cup)

1 small carrot, coarsely chopped
(½ cup)

1 small celery stalk, coarsely
chopped (⅓ cup)

**2 pounds raw ground lamb or
leftover cooked lamb,** trimmed
and finely chopped

¼ cup oil-cured black olives,
pitted and coarsely chopped
(2 ounces)

**1 (14½-ounce) can lower sodium
beef broth**

**1½ teaspoons ThickenThin
not/Starch thickener**

**1 tablespoon chopped fresh thyme
or 1 teaspoon dried**

½ teaspoon salt

¼ teaspoon pepper

1 tablespoon butter

**3 tablespoons grated Parmesan
cheese**

1 **For the topping:** Put potatoes and cauliflower in a large saucepan; cover
with cold salted water and bring to a boil. Reduce heat to low and simmer
until vegetables are tender, about 12 minutes. Drain. Mash with a potato
masher or put through a potato ricer. Add cream, butter, salt, and pepper.
Stir just until smooth. Adjust seasonings to taste.

2 **For the meat layer:** Meanwhile, heat oil in a large skillet over medium-
low heat. Add onion, carrot, and celery; cook, stirring occasionally, until

vegetables are tender, about 10 minutes. Add lamb and increase heat to medium. Cook, stirring and breaking up meat with a spoon, until lightly brown, about 10 minutes. Drain excess fat.

3 Heat oven to 400°F. Add olives, broth, thickener, thyme, and salt and pepper. Increase heat to medium-high, bring to a boil, and cook until sauce reduces and begins to thicken, about 10 minutes. Adjust seasonings to taste. Transfer mixture to a heat- and freezer-resistant 3- to 4-quart baking dish. Spread mashed vegetables evenly over top. Dot with butter and dust with cheese. Bake until bubbly, about 20 minutes. Put pie under broiler for a minute or two to brown, if desired.

To freeze: If freezing, do not bake ahead. Assemble in baking dish as instructed in recipe. Cool completely. Wrap well with heavy-duty foil.

To reheat: Defrost overnight in refrigerator. Unwrap and bake at 400°F until bubbly, about 20 minutes. Or, remove from freezer, remove foil, and bake at 400°F until bubbly and hot, 40 to 45 minutes.

tip

If you're a fan of mashed potatoes, remember this recipe. The topping (and step 1) yields a terrific version, with 8.5 grams of Net Carbs per serving. If this recipe is made without potatoes, it works for Induction and Ongoing Weight Loss.

Stuffed Peppers

2 Per serving: **NET CARBS: 9 GRAMS** ▪ Carbohydrates: 13 grams ▪ Fiber: 4 grams ▪ Protein: 34 grams ▪

3 4 Fat: 9.5 grams ▪ Calories: 466 ▪ **PREP TIME: 20 MINUTES** ▪ **COOK TIME: 40 MINUTES** ▪ **SERVINGS: 4**

For a festive presentation, use four different-colored sweet peppers—red, yellow, orange, and green. Choose a baking dish in which the peppers fit snugly; you want them to stand upright so the filling doesn't spill out.

3 tablespoons olive oil, plus more
  for baking dish

4 medium bell peppers

½ cup finely chopped onion

1¼ pounds ground turkey

½ cup low-carb tomato sauce

1 small (4-ounce) zucchini or
  yellow squash, diced or cut into
  half-moons (1 cup)

¾ teaspoon salt

¾ teaspoon dried thyme

¼ teaspoon pepper

2 large eggs, lightly beaten

¼ cup walnuts, coarsely chopped

tip

Blanching the peppers before stuffing them cuts down on the baking time so that the filling does not overcook.

1 Heat oven to 375°F. Oil a small baking dish.

2 Cut the top ½ inch from peppers; set aside. Scoop out seeds with a spoon. Bring a large pot of salted water to a boil; blanch peppers for 5 minutes. Remove and run under cold water. Pat dry inside and out.

3 Meanwhile, finely chop pepper tops. Heat oil in large skillet over medium-high heat. Add chopped peppers and onion and cook, stirring frequently, until softened, about 3 minutes. Add turkey and cook, stirring, until meat is no longer pink, about 5 minutes. Stir in tomato sauce, zucchini or yellow squash, salt, thyme, and pepper; continue to cook, stirring occasionally, until most of the liquid evaporates, 5 to 8 minutes. Remove pan from heat and stir until mixture cools slightly, about 1 minute. Stir in eggs.

4 Spoon mixture into peppers, place in baking dish. Sprinkle walnuts over filling. Bake until peppers are tender and filling is hot, about 20 minutes.

To freeze: Cool cooked stuffed peppers completely. Wrap in heavy-duty foil or place in freezer containers.

To reheat: Defrost overnight in refrigerator. Place in oiled baking dish into which they fit snugly. Cover with foil and reheat at 350°F until hot, about 30 minutes. Or, remove from freezer, remove foil, place in oiled baking dish, and bake at 350°F until hot, 40 to 50 minutes.

Vegetable and Tofu Lasagne

3 4 Per serving: **NET CARBS: 16.5 GRAMS** ▪ Carbohydrates: 20.5 grams ▪ Fiber: 4 grams ▪ Protein: 24 grams ▪ Fat: 21.5 grams ▪ Calories: 361 ▪ **PREP TIME: 35 MINUTES** ▪ **COOK TIME: 45 MINUTES** ▪ **SERVINGS: 8**

To make this a lower-carb vegetarian dish, substitute zucchini slices for some of the lasagne noodles. If you like, make the first layer all noodle, the second layer all zucchini, and the the third layer all noodle. Go all zucchini and this works for Ongoing Weight Loss. Using tofu instead of ricotta is an easy way to get soy protein into your diet. For photo, see page 197.

4 ounces whole-wheat lasagne noodles (about 6 noodles)

3 medium (6-ounce) zucchini, cut lengthwise into ¼-inch slices

2 tablespoons olive oil, plus more for baking dish

8 ounces sliced mushrooms (2 cups)

1½ cups low-carb tomato sauce

¼ teaspoon red pepper flakes

1 (16-ounce) package soft tofu

1 (10-ounce) box frozen leaf spinach, thawed and squeezed dry

1 large egg

1 cup grated Parmesan cheese, divided

½ teaspoon salt

1 pound mozzarella cheese, grated (4 cups)

1 Heat oven to 400°F. Lightly oil a 9- by 13-inch baking dish.

2 Bring a large pot of salted water to a boil. Add noodles and cook for 6 minutes; add zucchini and cook until noodles are *al dente* and zucchini is soft, about 4 minutes longer. Drain. Rinse under cold water and set aside.

3 Heat oil in a large skillet over medium heat. Add mushrooms and cook, stirring, until softened, about 5 minutes. Stir in tomato sauce and red pepper flakes. Remove from heat.

4 In a food processor fitted with a metal blade, process tofu, spinach, egg, ¼ cup of the Parmesan, and ½ teaspoon salt.

5 Arrange one-third of noodles and zucchini in an even layer in baking dish. Top with half of the tofu mixture, spreading in an even layer. Add one-third of mozzarella and one-third of tomato sauce. Arrange another one-third noodles and zucchini in a single layer over sauce. Spread with remaining

tofu mixture and another one-third each of sauce and mozzarella. Finish with remaining noodles and zucchini, sauce, and mozzarella. Sprinkle with remaining ¾ cup Parmesan cheese.

6 Bake until cheese is melted and sauce is bubbly, about 30 minutes. Let cool slightly before cutting and serving.

To freeze: Cool baked lasagne completely. Wrap well with heavy-duty foil.

To reheat: Defrost overnight in refrigerator. Cover with foil and reheat in 350°F oven until hot, about 30 minutes. Or remove from freezer, unwrap, and bake in 350°F oven until hot and bubbly, about 60 minutes.

safe thawing

Once you've frozen a food, you need to thaw it safely. Bacteria grow most rapidly between 40°F and 140°F, known as the "danger zone." Never thaw food at room temperature. Instead, thaw it in the refrigerator (allow up to 3 days, depending upon size), in the microwave (only if you are planning to use the food immediately after thawing), or immersed in cold water (change the water when it becomes lukewarm).

Is it possible to refreeze food once it's thawed? Technically, yes, if a few very specific conditions are met. However, freezing and thawing are tough on foods and can compromise their texture. The bigger problem is food poisoning. If foods are not thawed properly, refrozen properly, and then rethawed properly, bacteria can grow rapidly. You're better off preparing the thawed food.

Baked Ziti with Sausage and Peppers

2 Per serving: **NET CARBS: 10 GRAMS** ▪ Carbohydrates: 15.5 grams ▪ Fiber: 5.5 grams ▪ Protein: 33 grams ▪
3 4 Fat: 25 grams ▪ Calories: 426 ▪ **PREP TIME: 15 MINUTES** ▪ **COOK TIME: 1 HOUR** ▪ **SERVINGS: 6**

When the ziti is done baking, run it under the broiler for a minute or two, if you like a crusty top.

1½ pounds hot or sweet Italian-style pork sausage

2 medium red bell peppers or 1 red and 1 green bell pepper, diced (2 cups)

4 garlic cloves, minced (2 teaspoons)

1 (28-ounce) can diced tomatoes

¼ teaspoon red pepper flakes

Salt

3 ounces whole-wheat ziti or low-carb penne (1 cup)

1½ cups grated mozzarella cheese (6 ounces)

1 cup grated Parmesan cheese

tip

Green bell peppers are traditional in sausage and peppers, but red ones add considerable nutrition—they contain generous amounts of beta carotene and more than double the vitamin C of green peppers.

1 Heat a large skillet over medium heat. Add sausage and cook, turning, until brown on all sides, about 10 minutes. Prick sausage with a fork as it cooks to release juices. Remove sausage from skillet and let cool slightly; cut into ½-inch slices. (It's okay if sausage is not completely cooked through.)

2 Pour off all but 1 tablespoon fat. Add peppers and garlic; cook, stirring frequently, until softened, about 5 minutes. Return sausage to pan; add tomatoes and red pepper flakes. Bring to a boil, reduce heat to medium-low, and cook until thickened, 15 to 20 minutes. Season with salt to taste.

3 Meanwhile, cook pasta according to package directions. Drain, then stir into sausage and pepper mixture. Heat oven to 375°F.

4 Spread half of the sausage and pepper mixture in a 2½- to 3-quart baking dish. Cover with half of the mozzarella and Parmesan cheeses. Spread remaining sausage and peppers over cheeses. Cover with remaining cheeses. Bake until bubbly, about 15 minutes.

To freeze: If freezing, do not bake ahead. Assemble in baking dish as instructed in recipe. Cool completely. Wrap well with heavy-duty foil.

To reheat: Bake at 375°F until bubbly, about 15 minutes. Slide under broiler for 2 minutes if a crunchy top is desired. Or remove from freezer, unwrap, and bake in a 375°F oven until hot and bubbly, 35 to 40 minutes.

Baked Pasta with Ham and Swiss Chard

2 **3** **4** Per serving: **NET CARBS: 8 GRAMS** ▪ Carbohydrates: 13 grams ▪ Fiber: 5 grams ▪ Protein: 41.5 grams ▪ Fat: 42 grams ▪ Calories: 594 ▪ **PREP TIME: 30 MINUTES** ▪ **COOK TIME: 40 MINUTES** ▪ **SERVINGS: 6**

Jarlsberg is a Norwegian cheese; it looks like Swiss cheese—it has large holes—but its flavor is sweeter than Swiss and not as nutty. If your supermarket has a cheese section, you're likely to find it there, but use Swiss cheese if you can't.

3 tablespoons unsalted butter, divided, plus more for baking dish

1½ cups low-carb penne or rotini

½ pound Swiss chard, leaves cut into thin strips and stems chopped

2 medium leeks, white part only, rinsed thoroughly, halved, and thinly sliced (1 cup)

¾ teaspoon salt, divided

1½ cups heavy cream

½ cup water

1½ tablespoons ThickenThin not/Starch thickener

6 ounces Jarlsberg cheese, grated (1⅓ cups)

½ cup grated Parmesan cheese

1 teaspoon Dijon mustard

¼ teaspoon pepper

¾ pound ham, cut into ½-inch cubes

½ cup low-carb bread crumbs

1 Heat oven to 375°F. Lightly butter a 2½- to 3-quart baking dish. Cook pasta according to package directions.

2 Melt 2 tablespoons of the butter in large skillet over medium-low heat. Stir in Swiss chard, leeks, and ¼ teaspoon salt. Increase heat to medium and cook, stirring occasionally, until vegetables are tender, 7 to 8 minutes.

3 Whisk together cream, water, and thickener in a large saucepan. Set over medium heat and cook, whisking occasionally, until mixture simmers and thickens, 5 minutes. Add Jarlsberg and Parmesan cheeses; stir until blended. Stir in mustard, remaining ½ teaspoon salt, and pepper.

4 Add vegetables, pasta, and ham to cheese sauce and stir to combine. Transfer to baking dish, cover with foil, and bake 20 minutes.

5 Melt remaining tablespoon butter in a small skillet over medium heat. Add bread crumbs and cook until they begin to brown, about 2 minutes. Uncover pasta, sprinkle with bread crumbs, and bake until golden and bubbly, about 5 minutes longer.

To freeze: If freezing, do not bake ahead. Transfer pasta mixture to baking pan. Do not add crumb topping. Cool completely. Wrap well with heavy-duty foil.

To reheat: Defrost overnight in refrigerator. Cover with foil and bake at 375°F for 20 minutes. Make buttery crumb topping and sprinkle over pasta. Bake until golden and bubbly, about 5 minutes more. Or remove from freezer and bake in a 375°F oven for 40 minutes. Remove foil, top with crumb topping, and bake until golden and bubbly, 10 to 20 minutes longer.

tip

If you don't have low-carb bread crumbs on hand, put 1½ slices of low-carb bread in a toaster oven set at 300°F for 10 minutes to dry it out. Pulverize toasted bread in a food processor to make crumbs; store leftover crumbs in the freezer, in a tightly sealed jar.

Pork and Beef Chili

Per serving: **NET CARBS: 10.5 GRAMS** ▪ Carbohydrates: 15.5 grams ▪ Fiber: 5 grams ▪ Protein: 45 grams ▪

3 **4** Fat: 39 grams ▪ Calories: 604 ▪ **PREP TIME: 15 MINUTES** ▪ **COOK TIME: 1 HOUR** ▪ **SERVINGS: 6** (generous 1 cup each)

If you like, add hot sauce to taste at the table to make this dish as spicy as you please.

2 tablespoons vegetable oil

½ cup chopped onion

1½ pounds ground beef

1½ pounds ground pork

2 to 3 tablespoons chili powder

1 to 2 finely chopped fresh or canned jalapeños

2 teaspoons ground cumin

1 teaspoon dried oregano

1 (14½-ounce) can lower sodium beef broth, plus 1 can water

1 (14½-ounce) can diced tomatoes

1 teaspoon salt

½ teaspoon pepper

1 (15-ounce) can kidney beans, drained and rinsed

Grated cheddar cheese, for serving (optional)

Hot pepper sauce (such as Tabasco)

tip

Look beyond generic "chili powder," which is usually a blend of dried peppers and spices like cumin—some supermarkets sell chili powders made solely from ancho, chipotle, or even habanero chilies. These have a purer flavor than blends and their heat level varies considerably, but they can become muted during cooking.

1 Heat oil in a large saucepan over medium heat. Add onion and cook until almost tender, about 3 minutes. Add beef and pork and cook until no longer pink, about 8 minutes. Drain off excess fat.

2 Stir in chili powder, jalapeños, cumin, and oregano to coat meat. Add broth, tomatoes, salt, and pepper. Bring to a boil; reduce heat to low, partially cover, and simmer about 20 minutes. Stir in beans and simmer, uncovered, until flavors are blended and broth has thickened, about 15 minutes longer. Serve with grated cheddar cheese, if desired. Add hot sauce to taste.

To freeze: Cool chili completely. Place in airtight plastic container, allowing some space at the top for expansion.

To reheat: Defrost overnight in refrigerator. Place in saucepan and reheat, stirring occasionally, over medium heat until hot, about 20 minutes.

Quick Beef Stew

3 4 Per serving: **NET CARBS: 20 GRAMS** ▪ Carbohydrates: 26.5 grams ▪ Fiber 6.5 grams ▪ Protein: 45 grams ▪ Fat: 17 grams ▪ Calories: 442 ▪ **PREP TIME: 20 MINUTES** ▪ **COOK TIME: 35 MINUTES** ▪ **SERVINGS: 4** (1½ cups each)

A warming bowl of beef stew is just the ticket on a cold winter's night, but the best ones seem to take hours, if not days, to prepare—most stew meat is tough and requires long, slow cooking to become tender. Sirloin steak cooks quickly in this colorful, flavorful stew, and it can be on the table in less than an hour.

2 tablespoons olive oil, divided

1½ pounds sirloin steak, trimmed of fat and cut into ½-inch chunks

½ cup chopped onion

1 (14½-ounce) can whole tomatoes, drained

1 (14½-ounce) can lower sodium beef broth

2 teaspoons ThickenThin not/Starch thickener

1 small (4-ounce) sweet potato, peeled and diced

1 small (4-ounce) parsnip, peeled and diced

1 (10-ounce) box frozen peas, thawed (2 cups)

1 tablespoon chopped fresh thyme or ¼ teaspoon dried thyme

½ teaspoon salt

¼ teaspoon pepper

1 Heat 1 tablespoon oil in a large heavy skillet over medium-high heat. Add steak and brown on all sides. Transfer to a bowl.

2 Add remaining tablespoon oil and onion to skillet. Reduce heat to medium and cook, stirring occasionally, until softened, about 3 minutes. Crush tomatoes with your hands and add along with broth. Whisk in thickener. Stir in sweet potato and parsnip; bring to a boil. Reduce heat to low, cover, and simmer until vegetables are tender, 20 to 25 minutes.

3 Stir in peas, thyme, salt, and pepper. Cook until peas are heated through, 3 to 4 minutes. Return steak and any juices to skillet. Stir until heated through.

To freeze: Cool stew completely. Place in an airtight plastic container, allowing some space at the top for expansion.

To reheat: Defrost overnight in refrigerator. Place in saucepan and reheat, stirring occasionally, over medium heat until hot, about 20 minutes.

Chicken Tortilla Pie

2
3 **4**

Per serving: **NET CARBS: 9.5 GRAMS** ▪ Carbohydrates: 16.5 grams ▪ Fiber: 7 grams ▪ Protein: 53 grams ▪
Fat: 32 grams ▪ Calories: 560 ▪ **PREP TIME: 45 MINUTES** ▪ **COOK TIME: 1½ HOURS** ▪ **SERVINGS: 4**

*Wonderfully fragrant and deliciously savory, this puts the casseroles of your youth to
shame. Serve it with a salad of sliced red onion and oranges on a bed of greens.*

Cooking spray

1½ pounds boneless, skinless
chicken, finely chopped, or
ground chicken

1 teaspoon salt

⅛ teaspoon pepper

2 tablespoons olive oil

1 large onion, chopped (1 cup)

2 garlic cloves, minced
(1 teaspoon)

1 tablespoon chili powder

½ teaspoon dried oregano

1 (10-ounce) can diced tomatoes
with green chilies

1 cup chicken broth

1 small piece bay leaf

¾ cup grated cheddar cheese
(3 ounces)

¾ cup grated Monterey Jack
cheese (3 ounces)

4 (8-inch) low-carb tortillas, cut in
quarters

3 tablespoons sour cream

1 Spray an 8-inch square baking dish with cooking spray. Season the chicken
with salt and pepper.

2 Heat a large skillet over medium heat. Add oil and heat for 30 seconds.
Add chicken and cook, stirring frequently, until lightly browned, 7 to 8 minutes. Add onion and cook until translucent, 2 to 3 minutes. Add garlic and
cook until fragrant, 30 to 45 seconds. Reduce heat to medium-low, add chili
powder and oregano, and cook, stirring frequently, until meat is coated and
spices are aromatic, 2 to 3 minutes.

3 Add tomatoes, broth, and bay leaf; bring to a boil. Reduce heat, cover,
and simmer until chicken is tender, 25 to 30 minutes. Transfer to a bowl and
let cool.

4 Heat oven to 350°F.

5 Mix cheeses together. Spread 1⅓ cups chicken mixture in the baking dish
and top with 8 tortilla quarters. Add another 1⅓ cups chicken mixture,
topped with half of the cheese mixture. Top with remaining 8 tortilla quar-

ters and cover evenly with remaining chicken. Dot with sour cream, and cover with remaining cheese. Bake until cheeses are melted and sauce is bubbly, about 30 minutes.

To freeze: If freezing, do not bake ahead. Place a piece of waxed paper over the cheese and cover with foil. Place dish in a large freezer bag and freeze for up to 1 month.

To reheat: Defrost pie overnight in the refrigerator. Remove from freezer bag and bake at 350°F for 1 hour, then remove the foil and waxed paper and bake until top is golden brown, 10 minutes longer. Or remove from freezer, unwrap, and bake at 350°F until bubbly and hot, 1 to 1¼ hours. Cut into 4 squares and serve.

the low-carb freezer

Besides vegetables, you'll want to keep certain staple items in the freezer for convenience.

Whole grains contain oils that can go rancid quickly at room temperature. Keep low-carb breads; whole grains (including wild rice), and whole-grain flours in the freezer to help maintain freshness.

Frozen fruit, from berries to cantaloupe, mango, and peaches—all unsweetened, of course—are easy to find in most markets. Buy them in resealable bags and pour out only what you need before thawing (if necessary) for use in sauces, smoothies, and baked goods. Use them straight from the freezer in lieu of ice cubes in a tall drink on a hot day, or in a shake or smoothie.

Try freezing cooked meat. Raw meat contains more water in its cells than cooked meat. As the meat freezes, the water forms ice crystals. When the food thaws, the crystals can tear the cell walls, causing the water to escape. (This is why frozen meats usually have more liquid in the tray or packaging than meats that have never been frozen.) Leftover ham, roast chicken, and turkey all freeze beautifully and can be used in dishes like Chicken Tortilla Pie (see above) or quesadillas, with minimal loss of flavor or texture.

Make double or triple batches of soups and tomato sauces. Measure into freezer bags, then refrigerate. When cold, stack flat in your freezer so they form tiles. (They'll thaw more rapidly than fat little bundles.)

Hearty Italian Vegetable Soup with Tiny Veal Meatballs

2 **3 4** Per serving: **NET CARBS: 6.5 GRAMS** ▪ Carbohydrates: 13 grams ▪ Fiber: 6.5 grams ▪ Protein: 33 grams ▪ Fat: 10 grams ▪ Calories: 271 ▪ **PREP TIME: 20 MINUTES** ▪ **COOK TIME: 15 MINUTES** ▪ **SERVINGS: 6** (1½ cups each)

This satisfying soup is full of meatballs and plenty of vegetables—in fact, you might find that it's hearty enough without the pasta.

3 ounces low-carb rotini

1½ pounds ground veal

¼ cup grated Parmesan cheese, plus more for serving

2 large eggs, beaten

2¼ teaspoons salt, divided

½ teaspoon pepper, divided

2 (14½-ounce) cans lower sodium beef broth (4 cups)

1 small carrot, cut into ¼-inch dice (½ cup)

4 ounces fresh green beans, cut into ½-inch lengths (1 cup)

1 (14½-ounce) can whole tomatoes, drained

1 pound escarole, trimmed and thinly sliced crosswise (4 cups)

tip

Escarole is a part of the endive family, though it's less bitter than Belgian endive or curly endive (sometimes called frisée). Look for it near the lettuces and use it in soups or sautés. It's particularly tasty with cannellini beans.

1 Cook pasta according to package directions. Drain.

2 Mix together veal, cheese, eggs, 1¼ teaspoons of the salt, and ¼ teaspoon of the pepper in a large bowl. With wet hands, roll 1 to 1½ teaspoons of the mixture into balls and place on a large plate.

3 Put broth in a large saucepan. Add carrot and green beans and bring to a boil over high heat. Reduce heat to medium-low and simmer for 5 minutes.

4 Crush tomatoes with your hands and add them along with meatballs to broth. Bring to a boil and simmer until meatballs are cooked through, about 4 minutes. Stir in escarole and pasta. Season with remaining teaspoon salt and ¼ teaspoon pepper; cook until escarole wilts, about 1 minute. Serve with additional Parmesan cheese.

To freeze: Cool soup completely. Place in airtight plastic container, allowing some space at the top for expansion.

To reheat: Defrost overnight in refrigerator. Place in saucepan and reheat, stirring occasionally, over medium heat until hot, about 15 minutes.

freeze your own veggies

It's a wise cook who stockpiles boxes and bags of frozen produce. They're prewashed and trimmed, often pre-cooked, and are a convenient solution to hectic meals.

Although some frozen vegetables can be of high quality, others can warrant their reputation as a less than ideal substitute for fresh produce. When you buy frozen foods at the supermarket, you really have no way of knowing whether the items were kept at the appropriate temperature between packing plant and freezer case. Foods that thaw and are refrozen can suffer in texture. Freezing vegetables yourself guarantees optimum freshness and quality, and it isn't hard at all.

Start by choosing tender, young vegetables. Those that are high in water, such as cucumbers and onions, don't freeze well.

Blanch vegetables first. Plunge washed and trimmed vegetables into vigorously boiling water. Cook briefly, then cool them immediately and thoroughly. Drain and pat completely dry.

Freeze vegetables before you pack them. Line a jelly-roll pan with waxed paper, then arrange veggies in a single layer and put in the freezer. After they're frozen, transfer to heavy-duty freezer bags, pressing out as much air as possible. Label and date bags.

Use this chart to determine how long to blanch vegetables—remember to begin timing when the water returns to a boil.

Asparagus: 2 minutes for pencil-thin spears, 4 minutes for thick spears

Beans, green or wax (1½-inch pieces): 3 minutes

Broccoli (1½-inch pieces): 3 minutes

Cauliflower (1½-inch pieces): 3 minutes (add 1 tablespoon vinegar to water)

Collard greens, kale, Swiss chard: 2 minutes

Eggplant (⅓-inch slices): 4 minutes (add ½ cup lemon juice to water)

Sugar snap and snow peas: 1½ minutes for small pods, 2 minutes for large pods.

Yellow squash and zucchini (1½-inch pieces): 3 minutes

take a world tour

without leaving your backyard or terrace: Moroccan lamb, Italian pork, Vietnamese skewered beef, and North Carolina barbecue can be on your table tonight. Whether you're looking for a quick dish like Grilled Swordfish Kebabs or Grilled Butterflied Chicken with Herbs or one that's smoked slowly over coals, something casual like quesadillas or a show-stopping beef tenderloin, you'll find it here.

Grilled Tomato "Bruschetta," page 228
Grilled Sesame Asparagus, page 224
Brine-Spiced Grilled Shrimp, page 222

the great
outdoors

atkins cuisine lends itself perfectly to grilling, barbecuing, and smoking, and this relaxed way of eating is also a terrific way to spend quality time with friends and family during the warmer months of the year—or year-round if you are fortunate enough to live in the Sun Belt. On weekends at our country house, Dr. Atkins and I loved the combined experience of cooking outdoors followed by eating alfresco. Somehow, whatever is on the menu tastes better when it is served on the deck instead of in the dining room.

Part of what makes this cooking method so effortless is that the grill imparts its own delightful flavor to fresh whole foods, letting their natural taste shine through. After all, what could be tastier than a fire-grilled salmon steak or a juicy burger cooked on the patio? So you can certainly keep it simple—time-consuming basting and complicated marinades are rarely necessary. However, we also offer a slew of recipes to suit all of your barbecuing needs, including old standbys like Quick and Tasty Barbecued Chicken (page 238) and authentic fare such as Real North Carolina Barbecue Pork (page 230) with two sauces, as well as more exotic dishes like Italian Pork Chops with Leeks (page 226) and Grilled Duck with Pepper Jelly Glaze (page 234).

And don't forget—the grill isn't just for fish, meat, and poultry. Vegetables prepared on the grill are satisfying and delicious. Try Grilled Portobellos with Blue Cheese Butter (page 236), Grilled Tomato "Bruschetta" (page 228), and Grilled Sesame Asparagus (page 224). Even fruits, such as peaches or pineapple, are superb when you toss them on the grill for a few minutes, or try our Grilled Plums with Butter Pecan Ice Cream (page 153).

Vietnamese-Style Beef Skewers

2
3 4
Per serving (including slaw): **NET CARBS: 9 GRAMS** ▪ Carbohydrates: 13.5 grams ▪ Fiber: 4.5 grams ▪
Protein: 39.5 grams ▪ Fat: 16.5 grams ▪ Calories: 357 ▪ **PREP TIME: 35 MINUTES,** plus cooling ▪
MARINATE TIME: OVERNIGHT ▪ COOK TIME: 15 MINUTES ▪ SERVINGS: 4

Fish sauce is a thin, dark brown, very pungent sauce common in Vietnamese cooking; you may see it marketed as nuoc mam *or* nam pla *in the Asian food section of the supermarket. Although jalapeños and serrano chilies are associated with Mexican cooking, hot peppers are also used in Asian dishes; these two are readily available in most markets. For photo, see page 221.*

2 tablespoons dried lemongrass

1 tablespoon granular sugar substitute

1 tablespoon fish sauce, *nam pla*

1 tablespoon dark sesame oil

1 cup unseasoned rice wine vinegar

2 garlic cloves, minced (1 teaspoon)

1 jalapeño or serrano chile, seeded and minced (1 teaspoon)

1 teaspoon grated fresh ginger

1 tablespoon soy sauce

½ cup fresh lime juice

1½ pounds round or sirloin steak

4 cups Asian Slaw (Recipe follows)

2 tablespoons chopped peanuts

1 bunch chives, for garnish

8 (10-inch) wooden skewers

tip

Choose dried lemongrass with a fine texture like dillweed; otherwise, you'll want to crush it before adding it to the marinade.

1 Combine lemongrass, sugar substitute, fish sauce, oil, and vinegar in medium bowl. Stir in garlic, chile, ginger, soy sauce, and lime juice. Stir to combine.

2 Put steak in a zip-close plastic bag and pour in marinade. Close bag and turn several times to coat meat. Refrigerate 12 to 24 hours, turning bag over occasionally.

3 Soak skewers in water for 30 minutes. Prepare a medium-high-heat grill.

4 Remove meat from marinade and discard marinade; slice steak thinly. Weave steak strips onto skewers. Grill until done to taste, 1 to 2 minutes per side for medium.

5 To serve, scoop ½ cup of the slaw onto each plate, set skewers over slaw, and sprinkle with peanuts. Serve garnished with long pieces of chives.

Asian Slaw

2 **3** **4** Per serving: **NET CARBS: 7.5 GRAMS** ▪ Carbohydrates: 11.5 grams ▪ Fiber: 4 grams ▪ Protein: 2.5 grams ▪ Fat: 0.5 gram ▪ Calories: 51.5 ▪ **PREP TIME: 15 MINUTES,** plus cabbage salting time ▪ **SERVINGS: 4**

If you don't have champagne vinegar, use white wine vinegar or rice vinegar instead. Be sure to choose an unseasoned rice vinegar, however, because some brands contain added sugars.

1 small (1½-pound) head
  cabbage, thinly sliced (9 cups)

2 tablespoons kosher or sea salt

1 bunch chives, finely chopped
  (⅓ cup)

1 tablespoon chopped fresh mint

1 tablespoon chopped fresh
  cilantro

1 tablespoon chopped fresh basil

⅓ cup champagne vinegar

Toss cabbage with salt and let stand until wilted, about 30 minutes. Rinse cabbage and squeeze dry. Put in a medium bowl and toss with chives, mint, cilantro, basil, and vinegar.

tip

Kosher salt is completely free from any additives (table salt, for example, is fortified with iodine). Its crystals are large, but they are designed to melt almost instantly when they come into contact with liquid because kosher salt is used to brine poultry and meats.

Brine-Spiced Grilled Shrimp

1	2
3	4

Per serving: **NET CARBS: 0 GRAMS** ▪ Carbohydrates: 0 grams ▪ Fiber: 0 grams ▪ Protein: 19 grams ▪ Fat: 5.5 grams ▪ Calories: 133 ▪ **PREP TIME: 20 MINUTES** ▪ **MARINATE TIME: 1½ HOURS** ▪ **COOK TIME: 8 MINUTES** ▪ **SERVINGS: 6**

When they're cooked properly, grilled shrimp are a true treat. Unfortunately, most grilled shrimp come off the coals tough and rubbery. But brining the shrimp helps keep them plump and moist—and the additional spices add a subtle flavor. For photo, see page 217.

½ cup kosher salt

2 tablespoons coriander seeds

1 tablespoon black peppercorns

1 tablespoon granular sugar substitute

6 cups water

2 pounds extra-large shrimp (16 to 20 per pound)

2 tablespoons canola oil

6 (10-inch) wooden skewers

tip
Larger shrimp may be sold deveined— try to find them in your freezer section to save yourself some time.

1 Mix together salt, coriander, peppercorns, and sugar substitute in a large bowl. Add water.

2 With kitchen shears or a paring knife, cut down the center of shrimp peels along the outer curve until you reach the last section before the tail. Leave peel intact. Remove vein. Add shrimp to brine mixture; refrigerate for 1½ hours.

3 Soak skewers in water for 30 minutes. Prepare a medium-high-heat grill.

4 Remove shrimp from brine and pat dry. Thread shrimp onto skewers, threading each shrimp through the tail and top to prevent them from spinning on the skewers. Brush with oil. Grill shrimp until bright pink, 2 to 3 minutes per side.

Foolproof Grilled Fish

1 2 3 4 Per serving: **NET CARBS: 0.5 GRAM** ■ Carbohydrates: 0.5 gram ■ Fiber: 0 grams ■ Protein: 33 grams ■ Fat: 13 grams ■ Calories: 258 ■ **PREP TIME: 10 MINUTES** ■ **COOK TIME: 10 MINUTES** ■ **SERVINGS: 4**

Although this recipe calls for grouper, you can use any thick fillet. If necessary, adjust the cooking time: Figure 10 minutes per inch of thickness.

½ teaspoon ground cumin

½ teaspoon ground coriander

½ teaspoon kosher salt

⅛ teaspoon pepper

4 (6-ounce) grouper fillets, 1 inch thick

4 tablespoons mayonnaise

1 Prepare a medium-high-heat grill.

2 Mix cumin, coriander, salt, and pepper in a small bowl; season the fish.

3 Spread mayonnaise over top of each fillet. Grill fillets, mayonnaise-side up, for 6 minutes. Turn and cook until opaque, 2 to 4 minutes longer.

tip

Even experienced grill masters find the prospect of grilling fish more than a bit daunting. Three tricks: Start with a very clean grill to prevent fish from sticking, coat the fish with mayonnaise to help keep it moist, and use a wire basket so fish is easier to turn and does not stick to grill.

Grilled Sesame Asparagus

Per serving: **NET CARBS: 1.5 GRAMS** ▪ Carbohydrates: 3 grams ▪ Fiber: 1.5 grams ▪ Protein: 2.5 grams ▪ Fat: 13 grams ▪ Calories: 132 ▪ **PREP TIME: 5 MINUTES** ▪ **COOK TIME: 8 MINUTES** ▪ **SERVINGS: 4**

Grilled asparagus make great finger food at a party, but this can also double as a side dish for grilled fish or chicken. Using wooden skewers to make a "raft" makes turning easier and helps to prevent any from slipping through the grate. Use a mixture of black and white sesame seeds for dramatic effect. For photo, see page 217.

8 (6-inch) wooden skewers

1 tablespoon olive oil

2 **garlic cloves**, minced (1 teaspoon)

1 pound **fat asparagus**, woody ends trimmed

¼ teaspoon kosher salt

⅛ teaspoon pepper

2 tablespoons dark sesame oil

2 tablespoons sesame seeds

tip

Sesame seeds come in several colors. Creamy white seeds are the most common, but reddish brown are also cultivated. The red variety is most often used to make sesame oil, though you may see it in some specialty markets or natural foods stores. Black sesame seeds are smaller than the white ones and slightly more bitter.

1   Prepare a medium-high-heat grill. Soak skewers in water for 30 minutes.

2   Mix oil and garlic in a small bowl. Line up 5 to 6 asparagus. Insert skewer 2 to 3 inches below tips. Slide another skewer through them about 1 inch from root end. Repeat with remaining asparagus and skewers. Brush each "raft" with garlic oil and season with salt and pepper.

3   Grill asparagus for 5 minutes; turn and cook until tender and lightly charred, 5 minutes longer. Transfer rafts to a platter and remove skewers. Drizzle with sesame oil and scatter on sesame seeds.

Eggplant "Pizzas"

2 3 4 Per serving: **NET CARBS: 1 GRAM** ▪ Carbohydrates: 2 grams ▪ Fiber: 1 gram ▪ Protein: 4 grams ▪ Fat: 9.5 grams ▪ Calories: 107 ▪ **PREP TIME: 20 MINUTES** ▪ **COOK TIME: 10 MINUTES** ▪ **SERVINGS: 6**

Japanese eggplants are straight and very slender; most are a deep purple, though you may find some that are white or striped. They are slightly sweeter than American eggplant and tend to be less porous, which means they'll absorb less oil.

1 (6-ounce) Japanese eggplant, cut into 12 slices about ⅓ inch thick

1 tablespoon olive oil

1 tablespoon chopped fresh thyme

1 tablespoon chopped fresh chives

4 ounces (2½-inch piece) log-style goat cheese

1 tablespoon walnut or extra virgin olive oil

⅛ teaspoon salt

⅛ teaspoon pepper

1 tablespoon finely chopped walnuts

tip Cutting goat cheese with a knife can be frustrating—the cheese is so soft that it flattens and crumbles. You're much more likely to get tidy results using unwaxed dental floss, believe it or not. Wrap the floss around your fingers and pull it through the cheese.

1 Prepare a medium-high-heat grill.

2 Brush eggplant with olive oil.

3 Mix thyme and chives in a shallow plate. Brush sides of goat cheese lightly with walnut oil; roll in herbs, coating the rounded sides. Cut cheese into 12 slices. Set cheese slices on a baking sheet and season with salt and pepper. Pour any remaining walnut oil over cheese.

4 Set eggplant slices on grill. Cook, without moving, until nicely charred, about 5 minutes. Turn and top each eggplant round with cheese. Cook until cheese is warm and eggplant is slightly charred, 2 to 3 minutes longer. Sprinkle with walnuts and serve piping hot.

Italian Pork Chops with Leeks

3 4 Per serving: **NET CARBS: 13.5 GRAMS** ▪ Carbohydrates: 15.5 grams ▪ Fiber: 2 grams ▪ Protein: 43.5 grams ▪ Fat: 30.5 grams ▪ Calories: 516 ▪ **PREP TIME: 15 MINUTES** ▪ **MARINATE TIME: OVERNIGHT** ▪ **COOK TIME: 20 MINUTES**, plus resting ▪ **SERVINGS: 4**

Pork today is extremely lean; it lacks the external layer of fat that helps to baste the meat while it cooks, so it can become tough if overcooked. Use an instant-read thermometer to check the temperature and remove the pork when it hits 145°F to 150°F. If you use boneless chops, reduce the cooking time by a few minutes.

Chops:

¾ cup olive oil

4 garlic cloves, smashed with the side of a knife

2 teaspoons dried sage

1 teaspoon dried oregano

½ teaspoon dried thyme

½ teaspoon dried rosemary, crushed

1 tablespoon balsamic vinegar

4 (12- to 14-ounce) bone-in rib or loin pork chops, about 1 inch thick

4 medium leeks (1 pound)

½ teaspoon salt

¼ teaspoon pepper

Dressing:

2 tablespoons extra virgin olive oil

1 tablespoon balsamic vinegar

¼ teaspoon salt

¼ teaspoon pepper

tip
Don't know a loin chop from a rib chop? Loin chops are slightly larger; they look like a T-bone steak with meat on both sides of the bone. Rib chops have a large "eye" on one side of the bone. Rib chops tend to be fattier and are less likely to dry out than loin chops, but they tend to be a bit pricier, too. Whichever you choose, be sure that they're thick-sliced.

1 For the chops: Combine oil, garlic, sage, oregano, thyme, and rosemary in a medium bowl. Whisk in balsamic vinegar, and set 1 tablespoon of marinade aside. Add pork chops and turn to coat. Refrigerate overnight, turning the pork occasionally.

2 Prepare a high-heat grill.

3 Trim dark greens from leeks and discard. Cut leeks from tops almost to roots, leaving root end intact. Turn and make another cut, so leeks are cut in a crosshair pattern. Rinse leeks thoroughly and shake dry. Brush them lightly with reserved marinade.

4 Remove pork from the marinade, shaking off any excess. Season with salt and pepper. Set chops and leeks on grill. Cook the leeks until tender, about 15 minutes, turning every 2 to 3 minutes. Cook the chops for 3 minutes;

then give chops a quarter turn to make cross grill marks and continue to cook 6 minutes longer. Turn chops over and cook until no longer pink inside, 6 to 8 minutes longer. Transfer chops to a platter and let stand.

5 **For the dressing:** Whisk oil, vinegar, salt, and pepper in a small bowl.

6 Trim root end from cooked leeks and cut in half lengthwise. Set 2 halves on each of 4 plates and drizzle with the dressing. Top with chops.

the goods on ground meat

Summertime is synonymous with grilling, and for many, the quintessential grilled food is the burger. Burgers are less costly than steak, less messy than barbecue, and adaptable to a variety of palates. Beef, of course, is the traditional meat for burgers, and a quick trip through the meat department reveals several permutations of ground beef. The biggest difference is the amount of fat each contains. Once upon a time, ground round included 15 or less percent fat, ground sirloin contained 15 to 20 percent fat, ground chuck contained 20 to 25 percent fat, and ground beef contained about 30 percent fat.

Now, you're likely to see "ground beef" on the label regardless of which cut it comes from, and rather than percentage of fat, labels proclaim the percentage of lean meat. For the vast majority of recipes, 80 to 85 percent lean ground beef is best. It's high enough in fat to be flavorful and juicy, yet it isn't so high in fat that your dish will have an unpleasantly greasy feel. (Steer clear of products labeled "hamburger"—it can have fat or seasonings added to it. Better to buy ground beef and season it yourself.)

No matter which ground meat you use, be sure to handle it with caution. Bacteria only live on the surface of the meat. When you cook steaks or chops, the heat will kill any bacteria. When meat is ground, surface bacteria are mixed throughout. If you grind the meat yourself, be sure your food processor is scrupulously clean. Wash your hands, as well as knives and cutting boards, thoroughly, and don't forget to rinse off the meat and pat it dry before you grind it.

Refrigerate ground meats until just before cooking, and cook ground meats to an internal temperature of 160°F, or well done.

Grilled Tomato "Bruschetta"

1 2 3 4

Per serving: **NET CARBS: 3.5 GRAMS** ▪ Carbohydrates: 6 grams ▪ Fiber: 2.5 grams ▪ Protein: 4 grams ▪ Fat: 3.5 grams ▪ Calories: 67 ▪ **PREP TIME: 10 MINUTES** ▪ **COOK TIME: 10 MINUTES** ▪ **SERVINGS: 6**

Plum, or Roma, tomatoes are firmer than beefsteak tomatoes; tasty, good-quality ones tend to be readily available year-round (though you may wish to try this dish with beefsteaks at the end of summer, when they are at their peak). Use any leftover tomato mixture to fill an omelet. For photo, see page 216.

1 tablespoon olive oil

4 (2- to 3-ounce) large plum **tomatoes,** halved lengthwise

½ teaspoon kosher salt

3 slices low-carb multigrain bread

1 large garlic clove, peeled and halved

2 tablespoons chopped fresh basil

1 tablespoon red wine vinegar

⅛ teaspoon salt

⅛ teaspoon pepper

2 teaspoons extra virgin olive oil (optional)

tip

Seek out tomato products, such as paste and sauce, imported from Italy. They're less likely to contain added sugars than those from the United States.

1 Prepare a medium-high-heat grill.

2 Drizzle olive oil over tomatoes; sprinkle with salt. Set tomatoes, skin-side down, and bread on grill. Cook bread until golden, about 1 minute per side. Remove from the grill and rub toast with cut sides of garlic. Set toast aside; finely chop garlic.

3 Cook tomatoes until tender, 4 to 5 minutes per side. Transfer to a cutting board and coarsely chop. Transfer to a bowl and stir in basil, vinegar, and garlic. Season with salt and pepper.

4 Cut toast into quarters. Spoon about 1 tablespoon tomato mixture on each piece. Drizzle with extra virgin olive oil, if desired. Serve at room temperature.

Spicy Ground Lamb Kebabs

1 2 3 4 Per serving: **NET CARBS: 2.5 GRAMS** ▪ Carbohydrates: 3.5 grams ▪ Fiber: 1 gram ▪ Protein: 20.5 grams ▪ Fat: 27 grams ▪ Calories: 340 ▪ **PREP TIME: 15 MINUTES** ▪ **COOK TIME: 20 MINUTES** ▪ **SERVINGS: 4**

Kebabs are often chunks of food, typically meat, threaded onto skewers, but in Morocco you may find kebabs called keftedes made of ground meat, shaped like small footballs, and cooked on skewers. Make the yogurt sauce a day ahead, if you like, so the flavors can develop; serve any leftovers with chicken or fish. Served without the yogurt sauce, this dish is suitable for Induction.

4 (10-inch) wooden skewers

1 pound ground lamb

2 tablespoons minced onion

1 tablespoon Hungarian paprika

1 teaspoon ground cumin

1 teaspoon ground coriander

¼ teaspoon cayenne pepper

⅛ teaspoon ground cinnamon

Yogurt Sauce:

¼ cup plain whole-milk yogurt

¼ cup mayonnaise

¼ **cucumber,** peeled, seeded, and cut into a small dice (¼ cup)

1 tablespoon chopped fresh cilantro

1½ teaspoons chopped fresh mint

¼ teaspoon salt

⅛ teaspoon pepper

1 to 2 teaspoons distilled (white) vinegar

1 to 2 tablespoons water (optional)

tip

Meats that have a fair amount of fat, such as lamb, some cuts of beef, and duck with the skin on, can cause flare-ups as the fat hits the hot coals. Have a water bottle nearby to quench them when cooking outside.

1 Soak skewers in water for 30 minutes. Prepare a medium-high-heat grill.

2 Combine lamb, onion, paprika, cumin, coriander, cayenne, and cinnamon in a large bowl. With your hands, knead the ingredients thoroughly. Divide into 4 equal pieces and form each into a football shape about 6 inches long. Spear a skewer through each one lengthwise. Refrigerate until the grill is hot.

3 For the sauce: Combine yogurt and mayonnaise in a medium bowl. Stir in cucumber, cilantro, and mint, then add salt and pepper. Stir in 1 teaspoon of the vinegar and taste; add the second teaspoon if you prefer a sharper flavor. If necessary, stir in water to thin. Refrigerate until ready to serve.

4 Grill skewered lamb, turning every 5 minutes, until well browned and cooked through, about 20 minutes. Serve each kebab with 2 tablespoons yogurt sauce on the side.

Real North Carolina Barbecue Pork

1 2 3 4

Per serving with Eastern North Carolina Sauce: **NET CARBS: 5.5 GRAMS** ▪ Carbohydrates: 6 grams ▪ Fiber: 0.5 gram ▪ Protein: 33 grams ▪ Fat: 18 grams ▪ Calories: 320 ▪ **PREP TIME: 20 MINUTES** ▪ **COOK TIME: 7 HOURS** ▪ **SERVINGS: 12** ▪ Per serving with Lexington "Dip": **NET CARBS: 4 GRAMS** ▪ Carbohydrates: 4.5 grams ▪ Fiber: 0.5 gram ▪ Protein: 33 grams ▪ Fat: 18 grams ▪ Calories: 312

"Real" barbecue is defined differently throughout the South—not only from state to state, but even within states. If you use a charcoal grill, you'll need about 10 pounds of charcoal.

3 cups hickory wood chips

1 tablespoon Hungarian paprika

1 tablespoon brown sugar substitute (such as Sweet'N Low)

1 tablespoon kosher salt

1 tablespoon black pepper

1 teaspoon ground white pepper

1 teaspoon garlic powder

1 teaspoon dry mustard

1 (8-pound) Boston butt pork roast or pork shoulder

3 cups Eastern North Carolina Sauce or Lexington "Dip" (Recipes follow)

tip

In eastern North Carolina, the whole hog is slowly smoke-roasted and served with a vinegar sauce; near Lexington, only the shoulders are cooked and a little ketchup finds its way into the sauce, which is called a dip. Both of the sauces will pucker your mouth alone, but with the rich smoked pork they work wonderfully.

1 Soak wood chips in water for 1 hour. Mix paprika, sugar substitute, salt, black pepper, white pepper, garlic powder, and mustard in a small bowl. Rub all over pork until well coated. Set aside.

2 Preheat a gas grill for indirect cooking, or prepare a charcoal grill with the coals all on one side. Put 1 cup of the wood chips in a gas grill's smoker box, or sprinkle them over the charcoal. Set a disposable foil pan under the center of the grill to catch any fat and drippings. Cover grill until smoke appears. Set pork on the part of grill with no direct heat. Cover; turn the gas grill to low. If using charcoal close the vents almost completely. Every 1½ to 2 hours, add another cup of the chips and, if using a charcoal grill, about 10 briquettes. Continue to cook until pork is tender when pierced with a long fork and registers at least 175°F to 180°F on an instant-read thermometer, 4 to 7 hours (long, slow cooking imparts a smokier flavor). Transfer pork to a platter and let stand 20 minutes.

3 Remove the fat and skin from pork; discard. Pull off the meat in chunks (a pair of latex gloves is helpful), discarding any excess fat and membranes. Chop or shred meat. Put in a large pan and add 1 cup of the sauce, tossing with your hands. Serve with additional sauce on the side.

Eastern North Carolina Sauce

1 2 3 4 Per (¼ cup) serving: **NET CARBS: 5.5 GRAMS** ▪ Carbohydrates: 6 grams ▪ Fiber: 0.5 gram ▪ Protein: 0 grams ▪ Fat: 0.5 gram ▪ Calories: 15 ▪ **PREP TIME: 5 MINUTES** ▪ **YIELD: 3½ CUPS**

1½ cups cider vinegar

1½ cups distilled (white) vinegar

1 tablespoon granular sugar substitute

1 tablespoon red pepper flakes

1 tablespoon black pepper

1 tablespoon salt

1 tablespoon hot pepper sauce (such as Tabasco)

Mix cider vinegar, distilled vinegar, sugar substitute, red pepper flakes, black pepper, salt, and pepper sauce in a bowl, whisking until sugar substitute dissolves. Serve with pork, or cover and refrigerate for up to 2 months. Stir or shake before using.

Lexington "Dip"

1 2 3 4 Per (¼ cup) serving: **NET CARBS: 4 GRAMS** ▪ Carbohydrates: 4.5 grams ▪ Fiber: 0.5 gram ▪ Protein: 0 grams ▪ Fat: 0.5 gram ▪ Calories: 23 ▪ **PREP TIME: 5 MINUTES** ▪ **YIELD: ABOUT 3¼ CUPS**

2 cups cider vinegar

½ cup water

½ cup no-sugar-added ketchup

1½ to 2 tablespoons brown sugar substitute (such as Sweet'N Low)

1 tablespoon hot pepper sauce (such as Tabasco)

2 teaspoons red pepper flakes

2 teaspoons kosher salt

1 teaspoon black pepper

Mix vinegar, water, ketchup, sugar substitute, pepper sauce, red pepper flakes, salt, and black pepper in a medium bowl, whisking until sugar substitute dissolves. Serve with pork, or cover and refrigerate for up to 4 weeks. Stir or shake before using.

Grilled Butterflied Chicken with Herbs

Per serving: **NET CARBS: 1 GRAM** ■ Carbohydrates: 1 gram ■ Fiber: 0 grams ■ Protein: 56 grams ■ Fat: 34.5 grams ■ Calories: 551 ■ **PREP TIME: 20 MINUTES** ■ **MARINATE TIME: OVERNIGHT** ■ **COOK TIME: 30 MINUTES** ■ **SERVINGS: 4**

Roasting a chicken over indirect heat imparts a hint of smoke to the meat, but grilling a chicken over the direct heat of the fire gives you a deeper, smokier flavor that is hard to beat. Butterflying the bird makes it thin enough to cook evenly and rapidly; tongs and a large spatula simplify turning the bird.

1 (3½- to 4-pound) whole chicken

¼ teaspoon salt

¼ teaspoon pepper

¼ cup chopped fresh mixed herbs
  (such as thyme, oregano, basil,
  and rosemary)

¼ cup chopped fresh parsley

½ cup olive oil

½ cup fresh lemon juice
  (2 to 4 lemons)

tip

If you've ever tried to cut apart a chicken, you'll appreciate poultry shears. With one straight blade and one serrated blade, plus a notch for gripping bones, they make short work of butterflying chicken or duck.

1 Set chicken on a cutting board, breast-side down. Using poultry shears, cut alongside the backbone from neck to tail on both sides. Open bird up and press down on each side. Turn over and press on both sides again; you should hear a few joints pop and chicken should lie fairly flat. Turn chicken over again; make 2 slits toward the tail. Pull ends of drumsticks through each slit. Turn chicken back over and snip the wing tips, if desired. Season chicken with salt and pepper.

2 Combine mixed herbs and parsley in a medium bowl. Stir in oil and lemon juice. Put chicken in a 2-gallon zip-close plastic bag and pour in marinade. Refrigerate, turning bag occasionally but making sure chicken always lies flat, about 24 hours.

3 Prepare a medium-high-heat grill.

4 Remove chicken from marinade and pat it dry with paper towels; discard marinade. Grill chicken, skin-side down, for 12 to 15 minutes. Turn and cook until an instant-read thermometer registers 170°F when inserted into the thigh, not touching bone, 12 to 15 minutes longer. Transfer chicken to a cutting board. Let stand 10 minutes before cutting into serving pieces.

Grilled Duck with Pepper Jelly Glaze

1 2 3 4 Per serving: **NET CARBS: 6.5 GRAMS** ▪ Carbohydrates: 7 grams ▪ Fiber: 0.5 gram ▪ Protein: 57 grams ▪ Fat: 32 grams ▪ Calories: 554 ▪ **PREP TIME: 10 MINUTES** ▪ **MARINATE TIME: 6 HOURS** ▪ **COOK TIME: 30 MINUTES** ▪ **SERVINGS: 4**

Elegant, flavorful, and surprisingly simple, this dish is perfect for company. Look for no-sugar-added pepper jelly in the condiment section at gourmet markets or natural foods stores.

1 teaspoon salt

1 teaspoon pepper

2 teaspoons chopped fresh thyme

1 teaspoon chopped fresh rosemary

4 (8-ounce) duck breast halves, boned

1 large shallot, finely chopped (2 tablespoons)

3 tablespoons sherry vinegar

1 tablespoon finely chopped jalapeño

2 tablespoons no-sugar-added pepper jelly or ½ teaspoon granular sugar substitute and 2 tablespoons finely chopped red bell pepper

½ cup veal demi-glâce

2 tablespoons cold unsalted butter, cut into 4 pieces

1 Mix salt, pepper, thyme, and rosemary in a small bowl. Cut a few shallow slashes across the skin of the breasts. Rub the seasoning blend onto skin side of each breast. Cover and refrigerate for at least 4 but no more than 6 hours.

2 Prepare a medium-high-heat grill.

3 Grill duck, skin-side down, for 8 to 10 minutes. Turn breasts and cook until done to taste, 3 to 4 minutes longer for medium-rare or 5 to 6 minutes longer for well done. Remove from heat and let stand 5 minutes.

4 Meanwhile, combine shallot, vinegar, jalapeño, jelly, and demi-glâce in a small saucepan over medium-high heat. Bring to a boil; reduce heat to low, and simmer until reduced to ⅓ cup, 6 to 8 minutes. Remove from heat and whisk in butter. Spoon over duck and serve.

tip

Demi-glâce is veal stock that has been reduced to almost a syrup; it is full of flavor but can be difficult to find. Look for it in some larger supermarkets and specialty food stores in the frozen foods section or perhaps in the meat department or with soups. It is also available through many mail-order sources. Don't use powdered demi-glâce mixes, as they tend to be too salty. To make demi-glâce, boil 1 cup rich veal stock (or beef broth) until reduced to ½ cup, 4 to 5 minutes.

Grilled Squash Quesadillas

2
3 4
Per serving: **NET CARBS: 6 GRAMS** ▪ Carbohydrates: 13 grams ▪ Fiber: 7 grams ▪ Protein: 13.5 grams ▪ Fat: 19 grams ▪ Calories: 264 ▪ **PREP TIME: 20 MINUTES** ▪ **COOK TIME: 20 MINUTES** ▪ **SERVINGS: 8**

Usually fried or broiled, quesadillas are delicious when they're grilled. The grilled squashes are so tasty you may find yourself preparing them alone as a side dish; try serving them with Foolproof Grilled Fish (page 223) or Grilled Butterflied Chicken with Herbs (page 232). Quesadillas are a versatile snack, starter, or side.

2 tablespoons olive oil

2 **garlic cloves**, minced (1 teaspoon)

½ **teaspoon red pepper flakes**

3 **medium (6-ounce) zucchini**, cut into ¼-inch slices

3 **medium (6-ounce) yellow squash**, cut into ¼-inch slices

8 (8-inch) low-carb tortillas

½ cup chopped fresh cilantro

2 cups grated Monterey Jack or Colby cheese (8 ounces)

2 tablespoons unsalted butter, melted

Sour cream (optional)

tip
Colby cheese is a type of cheddar; it's quite mild in flavor and is higher in moisture than regular cheddars. Because its high water content means it spoils more rapidly, buy Colby cheese only in amounts you can consume quickly.

1 Prepare a medium-high-heat grill.

2 Combine oil, garlic, and red pepper flakes in a large bowl. Add zucchini and yellow squash; toss to coat.

3 Grill squash until lightly browned, about 4 minutes per side.

4 Put 2 or 3 slices each of the zucchini and yellow squash on one half of each tortilla; sprinkle each with 1 tablespoon cilantro and ¼ cup cheese. Fold tortillas in half and press gently to close. Grill quesadillas for 2 minutes; turn and brush with melted butter. Cook until the cheese is melted, 2 to 3 minutes longer. Cut each tortilla into 3 wedges and serve with sour cream, if desired.

Grilled Portobellos with Blue Cheese Butter

Per serving: **NET CARBS: 4.5 GRAMS** ▪ Carbohydrates: 6 grams ▪ Fiber: 1.5 grams ▪ Protein: 4 grams ▪ Fat: 14 grams ▪ Calories: 154 ▪ **PREP TIME: 20 MINUTES** ▪ **COOK TIME: 10 MINUTES** ▪ **SERVINGS: 6**

Portobello mushrooms have a meaty texture and a hearty flavor, and grilling them brings out their best. If you've been preparing this vegetable as a side, try it treated like a steak, as in this recipe.

4 tablespoons unsalted butter, at room temperature

1 ounce Roquefort cheese

1 teaspoon fresh thyme leaves

¼ teaspoon pepper, divided

6 large (6- to 8-inch) portobello **mushrooms,** stemmed and wiped with a damp paper towel

2 tablespoons extra virgin olive oil

1 teaspoon salt

1 Combine butter, cheese, thyme, and ⅛ teaspoon of the pepper in a small bowl, mashing with a fork to blend completely. Roll into a 3-inch log; wrap in plastic and refrigerate.

2 Prepare a high-heat grill.

3 Brush mushrooms on both sides with oil; season with salt and remaining ⅛ teaspoon pepper. Grill mushrooms, gill-side up, for 6 minutes. Flip and cook until firm to the touch with a bit of give, about 6 minutes longer. (If you cut into one to check for doneness, the inside should look moist.)

4 Cut butter into 6 slices. Serve mushrooms gill-side down, topped with seasoned butter.

tip

The juices from the mushrooms combine with the melting butter to make a delectable sauce. Use a high-quality Roquefort in the butter, preferably purchased in a block rather than crumbled.

Smoke-Roasted Turkey

Per serving: **NET CARBS: 0.5 GRAM** ▪ Carbohydrates: 0.5 gram ▪ Fiber: 0 grams ▪ Protein: 90 grams ▪ Fat: 18.5 grams ▪ Calories: 549 ▪ **PREP TIME: 20 MINUTES** ▪ **BRINING TIME: 48 HOURS** ▪ **COOK TIME: 3 HOURS** ▪ **SERVINGS: 8**

Grilled turkey has a hint of smoky flavor that makes oven-roasted turkey pale in comparison and is subtler than the slightly chemical taste of commercially smoked turkey. If you don't have the space or the time to brine the bird, skip that step. Instead, melt a stick of butter and brush the bird with it every 30 minutes or so. The scent of onion, thyme, and garlic perfumes the meat, but the aromatics are not served with the turkey.

1 gallon water

2 cups kosher salt

½ cup granular sugar substitute

1 (12- to 14-pound) fresh turkey, preferably free-range, giblets removed

1½ teaspoons pepper

2 onions, quartered but left unpeeled

1 bunch fresh thyme

10 garlic cloves, unpeeled

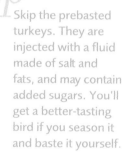

tip

Skip the prebasted turkeys. They are injected with a fluid made of salt and fats, and may contain added sugars. You'll get a better-tasting bird if you season it and baste it yourself.

1 Mix water, salt, and sugar substitute in a large container. If this container is large enough to hold the turkey and will fit in your refrigerator, add turkey and refrigerate. Otherwise, put turkey in a large plastic bag and pour in brine. Refrigerate for at least 24 hours but no longer than 48 hours.

2 Prepare a gas grill for indirect heat or build a fire on one side of a charcoal grill.

3 Remove turkey from brine. Rinse turkey and pat dry. Season turkey cavity with ½ teaspoon pepper and outside with 1 teaspoon pepper. Stuff onions, thyme, and garlic in cavity; set turkey on grill away from direct heat. Cover and grill until an instant-read thermometer inserted between breast and thigh registers 165° to 170°F, 2½ to 3 hours, turning 180 degrees every hour to promote even cooking. If you are using a charcoal grill you will need to add 5 to 6 briquettes every hour. Transfer turkey to a platter and let stand 15 minutes before carving.

Quick and Tasty Barbecued Chicken

1 2 3 4 Per serving: **NET CARBS: 6.5 GRAMS** ▪ Carbohydrates: 11.5 grams ▪ Fiber: 5 grams ▪ Protein: 46.5 grams ▪ Fat: 6 grams ▪ Calories: 306 ▪ **PREP TIME: 10 MINUTES** ▪ **COOK TIME: 30 MINUTES** ▪ **SERVINGS: 4**

Boneless, skinless chicken breasts are quick weeknight fare, but they tend to be boring at best and bland at worst. Cover them with a rub and glaze them with barbecue sauce, though, and you can fake a slow-cooked depth of flavor.

Sauce:

1 tablespoon olive oil

¼ cup finely chopped onion

2 garlic cloves, minced (1 teaspoon)

1 to 2 chipotles en adobo, finely chopped or mashed

1 cup no-sugar-added ketchup

2 tablespoons fresh lime juice

Rub for Barbecued Chicken:

1 tablespoon ground cumin

1 tablespoon paprika

1 teaspoon kosher salt

1 teaspoon garlic powder

1 teaspoon onion powder

½ teaspoon dried thyme

½ teaspoon dried oregano

½ teaspoon pepper

4 (6- to 8-ounce) boneless, skinless chicken breasts

tip

Make the sauce a few hours or a few days ahead; use the second chipotle if you like your food spicy. You'll have twice as much rub as you need, so refrigerate the extra in an airtight container for up to a month—use it on pork chops, ribs, or salmon.

1 Prepare a medium-high-heat grill.

2 **For the sauce:** Heat oil in a small saucepan over medium-low heat. Add onion and cook until softened, 3 to 4 minutes; add garlic and cook until very fragrant, about 1 minute longer. Stir in chipotles and ketchup. Bring to a simmer; reduce heat to low and cook until the flavors have blended and sauce is slightly thickened, 6 to 8 minutes. Add lime juice and remove from heat. Remove ¼ cup of the sauce to use for basting; reserve the rest for serving with the chicken.

3 **For the chicken:** Mix cumin, paprika, salt, garlic powder, onion powder, thyme, oregano, and pepper in a small bowl. Set chicken on a sheet of waxed paper. Season each breast with ½ teaspoon of the rub, turn over, and repeat.

4 Grill chicken until browned, about 8 minutes; turn and brush with some sauce. Cook 4 minutes longer, then brush with sauce; cook until just opaque in center, 1 to 2 minutes longer. Serve with the reserved sauce.

Pepper-Crusted Beef Tenderloin

1 2 3 4 Per serving: **NET CARBS: 0.5 GRAM** ▪ Carbohydrates: 1 gram ▪ Fiber: 0.5 gram ▪ Protein: 46 grams ▪ Fat: 18 grams ▪ Calories: 362 ▪ **PREP TIME: 10 MINUTES** ▪ **COOK TIME: 45 MINUTES** ▪ **SERVINGS: 10**

Tenderloins are extremely lean, meaning they don't have much flavor, so the seasoning rub helps to add punch. Coat the meat the day before to heighten the flavors and refrigerate; remove it from the refrigerator when you start the grill.

1 (4½- to 5-pound) trimmed beef tenderloin

2 tablespoons olive oil

1 tablespoon kosher salt

3 tablespoons black peppercorns, cracked

⅓ to ½ cup prepared horseradish (optional)

1 Set tenderloin on sheet of waxed paper; brush with oil and season with salt and pepper, rubbing them in. Turn meat to coat evenly.

2 Preheat a gas grill for indirect cooking, or build a fire on one side of a charcoal grill.

3 Grill tenderloin over direct heat or directly over the fire until seared on all sides and a crust has developed, about 10 minutes, turning halfway through cooking. Melting fat may cause flare-ups, so have a spray bottle of water handy. Move tenderloin away from direct heat and cover grill; cook until done to taste, 20 to 25 minutes longer for medium-rare (an instant-read thermometer will register 130°F). Let stand for 15 minutes before slicing. Serve with horseradish on the side, if desired.

tip

A tenderloin is full and round at one end and tapered at the other, which makes it ideal for gatherings where some prefer their beef rare and others well done; cook it so the middle is medium-rare and you'll have something to suit everyone's taste.

Grilled Swordfish Kebabs

1 2 3 4 Per serving: **NET CARBS: 0 GRAMS** ▪ Carbohydrates: 0 grams ▪ Fiber: 0 grams ▪ Protein: 23 grams ▪ Fat: 8 grams ▪ Calories: 171 ▪ **PREP TIME: 10 MINUTES** ▪ **COOK TIME: 12 MINUTES** ▪ **SERVINGS: 4**

Nothing could be tastier than simply cooked swordfish on the grill; be sure your grill grate is clean and oiled to keep the fish from sticking. Cook the fish through, but take care not to overcook it.

4 (6-inch) wooden skewers

1½ pounds swordfish steak, trimmed and cut into 1¼-inch chunks

1 tablespoon olive oil

1 teaspoon salt

½ teaspoon pepper

¼ teaspoon dried thyme leaves

4 lemon quarters

4 lime quarters

1 Soak skewers in water for 30 minutes. Prepare a medium-heat grill.

2 Divide swordfish among skewers. Brush with oil and season with salt, pepper, and thyme, turning to season all sides.

3 Grill kebabs until seared and cooked through, about 6 minutes; turn and cook until opaque throughout, about 6 minutes longer. Serve with lemon and lime.

BBQ gear

There are lots of nice-to-haves, but only a few real essentials:

A big—really big—spatula, and industrial-strength tongs. Flipping is the trickiest part of grilling, and it helps to have the right tools.

A chimney starter, which looks like a giant beer stein with holes around the base. You put newspaper at the bottom and pile your charcoal on top. Light the newspaper, and the updraft lights the coals. When they're going strong, pile them in the grill.

A grill basket. There are some foods that stick—primarily fish and vegetables. A basket is great for food that's small enough to fall through the grill.

cool and creamy

custards, rich frozen mousses and ice creams, crisp-crusted cheesecakes, or fruit-dappled tortes: Which dessert is your favorite? Our Delectable Desserts tend to take a little more time than those in the Sweet & Simple chapter—but they are well worth the effort when you bring them to the table and bask in your guests' appreciation of your culinary skills. Sophisticated flavor combinations like ginger with pear dress up ice cream, almond adds intrigue to chocolate pudding, and coffee elevates flan to elegant levels.

Almond Torte with Chocolate Sauce,
page 252

delectable
desserts

one of the delights of doing Atkins is that dessert is most definitely on the menu. And when you are entertaining, it's hard to imagine not ending the perfect meal with the perfect dessert. My sweet tooth is partial to chocolate, the darker the better. I know I am not alone, so we offer a variety of delights made with unsweetened baking chocolate, which contains no sugar, equally sugar-free low-carb chocolate, or unsweetened cocoa. Just wait until you tuck into our Dark Chocolate Sorbet (opposite) or Raspberry Chocolate Walnut Torte (page 254) , to name just two of our marvelous array of sweet endings.

Cheesecake was one of Dr. Atkins' favorite desserts, and we offer up a duo of mouthwatering options in the following pages: Pumpkin Pecan Cheesecake (page 249) and perfectly portioned Individual Cheesecakes with Strawberries (page 250). Other ingredients custom-made for the low-carb lifestyle include nut flours, particularly almond, walnut, and hazelnut, which make superb tortes and cakes. Creamy flans and custards based upon eggs are also Atkins-friendly. We've also come up with some wonderful frozen dessert recipes, including Ginger Ice Cream with Caramelized Pears (page 257) and Frozen Lime Mousse (page 253) .

Dessert may be one of life's pleasures, but like most things, it is best enjoyed in moderation. Eat such desserts occasionally, not on a regular basis. To assist with portion control, make desserts in individual containers whenever possible. Also, make sure that your portion matches the recommended serving size so you don't overdose on carbs. And most important of all, unless you are a paragon of self-control, when your guests bid you good night, make sure that they take any leftover pie or cake home with them!

Dark Chocolate Sorbet

Per serving: **NET CARBS: 1 GRAM** ▪ Carbohydrates: 1 gram ▪ Fiber: 0 grams ▪ Protein: 3.5 grams ▪ Fat: 2 grams ▪ Calories: 55 ▪ **PREP TIME: 10 MINUTES,** plus chilling ▪ **SERVINGS: 4**

The grownup version of a frozen fudgy ice pop, this sorbet is creamy, rich, and oh-so-chocolatey. Be sure the water and milk are very cold.

2 cups ice-cold water, divided

1 teaspoon unflavored gelatin

1¼ cups sugar-free chocolate syrup, divided

1 cup reduced-carb, whole-milk dairy beverage

2 to 3 tablespoons dark rum

1 Put 2 tablespoons of the water in a glass measuring cup. Sprinkle with gelatin. Microwave 10 to 20 seconds to melt, then stir until dissolved.

2 Put ¾ cup of the chocolate syrup, remaining 1⅞ cups water, dairy beverage, and rum in a bowl.

3 Whisk ½ cup of the chocolate syrup into the gelatin mixture, then whisk the gelatin mixture into milk mixture.

4 Pour mixture into an ice-cream maker and churn according to manufacturer's instructions. Transfer to an airtight container and freeze until ready to serve.

tip

Sorbets and granitas are ice cream's milkless cousins. Sorbet's made just like eggless ice cream—by dissolving sweetener in the liquid and then freezing it, keeping it in constant motion. A granita is an icier, flakier version of sorbet and requires very little motion—after freezing, a simple scrape with the tines of a fork is all that's needed. A useful trick is to lightly coat the inside of the ice-cream maker's canister with cooking spray, it will help prevent ice crystals from forming on the container's sides.

Coffee Flans with Whipped Cream

1 2
3 4
Per serving: **NET CARBS: 4 GRAMS** ▪ Carbohydrates: 4 grams ▪ Fiber: 0 grams ▪ Protein: 6 grams ▪ Fat: 27.5 grams ▪ Calories: 285 ▪ **PREP TIME: 20 MINUTES** ▪ **COOK TIME: 35 MINUTES**, plus chilling ▪ **SERVINGS: 4**

If you have an espresso maker, by all means use it to brew the espresso. Or use 3 tablespoons ground espresso beans and 2⅔ cup water in a coffeemaker, or 2 teaspoons of instant espresso powder and 2⅔ cup hot water. Be sure the espresso is decaf, as this is an Induction dessert.

1 cup heavy cream	Boiling water, for roasting pan
⅔ cup decaf espresso	¼ cup sugar-free caramel sauce
3 tablespoons granular sugar substitute	2 tablespoons heavy cream, whipped
3 large eggs	Espresso beans (optional)

tip

Custards, soufflés, and cheesecakes are often cooked in a water bath—that is, the pan that holds the food is placed in a larger pan of water. The water diffuses the heat and makes the food less likely to curdle or separate.

1 Heat oven to 325°F.

2 Combine cream, espresso, and sugar substitute in a heavy medium saucepan; heat until small bubbles appear around edge, about 3 minutes.

3 Whisk eggs in a medium bowl. Gradually whisk in about one-third of the cream mixture. Whisk egg mixture into cream mixture. Reduce heat to very low and cook, whisking, for 1 minute.

4 Pour into four 6-ounce ramekins or custard cups (if mixture looks lumpy, pour it through a strainer). Place cups in a large roasting pan. Place roasting pan in oven and carefully pour boiling water into pan until water comes halfway up sides of cups. Cover entire pan loosely with foil and bake until they are just set, about 35 minutes. Remove from the oven and let stand for 10 minutes. Remove flans from roasting pan and wipe dry; cover with plastic wrap, stretching the wrap so it does not touch the flans. Refrigerate until cold, at least 3 hours.

5 To serve, dip bottoms of cups into very hot water for a few seconds; run a sharp knife around edge to loosen. Set a dessert plate over the custard and invert, shaking gently to unmold.

6 Heat caramel sauce in a microwavable bowl on high to liquefy, about 10 seconds. Whip cream. Drizzle caramel over flans; serve with whipped cream on the side and a few espresso beans for garnish, if desired.

Pumpkin Pecan Cheesecake

2 3 4 Per serving: **NET CARBS: 7 GRAMS** ▪ Carbohydrates: 10 grams ▪ Fiber: 3 grams ▪ Protein: 9.5 grams ▪
Fat: 43.5 grams ▪ Calories: 457 ▪ **PREP TIME: 25 MINUTES** ▪ **COOK TIME: 45 MINUTES,** plus chilling ▪ **SERVINGS: 10**

*Ultra-creamy and so delicious, this cheesecake uses heavy cream in the cheese layer
and bakes at a lower temperature in place of using the more usual water bath.*

Crust:

1½ cups pecans, finely chopped

1 tablespoon granular sugar
substitute

½ teaspoon ground cinnamon

2 tablespoons unsalted butter,
melted

1 large egg white

Filling:

3 (8-ounce) packages cream
cheese, softened

⅔ cup granular sugar substitute

1 cup heavy cream

1 (15-ounce) can pumpkin purée

1 teaspoon vanilla extract

1 teaspoon pumpkin pie spice

3 large eggs

1 For the crust: Heat oven to 350°F. Combine pecans, sugar substitute,
and cinnamon in a food processor. Process until finely ground. Toss with
butter and egg white; press onto bottom of a 9-inch springform pan, round-
ing up to cover the pan seam. Bake until golden and set, 8 to 10 minutes.
Cool completely on a wire rack.

2 For the filling: Reduce oven to 325°F. Combine cream cheese, sugar
substitute, and cream in a large bowl. Beat until smooth with an electric
mixer at medium speed. Add pumpkin purée, vanilla, and pumpkin pie
spice, mixing to combine. Beat in eggs, one at a time, just until combined.

3 Pour batter over crust. Bake until just set, 45 to 50 minutes. Turn off oven
and let stand 10 minutes; transfer to a wire rack and cool completely. Cover
and refrigerate until chilled, 4 hours or overnight.

tip

No pumpkin pie spice on hand? Simply use ¾ teaspoon ground cinnamon,
¼ teaspoon ground nutmeg, and a pinch of ground cloves.

Individual Cheesecakes with Strawberries

Per serving: **NET CARBS: 11.5 GRAMS** ▪ Carbohydrates: 14 grams ▪ Fiber: 2.5 grams ▪ Protein: 20 grams ▪
Fat: 62.5 grams ▪ Calories: 682 ▪ **PREP TIME: 30 MINUTES** ▪ **COOK TIME: 40 MINUTES**, plus chilling ▪ **SERVINGS: 6**

3 4

Look for mini springform pans in kitchen-supply and gourmet stores—or in party or craft stores that carry baking and candy-making products. Alternatively, bake in an 8- or 9-inch springform pan for 45 to 50 minutes.

1¼ cups low-carb cereal flakes

½ cup raw almonds, lightly toasted

3 tablespoons unsalted butter, melted

1 large egg white

3 (8-ounce) packages cream cheese, at room temperature

⅔ cup granular sugar substitute

½ cup heavy cream

3 large eggs

1 teaspoon grated lemon zest

1 pint strawberries, hulled and sliced

1 tablespoon brandy (optional)

tip
If you bake this in one large springform pan, cut the cheesecake into 8—or even 10—slices. You'll cut the Net Carbs to 8.5 or 7 grams, respectively.

1 Heat oven to 350°F.

2 Combine cereal and nuts in a food processor and process until finely ground; add butter and egg white; process until blended. Distribute crumbs evenly over six 4-inch mini springform pans; press to cover bottoms, forming a crust. Bake until just golden, about 13 minutes; don't worry if the crust doesn't look dry. Set on a rack to cool. Reduce oven temperature to 325°F.

3 Meanwhile, combine cream cheese and sugar substitute in a large bowl. Beat with an electric mixer at medium-high speed until creamy, scraping down sides of bowl occasionally. Beat in cream, then reduce speed to medium and beat in eggs, one at a time, until just combined. Stir in zest. Set pans on baking sheet; pour batter into pans. Bake until lightly puffed and just set in center, 21 to 24 minutes. Cool on baking sheet for 15 minutes; transfer to rack and cool completely. Cover with plastic wrap and refrigerate until cold, about 3 hours.

4 When ready to serve, unlock sides of pans. Remove cheesecakes from pans and set on plates. Toss strawberries with brandy, if using, and spoon over cheesecakes.

Fresh Mint Chocolate Chip Ice Cream

3 4 Per serving: **NET CARBS: 10 GRAMS** ▪ Carbohydrates: 11 grams ▪ Fiber: 1 gram ▪ Protein: 4 grams ▪ Fat: 35.5 grams ▪ Calories: 369 ▪ **PREP TIME: 15 MINUTES** ▪ **COOK TIME: 10 MINUTES,** plus chilling ▪ **SERVINGS: 9** (⅔ cup each)

Be sure to use only the leaves from the mint. The stems can impart a woody flavor and should be discarded.

3 cups heavy cream

2 cups packed coarsely chopped fresh mint leaves

6 large egg yolks

⅔ cup granular sugar substitute

¼ teaspoon salt

1 teaspoon peppermint extract (optional)

2 (1-ounce) Atkins Endulge Chocolate Candy Bars, coarsely chopped

1 Bring cream to a simmer in a medium saucepan. Put mint in a large bowl and pour cream over. Let steep for 10 minutes. Strain cream back into the saucepan; return to low heat and bring back to a simmer.

2 Whisk yolks, sugar substitute, and salt in a bowl, then gradually whisk in half of the hot cream. Return to pan and cook over very low heat until mixture reaches 170°F on an instant-read thermometer or until thickened, about 1 minute; do not boil. Strain mixture through a fine mesh strainer into a bowl. Stir in peppermint extract, if using; cover and chill until cold.

3 Pour mixture into an ice-cream maker and churn according to manufacturer's instructions. Add the chocolate during the last 5 minutes of churning, when ice cream is thick and creamy. Transfer to a container and let the ice cream firm in the freezer for 1 hour before serving.

tip

Homemade ice creams can freeze more solidly than their commercial counterparts. If you're not serving them right after churning, you should put them in the freezer, but take them out a half hour to an hour before you plan to serve them so they can soften.

Almond Torte with Chocolate Sauce

Per serving: **NET CARBS: 8.5 GRAMS** ▪ Carbohydrates: 12.5 grams ▪ Fiber: 4 grams ▪ Protein: 9.5 grams ▪
Fat: 21 grams ▪ Calories: 257 ▪ **PREP TIME: 25 MINUTES** ▪ **COOK TIME: 20 MINUTES** ▪ **SERVINGS: 8**

3 4

Folding the nuts into the yolks alternately with the egg whites helps to keep this torte light in texture.

1 cup blanched whole almonds

1 slice low-carb multigrain bread

1 teaspoon baking powder

⅛ teaspoon cream of tartar

Cooking spray

5 large eggs, separated

½ cup granular sugar substitute, divided

2 ounces unsweetened chocolate, coarsely chopped

⅓ cup sugar-free hazelnut syrup

2 tablespoons heavy cream

2 tablespoons water

½ cup whipped cream

1½ cups sweet cherries, pitted and coarsely chopped, or 1 (10-ounce) bag no-sugar-added frozen sweet cherries, thawed

tip

If you don't have a double boiler to make the chocolate sauce, set a large heatproof bowl (Pyrex is ideal, because the glass allows you to keep an eye on the simmering water) over a saucepan with a slightly smaller diameter. Be sure the bottom of the bowl does not touch the water in the saucepan.

1 Heat oven to 350°F. Spread almonds on a baking sheet; toast until golden, about 10 minutes; cool. Transfer to a food processor and add bread, baking powder, and cream of tartar; process until finely ground.

2 Line a 9-inch springform pan with waxed paper. Lightly coat with cooking spray, then dust with about 1 teaspoon of the ground almonds.

3 Combine egg yolks and ¼ cup of the sugar substitute in a large bowl; beat with an electric mixer until light and fluffy, about 3 minutes.

4 Beat egg whites in another bowl until soft peaks form. Add remaining sugar substitute and beat until stiff peaks form.

5 Fold nuts into yolks in three additions, alternating with one-quarter of the whites each time; fold in remaining whites. Spread lightly in pan. Bake until a toothpick inserted in center comes out clean, 18 to 20 minutes. Cool in pan.

6 Combine chocolate, syrup, and cream in the top of a double boiler set over simmering water. Whisk until chocolate melts, then whisk in water.

7 To serve, run a sharp knife between torte and pan to loosen. Set a plate over the pan and invert torte onto plate. Peel off waxed paper, then invert again onto a serving plate. Cut torte into eight wedges; top with sauce. Spoon whipped cream next to torte and add fruit alongside.

Frozen Lime Mousse

2 Per serving: **NET CARBS: 5.5 GRAMS** ▪ Carbohydrates: 5.5 grams ▪ Fiber: 0 grams ▪ Protein: 5.5 grams ▪
3 4 Fat: 32.5 grams ▪ Calories: 329 ▪ **PREP TIME: 20 MINUTES,** plus chilling ▪ **SERVINGS: 6**

For an elegant dessert, freeze these in cocktail glasses or wineglasses. Drizzle with raspberry sauce and dust with toasted chopped pistachio nuts, if you like.

3 large eggs

½ cup granular sugar substitute

6 tablespoons unsalted butter, melted

½ cup fresh lime juice

1 (¼-ounce) envelope unflavored gelatin

1¼ cups heavy cream

1 teaspoon lime zest

1 Whisk eggs and sugar substitute in a heatproof bowl or the top of a double boiler until smooth. Whisk in butter and lime juice. Sprinkle with gelatin and let stand 1 minute.

2 Fill bottom of double boiler or a medium saucepan with 1 inch of water; bring to a low boil over medium-low heat. Set bowl or top of double boiler over simmering water and cook, whisking constantly, until just thickened, 2 to 3 minutes. Remove from heat and whisk to cool slightly. Transfer to a bowl, cover with plastic wrap directly on surface, and refrigerate for 30 minutes.

3 Beat cream with an electric mixer at medium-high speed until soft peaks form. Fold about one-third of whipped cream into lime mixture, then fold in remaining whipped cream and lime zest. Spoon into 6 dessert glasses; cover each with plastic wrap directly on surface, and freeze until solid. Transfer to refrigerator about 1 hour before serving.

tip

Although gelatin is best known for its properties as a thickener, it helps to impart a smooth, creamy texture to this mousse. It also helps to keep the cream from "weeping," or separating.

Raspberry Chocolate Walnut Torte

Per serving: **NET CARBS: 12.5 GRAMS** ▪ Carbohydrates: 17.5 grams ▪ Fiber: 5 grams ▪ Protein: 12 grams ▪
Fat: 31.5 grams ▪ Calories: 388 ▪ **PREP TIME: 30 MINUTES** ▪ **COOK TIME: 15 MINUTES,** plus chilling ▪ **SERVINGS: 8**

The combination of flavors in this torte makes for a sweet ending any time of year, but its flourless nut crust makes it right for Passover (when served without whipped cream). The chocolate and eggs must be warm for proper combining; have both at room temperature for 15 to 20 minutes before starting.

Cooking spray

2 (1-ounce) Atkins Endulge Chocolate Candy Bars, coarsely chopped

6 egg yolks

2 whole eggs

6 egg whites

¾ cup granular sugar substitute, plus 1 teaspoon for sweetening cream (optional)

2 cups finely ground walnuts

¼ cup heavy cream

¼ cup no-sugar-added raspberry jam

1 pint fresh raspberries

1 Heat oven to 350°F. Coat a 9-inch springform pan with cooking spray.

2 Heat chocolate in a double boiler over 1 inch of boiling water until melted (or heat in a microwavable bowl on medium power for 2½ minutes). Stir egg yolks and whole eggs into chocolate.

3 Beat egg whites in large bowl with an electric mixer at medium-high speed, gradually adding ¾ cup of the sugar substitute until soft peaks just form; fold in walnuts. Fold chocolate mixture into egg whites until evenly combined. Pour into pan. Bake until toothpick inserted in center comes out clean, 13 to 15 minutes. Cool 5 minutes; loosen rim with sharp knife, remove, and cool torte completely.

4 Combine cream and 1 teaspoon sugar substitute, if using, in a bowl and whip. Heat jam in microwave until softened, about 1 minute. Spread jam over torte and cover with raspberries. Serve with whipped cream.

Chocolate Almond Pudding

2 3 4 Per serving: **NET CARBS: 6 GRAMS** ▪ Carbohydrates: 7.5 grams ▪ Fiber: 1.5 grams ▪ Protein: 5.5 grams ▪ Fat: 37 grams ▪ Calories: 374 ▪ **PREP TIME: 10 MINUTES** ▪ **COOK TIME: 8 MINUTES,** plus chilling ▪ **SERVINGS: 6** (½ cup each)

This homemade pudding requires a bit more effort than the stuff from a mix—but the rich, silky-smooth result is worth every extra moment. This is definitely for dark-chocolate aficionados.

2 cups heavy cream

2 ounces unsweetened chocolate, chopped

3 eggs

½ cup granular sugar substitute

1 teaspoon almond extract

1 tablespoon ThickenThin not/ Starch thickener

1 tablespoon toasted sliced almonds (optional)

1 Bring cream to a simmer in a medium saucepan over low heat. Put chocolate in a bowl and pour in ⅓ cup of the cream; let stand until melted, then stir until smooth.

2 Meanwhile, whisk together eggs and sugar substitute in another bowl. Gradually whisk half of the remaining cream into eggs; return to saucepan. Whisk in chocolate, almond extract, and thickener. Bring to a boil over medium heat, stirring constantly, and cook until just thick, 3 to 4 minutes.

3 Pour into a bowl; cover with plastic wrap directly on surface, and refrigerate until cold. Spoon into bowls and serve, topped with almonds, if using.

tip

Just because chocolate is bittersweet or semisweet doesn't mean it is acceptable on Atkins. Look for chocolate that is sweetened with sucralose, or use unsweetened baking chocolate or cocoa powder.

Ginger Ice Cream with Caramelized Pears

Per serving: **NET CARBS: 5.5 GRAMS** ■ Carbohydrates: 6.5 grams ■ Fiber: 1 gram ■ Protein: 3.5 grams ■ Fat: 35.5 grams ■ Calories: 352 ■ **PREP TIME: 20 MINUTES** ■ **COOK TIME: 10 MINUTES,** plus chilling ■ **SERVINGS: 10** (½ cup each)

Hot ginger lends a sharp note to the caramel-coated pear and rich ice cream.

3½ cups heavy cream

½ cup water

¼ cup grated fresh ginger

7 large egg yolks

⅔ cup granular sugar substitute

2 teaspoons unsalted butter

1 small pear, peeled, cored, and cut into ¼-inch dice

¾ cup sugar-free vanilla syrup

1 Combine cream, water, and ginger in a medium saucepan over medium heat. Bring almost to a boil; remove from the heat and let stand 10 minutes.

2 Whisk egg yolks and sugar substitute in a large bowl until lightened and thick. Gradually whisk half of the hot cream into egg mixture; return mixture to pan. Cook, stirring constantly, over medium heat until mixture registers 170°F on an instant-read thermometer or is thick enough to coat the back of a spoon. Strain through a fine mesh strainer into an airtight container, pressing with a spoon to extract liquid from ginger solids. Cover and refrigerate until cold.

3 Pour mixture into an ice-cream maker and churn according to manufacturer's instructions. Transfer to an airtight container and freeze until ready to serve.

4 Just before serving, melt butter in a small skillet over high heat; add diced pear and cook until tender and lightly browned, 3 to 4 minutes. Pour syrup into a small serving bowl; stir pear into syrup. Scoop ice cream into bowls; top with pears.

party and holiday menus

party and holiday menus

Whether I'm hosting a cocktail party buffet or a formal sit-down dinner, I have always taken particular pleasure in entertaining during the holidays and other special occasions. For one thing, the luscious foods you can savor when you are doing Atkins taste even better when they are shared with family and cherished friends. I especially enjoy the inevitable reaction of first-time guests, who are always pleased to discover that dining at my house doesn't mean forgoing their favorite once-a-year treats!

If your family traditions include treasured recipes handed down for generations and you're worried that your new healthier way of eating means those dishes must be relegated to the back of your recipe box, take a moment to flip through the magnificent menus in the following pages. Atkins-friendly Thanksgiving side dishes like Wild Rice, Sausage, and Cherry Stuffing and Butternut Squash Soup will quickly put to rest your concerns about a flavorless holiday season. All of the major holidays—as well as those fun events like Super Bowl Sunday and Oscar Night—are covered here, too, so you'll never be at a loss for something festive, great-tasting, *and* low in carbs.

Here's a hint of what else is in store: On Easter, sup on Mustard-and-Pepper-Coated Ham with Spring Vegetable Barley Risotto and Asparagus with Toasted Hazelnuts; make your 4th of July explode with flavor by serving up Buttery Shrimp and Lobster Rolls and Vanilla Fudge Ice Cream with Berry Sauce; and enjoy traditional dishes like Oven-Braised Brisket with Horseradish Sauce and Chicken Soup with Dilled Mini Matzo Balls for Passover dinner.

When it comes to putting together a successful occasion, let me share my experience with a few tricks for hosting an event that is a pleasure for both host and guests, while it stays true to the principles of the Atkins Nutritional Approach. And it needn't be time-consuming or complicated to be exciting and delicious. For example, simply set up bowls brimming with mixed or seasoned nuts as well as those containing a wonderful array of olives—from meaty green Spanish olives to wrinkly, rich-tasting Moroccan olives—for guests to enjoy with cocktails. It's an easy, appetizing way to prepare the palate for the main course.

Another tip: If the main dish is reasonably complicated, make sure that the side dishes are simple (all of those here qualify), not just to make your preparation chores easier, but so that there are not too many flavors competing for attention when they meet up on the same plate. Or if a dish is lacking in color, such as sautéed mushrooms, for example, toss in a handful of parsley to add visual interest.

Your holidays and special meals can be even better with Atkins. But don't take my word for it—let your family and friends confirm it with their satisfied smiles!

On the Menu

Butternut Squash Soup

Thanksgiving Turkey with Gravy

Wild Rice, Sausage, and Cherry Stuffing

Swiss Chard with Garlic Butter

Mashed Autumn Vegetables with Bacon and Scallions

Pumpkin-Pecan Cheesecake (page 249)

thanksgiving

Butternut Squash Soup

Per serving: **NET CARBS: 11 GRAMS** ▪ Carbohydrates: 15.5 grams ▪ Fiber: 4.5 grams ▪ Protein: 3.5 grams ▪

3 4 Fat: 4.5 grams ▪ Calories: 108 ▪ **PREP TIME: 20 MINUTES** ▪ **COOK TIME: 35 MINUTES** ▪ **SERVINGS: 8**

Vibrantly colored, subtly sweet, and light in texture, this soup is a perfect first course for a holiday meal; or serve it with Open-Faced Roasted Chicken Sandwich (page 64) or Pear, Boursin, and Watercress on Pumpernickel (page 88) for a light meal any time of year.

2 tablespoons vegetable oil

1 **medium onion,** halved and thinly sliced (¾ cup)

4 **garlic cloves,** minced (2 teaspoons)

4 **celery stalks with leaves,** sliced on the diagonal (2½ cups)

2 **large carrots,** sliced on the diagonal (2 cups)

¾ teaspoon dried thyme

¼ teaspoon ground nutmeg

¼ teaspoon salt

¼ teaspoon pepper

2 (14½-ounce) cans lower sodium chicken broth

1½ cups water

1 (1¼-pound) **butternut squash,** peeled, quartered lengthwise, seeded, and cut into ¼-inch slices

1½ **cups green beans,** trimmed and cut into 1-inch pieces

tip

Whether you're watching your sodium intake or not, opt for lower sodium chicken and beef broth for your recipes. The regular varieties are so high in salt that it can overwhelm other flavors.

1 Heat oil in a large, heavy saucepan over medium heat. Add onion and garlic; cook, stirring often, until softened, 2 to 3 minutes. Stir in celery, carrots, thyme, nutmeg, salt, and pepper. Cover and cook until the celery turns a brighter green, about 2 minutes. Add broth, water, squash, and beans. Cover and bring to a boil. Reduce heat to low and simmer until the vegetables are tender, about 15 minutes.

2 Season with additional salt and pepper, if desired, and serve.

Swiss Chard with Garlic Butter

1 2
3 4
Per serving: **NET CARBS: 3 GRAMS** ■ Carbohydrates: 4.5 grams ■ Fiber: 1.5 grams ■ Protein: 2 grams ■
Fat: 5 grams ■ Calories: 63 ■ **PREP TIME: 15 MINUTES** ■ **COOK TIME: 15 MINUTES** ■ **SERVINGS: 8**

*For the greatest visual impact, use ruby chard or rainbow chard—the brightly colored
stems contrast beautifully with the deep green leaves (shown on page 263).*

2 pounds Swiss chard, cleaned and
  trimmed

2 tablespoons unsalted butter

1 tablespoon olive oil

4 garlic cloves, minced
  (2 teaspoons)

½ teaspoon salt

¼ teaspoon pepper

1 Cut chard stems crosswise into ½-inch pieces. Cut chard leaves in half
lengthwise; stack them and cut crosswise into 2-inch pieces.

2 Heat butter and olive oil in a large saucepan over medium heat. Add garlic and cook, stirring, until just fragrant, about 30 seconds. Add chard stems;
cover and cook, stirring occasionally, until crisp-tender, about 4 minutes.

3 Add chard leaves in batches, tossing to coat; season with salt and pepper.
Cover and cook, stirring once, until stems are tender and leaves are wilted,
4 to 5 minutes.

tip

Prepare your vegetables earlier in the day, then cook them while the
turkey rests. Take care not to do it too far in advance, though, as veggies
can lose nutrients once they're cut. Wrap in damp paper towels and store
in plastic bags in the fridge.

Thanksgiving Turkey with Gravy

1 2
3 4
Per serving: **NET CARBS: 0.5 GRAM** ▪ Carbohydrates: 0.5 gram ▪ Fiber: 0 grams ▪ Protein: 69.5 grams ▪
Fat: 23.5 grams ▪ Calories: 510 ▪ **PREP TIME: 15 MINUTES** ▪ **COOK TIME: 4 HOURS** ▪ **SERVING: 8** plus leftovers

If you buy your turkey a few days ahead, remove the giblets and cook the broth up to three days before Thanksgiving; refrigerate it until ready to use. You'll have enough leftovers for five additional servings, so although this menu (shown on page 262) serves eight the nutrient analysis reflects 13 servings.

1 (12- to 13-pound) turkey, rinsed and patted dry, with giblets

2 oranges or lemons, cut into quarters

1 onion, quartered

10 parsley sprigs, divided

Salt and pepper

6 cups water, divided

½ celery stalk, halved

2 garlic cloves, smashed

1 bay leaf

4 black peppercorns

1 cup lower sodium chicken broth (if needed)

1 tablespoon ThickenThin not/Starch thickener

tip Oranges, lemons, onion, and parsley infuse the bird with a wonderful flavor while it's roasting, and because the fruit is discarded, this turkey is fine for the Induction and Ongoing Weight Loss phases of Atkins.

1 Heat oven to 325°F. Remove giblets from turkey and reserve. Fill large turkey cavity with oranges or lemons, onion, and 7 of the parsley sprigs. Place on a rack in a large shallow roasting pan. Season turkey generously with salt and pepper. Add 1 cup of the water to pan. Roast, basting occasionally with pan drippings and adding more water if pan gets dry, until an instant-read thermometer inserted into the thigh, not touching bone, registers 175° to 180°F, about 3 to 3½ hours. If necessary, cover turkey loosely with heavy-duty foil during the last hour of roasting so it doesn't get too brown. Transfer turkey to cutting board, cover loosely with foil, and let stand at least 20 minutes before carving.

2 While turkey is roasting, make broth for gravy: Combine reserved giblets, remaining 5 cups water, celery, garlic, remaining 3 parsley sprigs, bay leaf, and peppercorns in a large saucepan. Bring to a boil over high heat. Skim off the foam that rises to the surface. Reduce heat to very low and simmer until reduced to about 2 cups, 3 to 4 hours. If you like, dice the giblets and remove the meat from the neck to add to gravy. Wrap in plastic. Refrigerate broth and giblets until ready to use.

3 Pour juices from roasting pan into a fat separator or glass measure; skim off fat. Add giblet broth to measure 3 cups. Add chicken broth, if needed; if you have more than you need, reserve for another use.

4 Place roasting pan on the stovetop over 2 burners. Add broth and bring to a boil over medium heat, scraping up browned bits from bottom of pan. Stir in thickener and giblets and neck meat, if desired. Bring to a boil, stirring often. Reduce heat to low and simmer until thick and flavors are blended, about 5 minutes. Season with salt and pepper to taste.

5 Remove and discard oranges or lemons, onion, and parsley. Carve turkey and serve with gravy.

talking turkey

It's the centerpiece of the menu, but all too often the majestic turkey languishes while the humble sides are devoured. And that's too bad, because turkey is an excellent, versatile source of protein. The trouble is that turkeys cook unevenly—breasts tend to be overcooked by the time the thighs are done. Short of buying turkey parts and cooking them for the times they require, what can be done to ensure a tender, juicy bird?

Larger birds have a higher meat-to-bone ratio: A 20-pound turkey has considerably more meat than a 2-pounder, but the 20-pounder doesn't have that much more bone than the 12-pound bird. That extra meat is usually concentrated in the breast area, and denser meat takes longer to cook.

That so-called "fresh" turkey in your cart may have been frozen; in poultry processing, *fresh* birds can be stored at 26°F or above. *Frozen* means it has been kept at 0°F. Once cooked, fresh turkeys will have a juicier texture.

Natural turkeys have not been injected with artificial flavorings or basting mixtures. *Free-range* birds have the opportunity to roam. *Kosher* turkeys can be frozen, fresh, or natural, but they're never free-range: they roam indoors in special pens to keep them from eating nonkosher foods. Kosher turkeys are always brined, so they tend to be moister than nonkosher ones.

If you buy a frozen turkey, give it three to four days to thaw completely in the refrigerator. Or buy a fresh turkey a day or two ahead and store it in the coldest part of the fridge (usually the bottom shelf, on the same side as the door hinge). Never defrost a turkey at room temperature or in the microwave.

Wild Rice, Sausage, and Cherry Stuffing

Per serving: **NET CARBS: 8 GRAMS** ▪ Carbohydrates: 10.5 grams ▪ Fiber: 2.5 grams ▪ Protein: 6 grams ▪ Fat: 7.5 grams ▪ Calories: 133 ▪ **PREP TIME: 1 HOUR** ▪ **COOK TIME: 45 MINUTES** ▪ **SERVINGS: 8** plus leftovers

Wild rice (shown on page 263) is actually an aquatic grass; at 16 grams per half-cup, it's considerably lower in Net Carbs than white or even brown rice.

⅓ cup uncooked wild rice, picked over and rinsed

2½ cups water, divided

Salt

4 slices low-carb white bread, cut into ½-inch cubes

12 ounces sweet Italian sausage

4 tablespoons (½ stick) unsalted butter

3 celery stalks with leaves, finely diced (1½ cups)

¾ cup chopped onion

½ cup chopped fresh parsley

⅓ cup dried sour cherries

1 tablespoon poultry seasoning

½ teaspoon pepper

1 to 1¼ cups lower sodium chicken broth

1   Combine wild rice, 1½ cups of the water, and a generous pinch of salt in a small saucepan; bring to a boil over high heat. Reduce heat to low, cover, and simmer until tender, 40 to 45 minutes. Drain and set aside.

2   Heat oven to 350°F. Set bread cubes on a jelly-roll pan in a single layer. Bake, stirring once, until crispy, 10 to 14 minutes. Transfer to a large bowl.

3   Meanwhile, remove sausage from casing; crumble into a large nonstick skillet over medium heat. Cook, stirring frequently to break up clumps, until cooked through and lightly browned, about 12 minutes. Add to bread.

4   Return skillet to medium heat; add butter. When melted, add celery and onion; cook, stirring frequently, until tender, about 10 minutes. Add to bread mixture, then stir in parsley, cherries, poultry seasoning, pepper, and wild rice. Mix well. Stir in 1 cup of the chicken broth; add more if the stuffing still looks dry.

5   Transfer the stuffing to a large baking dish. Cover with foil and bake 30 minutes, then uncover and continue baking until lightly browned and heated through, 15 minutes longer.

Mashed Autumn Vegetables with Bacon and Scallions

3 4 Per serving: **NET CARBS: 9.5 GRAMS** ▪ Carbohydrates: 12 grams ▪ Fiber: 2.5 grams ▪ Protein: 4 grams ▪ Fat: 6 grams ▪ Calories: 118 ▪ **PREP TIME: 12 MINUTES** ▪ **COOK TIME: 35 MINUTES** ▪ **SERVINGS: 8**

Sweet potatoes benefit from savory toppings like bacon and scallions far more than treacly-sweet marshmallows. Cook the vegetables (shown on page 263) a day ahead and reheat in the microwave or oven; don't cook the bacon until just before serving, though, as its texture is less than ideal when it's cold.

1½ pounds turnips, peeled and cut into 1-inch chunks

1 pound sweet potatoes, peeled and cut into 1-inch chunks

Salt

4 slices bacon

1 tablespoon unsalted butter, at room temperature

⅛ teaspoon ground cinnamon

¼ teaspoon pepper

2 scallions, thinly sliced (2 tablespoons)

tip
Seek out bacon made without nitrates; some supermarkets sell it, though you may have to go to a butcher shop.

1 Put turnips and sweet potatoes in a large saucepan. Add cold water to cover and salt generously. Cover and bring to a boil over high heat. Reduce heat to medium-low and simmer until very tender, 10 to 12 minutes. Drain. If making ahead, cover and refrigerate. Thirty minutes before serving, reheat. Beat with an electric mixer or mash with a potato masher until fairly smooth.

2 Meanwhile, cook bacon in a medium skillet over medium heat until crisp. Drain on paper towels and coarsely crumble. Reserve drippings.

3 Add butter and bacon drippings to vegetables. Stir in cinnamon and pepper. Spoon into a serving dish and top with scallions and bacon.

On the Menu

christmas

Angelic Eggnog

2 Per serving: **NET CARBS: 3 GRAMS** ▪ Carbohydrates: 3 grams ▪ Fiber: 0 grams ▪ Protein: 7 grams ▪ Fat: 21 grams ▪
3 4 Calories: 262 ▪ **PREP TIME: 10 MINUTES** ▪ **COOK TIME: 5 MINUTES**, plus chilling ▪ **SERVINGS: 8** (½ cup each)

Be sure to bring the eggs to 175°F to reduce the risk of foodborne illness. If you exceed the temperature and your eggs scramble, don't worry—you can strain them.

4 large eggs

2 cups reduced-carb, whole-milk
  dairy beverage

¼ teaspoon ground cinnamon or
  1 (3-inch) cinnamon stick

¼ cup granular sugar substitute

½ cup brandy or dark rum

1½ cups heavy cream

1 teaspoon vanilla extract

Freshly grated nutmeg

1 Lightly beat eggs in a medium bowl.

2 Combine dairy beverage and cinnamon in a medium saucepan over medium heat. Bring just to a simmer, then gradually whisk into eggs. Return mixture to saucepan and reduce heat to low. Cook, whisking constantly, until mixture reaches 175°F on an instant-read thermometer, 1 to 2 minutes.

3 Remove from heat; whisk in sugar substitute, brandy or rum, cream, and vanilla. Let cool to room temperature; cover and refrigerate until cold, about 1 hour. Pour into cups and dust with nutmeg.

tip

If you'll be serving this to eggnog-loving children (or if you're in Induction), don't whisk in the brandy in step 3. Rather, pour a tablespoon (or half a shot) into the glasses of adults who choose to imbibe.

Filet Mignon Stuffed with Shiitake Mushrooms

1 2 3 4

Per serving: **NET CARBS: 3 GRAMS** ▪ Carbohydrates: 3.5 grams ▪ Fiber: 0.5 gram ▪ Protein: 34 grams ▪ Fat: 18 grams ▪ Calories: 321 ▪ **PREP TIME: 20 MINUTES** ▪ **COOK TIME: 20 MINUTES** ▪ **SERVINGS: 8**

Looking to gild the lily? Sprinkle the steaks (shown on page 271) with a tablespoon of crumbled blue cheese five minutes before you remove them from the oven. Slice any leftover steak and add to a green salad.

2 tablespoons extra virgin olive oil, divided

2 tablespoons unsalted butter, divided

1 pound shiitake mushrooms, stems trimmed (3½ cups)

2 teaspoons balsamic vinegar

Salt and pepper

8 (5- to 6-ounce) filet mignon steaks

tip

Take the time to seek out shiitake mushrooms that are uniform in size; if you can't find enough, use portobellos or the large white mushrooms sold for stuffing. Be sure the pan is very hot so the mushrooms brown.

1 Heat 1 tablespoon of the oil and 1 tablespoon of the butter in a medium nonstick skillet over medium-high heat. Add half of the mushrooms in a single layer and season with 1 teaspoon of the vinegar, salt, and pepper; cook, turning occasionally, until golden brown and tender, about 8 minutes. Transfer to a plate. Repeat with remaining mushrooms and vinegar, seasoning with salt and pepper. Let cool.

2 Lay filets flat on a work surface. With a small sharp knife, cut a slit in the center of each steak to make a pocket, cutting as far as possible into meat without cutting through.

3 Reserve 8 mushrooms to use as an edible garnish. Divide remaining mushrooms among the 8 steaks; stuff each steak, laying mushrooms flat and overlapping them. Press on steaks to close, then thread each with 2 to 3 toothpicks.

4 Heat oven to 450°F. Set a rack on a jelly-roll pan.

5 Heat skillet over medium-high heat. Add remaining tablespoon oil and remaining tablespoon butter. Season steaks on both sides with salt and pepper, and then add 4 steaks to pan. Cook, turning once, until nicely seared, about 2 minutes per side. Transfer to prepared pan. Repeat with remaining steaks. Roast steaks until done to taste, about 12 minutes for medium-rare. Serve steaks, drizzled with any juices they release during oven time, garnished with reserved mushrooms.

Sautéed Mussels in Tomato-Wine Broth

3 4 Per serving: **NET CARBS: 10.5 GRAMS** ▪ Carbohydrates: 11.5 grams ▪ Fiber: 1 gram ▪ Protein: 24 grams ▪ Fat: 9 grams ▪ Calories: 228 ▪ **PREP TIME: 25 MINUTES** ▪ **COOK TIME: 10 MINUTES** ▪ **SERVINGS: 8**

Serve this first course in shallow soup bowls. Toast some low-carb bread and cut it into triangles to dip in the flavorsome broth, or serve the broth separately in a cup to sip or eat with a spoon.

2 tablespoons extra virgin olive oil

⅓ cup finely chopped fennel

2 shallots, minced (⅓ cup)

4 garlic cloves, smashed and peeled

¼ to ½ teaspoon red pepper flakes

1 (14½-ounce) can diced tomatoes, drained

1 cup dry white wine

1 (8-ounce) bottle clam juice

¾ cup water

2 (2-pound) bags mussels, scrubbed and debearded (8 dozen mussels)

¼ cup chopped fresh parsley

1 tablespoon unsalted butter

Salt and pepper

1 Heat oil in an 8-quart or larger pot with lid over medium-low heat. Add fennel, shallots, garlic, and red pepper flakes; cook, stirring occasionally, until fennel is tender, about 5 minutes. Add tomatoes and cook, stirring, 2 minutes. Stir in wine, clam juice, and water. Add mussels; cover and cook, stirring once or twice, until shells open, 4 to 5 minutes.

2 Arrange open mussels in shallow bowls. Add parsley and butter to broth, stirring until butter melts; season with salt and pepper before ladling into bowls over mussels.

tip

Mussels should be alive when you purchase them. Discard any that are agape or don't snap shut when tapped, or that have cracked or broken shells. Similarly, don't eat any mussels that remain closed after cooking.

Butternut Squash and Escarole Gratin

Per serving: **NET CARBS: 16 GRAMS** ■ Carbohydrates: 23 grams ■ Fiber: 7 grams ■ Protein: 7 grams ■
Fat: 19 grams ■ Calories: 276 ■ **PREP TIME: 30 MINUTES** ■ **COOK TIME: 1 HOUR** ■ **SERVINGS: 8**

3   4

*If you know your day will be hectic, prepare the gratin (shown on page 271) a day
ahead, but cover and chill it without baking. Remove it from the refrigerator an hour
before you plan to put it in the oven.*

3 tablespoons unsalted butter,
  divided, plus more for baking
  dish

1 pound escarole, cleaned,
  trimmed, and cut crosswise into
  ½-inch strips (8 cups)

1 (3-pound) butternut squash,
  peeled, seeded, and cut into
  ½-inch pieces (4 cups), divided

¾ teaspoon salt, divided

¼ teaspoon pepper, divided

3 medium leeks, cleaned and thinly
  sliced crosswise (3 cups)

2 tablespoons water

1 cup heavy cream

½ cup canned lower sodium
  chicken broth

2 teaspoons ThickenThin
  not/Starch thickener

3 ounces Swiss cheese, grated
  (1 cup lightly packed)

2 tablespoons finely grated
  Parmesan cheese

tip
You'll get the best
flavor if you use top-
quality cheese. Seek
out Gruyère and
authentic Parmigiano-
Reggiano, and grate
them yourself.

1   Butter a 6- to 8-cup baking dish. Set oven rack in upper third of oven and
heat oven to 400°F.

2   Bring 3 inches of water to boil in a large saucepan. Add escarole and cook,
stirring, until tender, 3 to 5 minutes. Drain in a colander and rinse under cold
running water. Gently squeeze to remove as much moisture as possible.

3   Melt 1 tablespoon of the butter in a medium nonstick skillet over medium-
high heat. Add half of the squash and season with ¼ teaspoon of the salt and
⅛ teaspoon of the pepper; cook, turning occasionally, until lightly browned
and nearly tender, about 8 minutes. Transfer to baking dish. Repeat and
reserve.

4   Melt remaining tablespoon butter in skillet over medium-low heat. Add
leeks and season with ¼ teaspoon of the salt; cook, stirring, 3 minutes. Add
water, cover, and cook, stirring occasionally, until tender, about 3 minutes.
Stir in escarole and cook until heated through; spoon over squash in baking
dish. Top with reserved squash. Wipe out skillet.

5 Combine cream, broth, and thickener in skillet, whisking until blended. Cook over medium heat, stirring, until thickened, about 2 minutes. Remove from heat and stir in Swiss cheese until melted. Pour sauce over vegetables, spreading evenly. Sprinkle Parmesan on top and bake until bubbly and golden brown on top, about 30 minutes. Let stand 10 minutes before serving.

wonderful winter squash

At at time when most produce looks rather peaked, winter squashes are at their peak. They're harvested a little later than summer squash, and their very thick skin helps to preserve them. Most are a superb source of fiber, potassium, beta carotene, and vitamin C, and supply respectable amounts of folate, vitamin E, and B vitamins. They also supply alpha carotene and lutein.

Look for one of the following in your market; many can be used interchangeably. Spagetti squash, hubbards, and pumpkin are fine in Induction and Ongoing Weight Loss phases; save the acorn and butternut for the maintenance phases.

Acorn. High in fiber and beta carotene, acorn squash also supplies generous amounts of thiamin, vitamin C, iron, potassium, folate, and vitamin E.

Butternut. Butternut squash is an excellent source of beta carotene and vitamin C.

Hubbard. These blue-gray squash tend to be enormous, so you may find them precut in your market.

Pumpkin. If you need mashed pumpkin, it's much easier to use canned—it's been cooked down enough so that it won't become watery in most recipes. Otherwise, use pumpkin as you would another winter squash. It's very high in carotenoids, particularly beta carotene, alpha carotene, and lutein.

Spaghetti. Preparing spaghetti squash tends to be time-consuming, but its similarities to strands of spaghetti is astonishing. Make some on the weekend and heat it up with your favorite pasta sauce.

On the Menu

Israeli Salad

*Mediterranean Turkey Breast
with Lemon and Garlic*

Carrot-Zucchini Latkes

Sesame Seed Cookies

hanukkah

Israeli Salad

1 **2**
3 **4**

Per serving: **NET CARBS: 3 GRAMS** ■ Carbohydrates: 4 grams ■ Fiber: 1 gram ■ Protein: 0.5 gram ■
Fat: 7 grams ■ Calories: 77 ■ **PREP TIME: 15 MINUTES** ■ **SERVINGS: 8**

Make the dressing ahead, if you like, and refrigerate it, but don't toss the salad until just before serving; this way the vegetables remain crisp.

4 plum tomatoes, cored, seeded, and finely diced (1 cup)

1 small (12-ounce) English cucumber, finely diced

1 yellow bell pepper, diced (1 cup)

4 scallions, thinly sliced (¼ cup)

3 tablespoons fresh lime or lemon juice

¼ cup extra virgin olive oil

¾ teaspoon salt

½ teaspoon pepper

1 Combine tomatoes, cucumber, bell pepper, and scallions in a bowl.

2 Combine lime or lemon juice and oil in a small bowl, whisking to blend. Add salt and pepper. Pour dressing over vegetables and toss to coat.

updating hanukkah

Hanukkah lasts for eight nights, but it doesn't have to be eight food-centric nights. Instead of celebrating and exchanging gifts every evening, consider adopting a new tradition: Swap gifts only on the last night, but spend quality time with your family the other nights. Volunteer at a local hospital or soup kitchen, shop for toys or clothing to donate to charities or shelters, or visit a nursing home or assisted living center.

Consider renovating your recipes, too. Rather than make latkes with the usual potatoes, make Carrot-Zucchini Latkes (page 282), or use leeks or eggplant. Serve them with delicious low-carb extras, sour cream and caviar, for a special treat.

Change the way you entertain. If your gathering is informal, devise a theme, such as a soup tasting, and have guests bring their favorite low-carb potage. All you'll need is a wonderful salad dressed in a tasty vinaigrette to complete the meal.

Avoid gelt guilt: At your house, substitute silver dollars or other coins when playing dreidel; the religious symbolism will remain, but you'll cut down on the little ones' sugar consumption.

Mediterranean Turkey Breast with Lemon and Garlic

1 2 3 4

Per serving: **NET CARBS: 2 GRAMS** ■ Carbohydrates: 2 grams ■ Fiber: 0 grams ■ Protein: 60 grams ■ Fat: 15.5 grams ■ Calories: 399 ■ **PREP TIME: 10 MINUTES** ■ **MARINATE TIME: 1 HOUR** ■ **COOK TIME: 45 MINUTES** ■ **SERVINGS: 8**

If you can't find skinless turkey breasts, roast a whole breast. Purchase one that weighs about 7 pounds and increase the cooking time by half.

½ cup olive oil

2 to 3 teaspoons grated lemon zest

¼ cup fresh lemon juice

6 large garlic cloves, coarsely chopped (2 tablespoons)

1 teaspoon salt

½ teaspoon pepper

2 (1-pound) boneless, skinless turkey breast halves

1½ cups lower sodium chicken broth

Salt and pepper

tip

Now readily available at most supermarkets, boneless, skinless turkey breasts cook quickly and are a nice alternative to the old standby of chicken breasts, which they can replace in most recipes.

1 Combine oil, zest, lemon juice, garlic, salt, and pepper in a gallon-size zip-close bag. Seal bag and shake to mix. Add turkey, seal bag again, and turn over several times to coat turkey with marinade. Refrigerate for 1 hour, turning the bag frequently to keep turkey coated.

2 Heat oven to 450°F. Heat a large cast-iron or other ovenproof skillet over medium-high heat. Add turkey, skinned sides down, and cook until browned, 4 to 5 minutes. Turn turkey and pour in marinade. Transfer skillet to oven and roast for 15 minutes. Reduce heat to 375°F and continue to roast, brushing occasionally with marinade, until an instant-read thermometer inserted into meat registers 165°F, 25 to 30 minutes.

3 Transfer turkey to a cutting board and cover loosely with foil to keep warm. Pour juices from skillet into a fat separator or glass measure; skim off fat. Set skillet over medium-high heat; return pan juices to skillet and add broth. Bring to a boil, scraping pan to loosen browned bits, and boil until reduced to 1 cup, 3 to 5 minutes. Add any juices that have accumulated on cutting board. Season sauce with salt and pepper to taste. Slice turkey and serve with sauce.

Carrot-Zucchini Latkes

Per serving: **NET CARBS: 5 GRAMS** ▪ Carbohydrates: 7.5 grams ▪ Fiber: 2.5 grams ▪ Protein: 5.5 grams ▪

3 4 Fat: 16.5 grams ▪ Calories: 197 ▪ **PREP TIME: 15 MINUTES** ▪ **COOK TIME: 40 MINUTES** ▪ **SERVINGS: 8** (3 latkes each)

Pop these tasty latkes (shown on page 279) in a 300°F oven as you make them so they'll stay warm until serving time. You can also do the frying in two pans at once to cut your cooking time in half.

2 medium (6-ounce) zucchini

¾ **teaspoon salt,** divided

5 medium (2-ounce) carrots,
   peeled

1 small onion

1½ slices low-carb white bread

4 large eggs, beaten

½ teaspoon pepper

Vegetable oil for frying

Sour cream or lemon wedges
   (optional)

tip
Traditional latkes, which are made with potatoes, can have more than three times the carbohydrates of Carrot-Zucchini Latkes. It isn't unusual to see 25 to 30 grams of carbohydrates for three pancakes.

1 Heat oven to 300°F. Set a rack on a baking sheet.

2 Grate zucchini in a food processor fitted with shredding blade or with a box grater using the side with the largest holes. Transfer to a bowl; sprinkle with ¼ teaspoon of the salt and toss. Let stand while you prepare the remaining ingredients.

3 Grate carrots and onion in food processor or with grater. Transfer to a large bowl.

4 Put bread on a baking sheet and toast in the oven until dried out, 10 to 14 minutes. Leave oven on. Transfer bread to food processor and pulverize to make crumbs. Add crumbs, eggs, remaining ½ teaspoon salt, and pepper to carrots.

5 Transfer zucchini to a clean dish towel and squeeze out excess liquid. Add zucchini to carrot mixture and stir well to combine.

6 Heat ¼ inch of vegetable oil in a large skillet over medium heat until very hot. Drop batter by heaping tablespoons into oil and flatten to 3-inch pancakes; do not crowd pan. Cook until golden brown, 3 to 4 minutes per side. Transfer to paper towels to drain; then set on prepared baking sheet and keep latkes warm in the oven. Repeat, adding more oil if necessary, making a total of 24 latkes. Serve with sour cream or a squeeze of lemon, if desired.

Sesame Seed Cookies

3 4 Per serving: **NET CARBS: 5 GRAMS** ▪ Carbohydrates: 7 grams ▪ Fiber: 2 grams ▪ Protein: 5.5 grams ▪
Fat: 19 grams ▪ Calories: 213 ▪ **PREP TIME: 10 MINUTES** ▪ **COOK TIME: 30 MINUTES** ▪ **SERVINGS: 8** (3 cookies)

*Although these cookies are tasty made with butter, you may wish to use margarine
so they conform to Jewish dietary laws. Use a stick margarine, not a tub margarine,
and be sure it contains no hydrogenated oils.*

⅔ cup sesame seeds

⅓ cup soy flour

⅓ cup whole-wheat pastry flour

¼ teaspoon salt

½ cup trans fat–free margarine,
at room temperature

⅓ cup granular sugar substitute

½ teaspoon vanilla extract

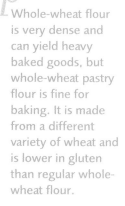

tip

Whole-wheat flour is very dense and can yield heavy baked goods, but whole-wheat pastry flour is fine for baking. It is made from a different variety of wheat and is lower in gluten than regular whole-wheat flour.

1 Heat oven to 350°F. Spread sesame seeds on a jelly-roll pan. Bake until toasted, 8 to 10 minutes, stirring or shaking the pan once or twice. Pour into a medium bowl and let cool briefly.

2 Add soy flour, pastry flour, and salt to sesame seeds; stir to combine.

3 Combine margarine and sugar substitute in another medium bowl. Beat with an electric mixer at medium speed until pale and creamy. Beat in vanilla. Add flour mixture and beat at medium-low speed until combined.

4 Pinch off walnut-size pieces of dough. Roll into 1-inch balls and set on ungreased baking sheets, making 24 balls. Dip a drinking glass into flour and flatten balls into 2-inch disks. Bake until golden brown, 8 to 10 minutes. Cool on baking sheets for 2 minutes, then transfer to a rack and cool completely. Handle cookies carefully, as they are fragile.

On the Menu

Dare-Deviled Eggs

*Mediterranean Pork and
Vegetable Skewers*

*Portobellos Stuffed with Crab
and Artichoke*

*Shrimp and Asparagus in
Blankets*

*Angel Food Cake (page 336)
with Black Forest Cherry Sauce*

Rum Punch

new year's eve

Dare-Deviled Eggs

1 **2** **3** **4** Per serving: **NET CARBS: 1 GRAM** ▪ Carbohydrates: 1 gram ▪ Fiber: 0 grams ▪ Protein: 7 grams ▪ Fat: 16 grams ▪ Calories: 178 ▪ **PREP TIME: 25 MINUTES** ▪ **COOK TIME: 18 MINUTES** ▪ **SERVINGS: 10**

With a potent kick of wasabi and a lavish garnish of caviar, these are not your typical deviled eggs (shown on page 285). Cook a few extra eggs as insurance against yolks that aren't centered or eggs that don't peel tidily. Make the eggs up to 12 hours ahead; cover tightly with plastic wrap and refrigerate.

10 large eggs

4 tablespoons cream cheese,
    at room temperature

2 teaspoons wasabi paste

½ cup mayonnaise

2 tablespoons minced fresh chives

Pepper

1½ ounces caviar

1 Put eggs in a single layer in a large saucepan and add cold water to cover. Bring to a boil. Turn off heat; cover and let stand 18 minutes. Drain and cover with the ice water until cold.

2 Peel eggs and cut in half lengthwise with a sharp knife.

3 Push yolks through a strainer and into a bowl. Cut cream cheese into pieces; add to yolks with wasabi paste. Mash with a fork until no flecks of white remain. Stir in mayonnaise and chives, season with pepper to taste.

4 Transfer yolk mixture to a pastry bag with a medium star tip and pipe yolk mixture into whites in a circular motion, mounding the filling generously in each egg half. Alternatively, use a spoon to stuff into whites.

5 Just before serving, spoon about ¼ teaspoon of caviar over each egg.

tip

If you're looking to splurge, purchase caviar from sturgeon. Beluga, osetra, and sevruga are all top quality and have prices to match—dusting the roe over deviled eggs is a way to stretch them. Lumpfish, golden, and red caviars are more affordable, but their flavors can't compare. If you choose not to use caviar, add about ½ teaspoon of salt with the chives and pepper.

Mediterranean Pork and Vegetable Skewers

Per serving: **NET CARBS: 9 GRAMS** ■ Carbohydrates: 12.5 grams ■ Fiber: 3.5 grams ■ Protein: 27 grams ■ Fat: 5.5 grams
■ Calories: 164 ■ **PREP TIME: 30 MINUTES** ■ **MARINATE TIME: 8 HOURS** ■ **COOK TIME: 12 MINUTES** ■ **SERVINGS: 10**

To ensure even cooking and consistent presentation, the number of pieces and the size you cut the vegetables is important. Cut the zucchini into 40 pieces; try to get them about the same size as the pork. The onions should be about two inches square and a few layers thick.

½ cup olive oil

¼ cup fresh lemon juice

8 **garlic cloves,** minced
(4 teaspoons)

1 **teaspoon dried oregano,**
crumbled

½ **teaspoon red pepper flakes**

½ **teaspoon salt**

½ **teaspoon pepper**

40 **cherry tomatoes**

5 **small onions,** quartered

1½ **pounds pork tenderloin,**
cut into 40 chunks

6 **small (4-ounce) zucchini,** cut into
40 (½-inch) rounds

4 **large bell peppers,** trimmed and
cut into 40 (1-inch) pieces

20 **(6-inch) bamboo skewers**

tip Choose vegetables of varying colors. Different-colored bell peppers, red or yellow tomatoes, and red onions look pretty with the zucchini.

1 Whisk together oil, lemon juice, garlic, oregano, red pepper flakes, salt, and pepper in a small bowl. Add tomatoes, onions, pork, zucchini, and bell peppers. Cover and refrigerate, stirring occasionally, for 1 to 8 hours.

2 Half an hour before cooking, soak skewers in water for 30 minutes. Set an oven rack 6 inches from the broiler element. Heat broiler.

3 Thread pork and vegetables onto skewers: Alternate zucchini and bell pepper, and end each skewer with pork and a cherry tomato or onion wedge.

4 Broil skewers, turning occasionally, until pork is completely cooked through and vegetables are slightly charred and tender, about 12 minutes. Serve warm or at room temperature.

Shrimp and Asparagus in Blankets

1 2 3 4 Per serving: **NET CARBS: 2.5 GRAMS** ▪ Carbohydrates: 5 grams ▪ Fiber: 2.5 grams ▪ Protein: 9 grams ▪ Fat: 5.5 grams ▪ Calories: 99 ▪ **PREP TIME: 25 MINUTES,** plus chilling ▪ **COOK TIME: 20 MINUTES** ▪ **SERVINGS: 10**

Like pigs in blankets for grown-ups' palates, these savory appetizers are ideal as passed hors d'oeuvres or as part of a buffet.

1 cup Atkins Quick Quisine Bake Mix

4 tablespoons (½ stick) unsalted **butter,** melted and cooled

¼ cup water

10 thin asparagus spears, ends trimmed

20 large shrimp, peeled and deveined (about 1 pound)

5 paper-thin prosciutto slices, cut crosswise into 20 strips

⅔ cup no-sugar-added tomato sauce, warmed

1 Combine bake mix, butter, and water in a medium bowl, stirring until the dough comes together. Transfer dough and loose flour onto a board or counter and knead until blended. Wrap in plastic wrap and refrigerate about 30 minutes.

2 Heat oven to 375°F.

3 Cut asparagus spears into 2 pieces that are as long as shrimp; discard any leftover pieces. Wrap 1 prosciutto strip around 1 asparagus piece and 1 shrimp; set aside and repeat with remaining prosciutto, asparagus, and shrimp.

4 Cut dough into 20 equal pieces. Roll each piece into a 3-inch circle. Set prosciutto bundles onto circles and roll up (shrimp and asparagus will stick out), pressing seam gently. Set, seam-side down, on a baking sheet. Bake until asparagus is tender, shrimp is pink, and dough is golden and puffed, about 20 minutes. Serve with the tomato sauce.

tip

If your asparagus are on the thick side, blanch them in boiling water for about 3 minutes, until they are just crisp-tender, before wrapping them.

Portobellos Stuffed with Crab and Artichoke

Per serving: **NET CARBS: 2.5 GRAMS** ▪ Carbohydrates: 4.5 grams ▪ Fiber: 2 grams ▪ Protein: 11 grams ▪ Fat: 17.5 grams ▪ Calories: 216 ▪ **PREP TIME: 20 MINUTES** ▪ **COOK TIME: 35 MINUTES** ▪ **SERVINGS: 10**

Select mushroom caps that are of fairly uniform size. If you can't find enough portobellos (shown on page 285), use large white mushrooms meant for stuffing. Depending on their size and the size of your skillet, you may have to cook them in batches.

20 medium portobello mushroom caps or 3 (6-ounce) packages

Cooking spray

1 cup chopped artichoke hearts, thawed if frozen

10 ounces lump crabmeat, picked over to remove cartilage and shells

4 ounces Gruyère cheese, grated (1½ cups)

¾ cup mayonnaise

½ teaspoon salt

½ teaspoon pepper

1 Heat oven to 400°F. Scrape gills out of mushroom caps with a soup spoon.

2 Heat a medium nonstick skillet or ridged grill pan over medium heat until hot; lightly coat with cooking spray. Add mushrooms, top-side down, in batches if necessary; partially cover and cook until juices collect on top, 3 to 4 minutes. Turn and cook 3 minutes longer. Transfer to a jelly-roll pan.

3 Combine artichoke hearts, crab, and cheese in a bowl. Stir in mayonnaise, salt, and pepper; stuff mushroom caps with a heaping tablespoon, mounding in center.

4 Bake mushrooms until hot and lightly browned, about 20 minutes; if you prefer a bit of a crust, broil for 2 to 3 minutes. Serve hot.

tip

Serve each mushroom on top of a handful of baby arugula. You'll have extra filling; warm it and serve as a dip with crudités. Back fin crab is best if your budget permits, but less expensive kinds are tasty, too.

Black Forest Cherry Sauce

3 4 Per serving: **NET CARBS: 9.5 GRAMS** ■ Carbohydrates: 8 grams ■ Fiber: 1.5 grams ■ Protein: 0.5 gram ■ Fat: 0.5 gram ■ Calories: 64 ■ **PREP TIME: 3 MINUTES** ■ **COOK TIME: 15 MINUTES** ■ **SERVINGS: 10** (generous 2 tablespoons)

You'll find this sauce far too tasty to reserve just for Angel Food Cake (page 336). Spoon it over Dark Chocolate Sorbet (page 245) or Vanilla Fudge Ice Cream (page 352), or find your favorite use for it. Note that the alcohol doesn't cook long enough to evaporate.

2 (10-ounce) bags no-sugar-added frozen sweet cherries, thawed and juices reserved

⅓ cup cognac or brandy

2 tablespoons sugar-free cherry syrup

1½ tablespoons chocolate extract

Combine cherries, their juices, cognac, and syrup in a large skillet. Bring to a boil over high heat; turn down heat to medium and simmer for 10 to 15 minutes, until cherries are very soft and juices are slightly thickened. Turn off heat and stir in chocolate extract. Serve hot over ice cream.

Rum Punch

2 **3 4** Per serving: **NET CARBS: 5.5 GRAMS** ■ Carbohydrates: 5.5 grams ■ Fiber: 0 grams ■ Protein: 0.5 gram ■ Fat: 0 grams ■ Calories: 124 ■ **PREP TIME: 10 MINUTES** ■ **SERVINGS: 10** (½ cup each)

The combination of sugar-free fruit-flavored syrups blends to provide a depth of flavor that one syrup simply cannot match in this festive drink (shown on page 289).

2 cups amber rum

1½ cups fresh orange juice

¾ cup fresh lemon juice (6 lemons)

¼ cup sugar-free strawberry syrup

¼ cup sugar-free raspberry syrup

¼ cup sugar-free cherry syrup

Crushed ice

1 orange, cut into slices for garnish (optional)

Combine all ingredients in a large pitcher or punch bowl. Serve with crushed ice and, if desired, orange slices.

On the Menu

Pomegranate Guacamole

Nifty Nachos

Texas Chili Cornbread Cobbler

South-of-the-Border Salad

Mexican Brownie Cheesecake Pie

Fresh Frozen Margaritas

super bowl
sunday

Pomegranate Guacamole

2 **3 4** Per serving: **NET CARBS: 3 GRAMS** ▪ Carbohydrates: 8 grams ▪ Fiber: 5 grams ▪ Protein: 2 grams ▪ Fat: 17 grams ▪ Calories: 177 ▪ **PREP TIME: 10 MINUTES** ▪ **SERVINGS: 10**

This surprising combination of tart, bright pomegranate seeds and creamy avocado refreshes your palate with every bite. Try these with Tortilla Chips (page 140) or mixed vegetables for dipping.

3 large Haas avocados

3 tablespoons fresh lemon juice

1½ tablespoons fresh lime juice

1 scallion, thinly sliced (1 tablespoon)

2 teaspoons minced jalapeño

Salt and pepper

⅓ cup pomegranate seeds

Halve and pit avocados and scoop flesh into a bowl. Stir or mash in lemon and lime juices. Add scallion, jalapeño, and salt and pepper to taste. Fold in pomegranate seeds.

the perfect pomegranate

Pomegranates require *patience*. First off, fans of this tropical fruit must wait until it is in season to enjoy it, generally from fall to early winter.

Obtaining the sweet-tart, crimson seeds from this fruit is best done at a leisurely pace, too. Pomegranates have a thick, leathery skin. Make a shallow cut at the blossom end, removing some of the pith; use the side of a teaspoon, if you like, as it's less likely to rupture the seeds. Use a knife to score the peel, then break the pomegranate apart along the score lines. Pick the seed sacs out of the pith.

Whole pomegranates keep in the fridge for about three months; seeds will keep for two months in a tightly sealed container in the freezer. Thaw them, then scatter them into salads, over low-carb ice cream, or even over meat dishes.

Pomegranates are high in anthocyanins, the same compounds that make blueberries so beneficial—and they're higher in antioxidant potency than green tea or red wine. One fourth of a pomegranate supplies 6.4 grams of Net Carbs.

Texas Chili Cornbread Cobbler

Per serving: **NET CARBS: 16.5 GRAMS** ▪ Carbohydrates: 23.5 grams ▪ Fiber: 7 grams ▪ Protein: 43 grams ▪
Fat: 34 grams ▪ Calories: 567 ▪ **PREP TIME: 20 MINUTES** ▪ **COOK TIME: 4 HOURS** (mostly unattended) ▪ **SERVINGS: 10**

3 4

Hearty shredded-meat chili is even better with a cornbread topping. The meat mixture is not super-spicy; let diners season it to their liking with hot sauce.

Chili:

2 tablespoons safflower oil, divided

Salt and pepper

3 pounds lean boneless beef chuck, cut into 1½-inch cubes

1½ cups finely chopped onion

3 garlic cloves, minced (1½ teaspoons)

2 poblano chilies, seeded and minced

1 tablespoon chili powder, preferably ancho

1 teaspoon ground cumin

¾ cup canned crushed tomatoes

2½ cups lower sodium beef broth

1 (15½-ounce) can pinto beans, drained and rinsed

1 bunch (6 to 8) scallions, sliced (1 cup)

Cornbread:

¾ cup Atkins Quick Quisine Deluxe Corn Muffin and Bread Mix

½ cup heavy cream

¼ cup water

1½ tablespoons safflower oil

1 large egg

1 large jalapeño, chopped (2 tablespoons)

6 ounces grated extra-sharp cheddar cheese (1½ cups)

tip

Poblanos are the dark green chilies commonly used in chiles rellenos. They're fairly mild, but the darkest ones have the richest flavor. Choose ones that are almost black.

1 For the chili: Heat 1 tablespoon of the oil in a large saucepan or Dutch oven over medium heat. Add one-third of the beef and season with salt and pepper; cook, turning frequently, until browned on all sides, about 8 minutes. Transfer to a plate. Repeat with remaining beef in 2 batches.

2 Add remaining tablespoon oil to saucepan. Add onions, garlic, and chilies; cook, stirring, until onions begin to soften, about 3 minutes. Add chili powder and cumin; cook, stirring, until vegetables are coated and spices are aromatic, about 3 minutes. Return meat to saucepan, then add tomatoes and broth; bring to a boil. Reduce heat to low, partially cover, and simmer gently, stirring occasionally, until beef is tender, 2½ to 3 hours.

3 Transfer beef cubes to a plate. When cool enough to handle, pull meat into shreds and return to saucepan. Stir in beans and scallions and cook until heated through.

4 Meanwhile, heat oven to 350°F. Spoon hot chili into a 9-inch deep-dish pie pan or 3-quart casserole and cover loosely with foil to keep warm.

5 **For the cornbread:** Combine cornbread mix, cream, water, oil, egg, and chopped jalapeño in a bowl, whisking to blend. Sprinkle cheese over chili, and then spoon batter over cheese, spreading evenly and leaving a ½-inch border between batter and pan. Bake until edge of chili is bubbly and cornbread is springy to the touch, 20 to 25 minutes.

smart super bowl snacks

Between the pregame festivities and the game itself, Super Bowl Sunday can be one giant eating competition: High-carb chips, honey barbecue wings, and lots of beer to wash it all down can make it a carb counter's nightmare.

If you've been invited to a Super Bowl party, offer to bring "chips" and dip or crackers and cheese to ensure you have noshes that fit your eating plan (odds are high that other guests will appreciate your contributions!). Here are a few vegetable stand-ins for potato chips and high-carb tortilla chips or crackers. Reach beyond the typical zucchini rounds for less common vegetables—or for common ones presented in uncommon ways:

Bell peppers. Instead of slicing into strips, cut them into panels so they can double for crackers. Hold the pepper by the stem upright on a cutting board; cut down the sides so they fall off into panels (the core and seeds should stay in one tidy bundle to discard). Cut the panels into 1½-to 2-inch squares or rectangles and serve with a soft, spreadable cheese; garlic-and-herb Boursin provides a savory contrast to the sweet pepper.

Jicama. Once peeled, this Mexican vegetable is a dead ringer for raw potato except for two critical characteristics: It tastes great (crunchy yet juicy and quite sweet) and it has a fraction of the Net Carbs (2.5 grams per ½ cup raw). Jicama are fairly large, but buy the smallest you can find. Peel them and cut them into ⅛-inch slices. Serve with a zesty guacamole.

Fennel. Cut fennel bulbs into thin wedges, or cut smaller bulbs into rounds. With its subtle anise flavor, fennel is best with blander cheeses and spinach dip.

Belgian endive. Separate the leaves from the core of this slightly bitter, elegantly pale winter vegetable, then give them a quick rinse. Their slightly scooped shape makes them perfect for dipping.

Nifty Nachos

2 3 4 Per serving: **NET CARBS: 6.5 GRAMS** ▪ Carbohydrates: 11 grams ▪ Fiber: 4.5 grams ▪ Protein: 20 grams ▪ Fat: 21 grams ▪ Calories: 306 ▪ **PREP TIME: 5 MINUTES** ▪ **COOK TIME: 2 MINUTES** ▪ **SERVINGS: 10**

Low-carb soy chips are a great stand-in for tortilla chips, but watch closely as they burn easily. Mist the foil with cooking spray to make it easy to transfer the nachos (shown on page 293) to a pretty platter.

Cooking spray

8 (1-ounce) bags low-carb soy chips

1 cup sliced black olives

1 (4½-ounce) can chopped mild green chilies

12 ounces sharp cheddar cheese, grated (3 cups)

⅔ cup sour cream

⅔ cup salsa

1 Set an oven rack 6 inches from the broiler element. Heat broiler. Line 2 baking sheets or jelly-roll pans with foil and lightly coat with cooking spray.

2 Arrange snack chips on baking sheets in a single layer. Top with olives and chilies; sprinkle with cheese. Broil, one baking sheet at a time, until cheese is melted, 30 to 60 seconds. Transfer nachos to a platter and serve right away with sour cream and salsa.

tip

Use up the jar of mayo in your fridge, but when you replace it, look for a brand that's sugar-free. Even though most varieties have a small amount of sugar, there are now a few brands without any.

South-of-the-Border Salad

1 2 3 4

Per serving: **NET CARBS: 3 GRAMS** ■ Carbohydrates: 4.5 grams ■ Fiber: 1.5 grams ■ Protein: 1 gram ■ Fat: 5.5 grams ■ Calories: 71 ■ **PREP TIME: 15 MINUTES** ■ **SERVINGS: 10**

Jicama adds a sweet note and plenty of crunch to this refreshing salad. You can make the dressing ahead; store any leftovers in the refrigerator in a sealed jar for five days.

Dressing:

¼ teaspoon cumin seeds

¼ cup mayonnaise

¼ cup sour cream

2 tablespoons fresh lime juice

1 teaspoon grated lime zest

1 tablespoon water

2 tablespoons minced fresh chives

Salt and pepper

Salad:

1 pound green leaf lettuce, trimmed and torn into bite-size pieces

¼ cup cilantro leaves

1 medium cucumber, peeled, halved, seeded, and thinly sliced (1 cup)

1 (4-ounce) piece jicama, peeled, thinly sliced, and cut into thin strips (1 cup)

1 cup grape tomatoes, halved lengthwise

tip
Toasting the cumin seeds intensifies their flavor. If you only find ground cumin in your spice rack, don't worry. Use about the same amount, but skip the toasting and grinding in step 1.

1 For the dressing: Roast cumin seeds in a small dry skillet over medium heat, shaking pan constantly, until fragrant and toasted, 20 to 30 seconds. Transfer to a mortar and pestle or spice grinder and grind.

2 Whisk mayonnaise, sour cream, lime juice, and zest in a small bowl. Whisk in water, cumin, and chives. Season with salt and pepper to taste.

3 For the salad: Combine lettuce, cilantro, cucumber, jicama, and tomatoes in a large bowl. Just before serving, add dressing and toss to coat.

Mexican Brownie Cheesecake Pie

Per serving: **NET CARBS: 15 GRAMS** ▪ Carbohydrates: 18 grams ▪ Fiber: 3 grams ▪ Protein: 6 grams ▪
3 4 Fat: 20 grams ▪ Calories: 256 ▪ **PREP TIME: 20 MINUTES** ▪ **COOK TIME: 40 MINUTES,** plus cooling ▪ **SERVINGS: 12**

A subtle hint of cinnamon is a nod to spiced Mexican chocolate. If you like, put a teaspoon of unsweetened cocoa powder into a fine-mesh strainer and shake it over the finished pie. Make the pie up to two days ahead and keep it in the refrigerator, covered loosely with plastic wrap.

Brownie Layer:

Cooking spray

1 (8.5-ounce) package Atkins
    Quick Quisine Deluxe Fudge
    Brownie Mix

⅓ cup unsalted butter, melted

⅓ cup water

1 large egg

¼ teaspoon ground cinnamon

Cheesecake Layer:

2 (8-ounce) packages cream
    cheese, at room temperature

2 large eggs

1 large egg white

⅓ cup granular sugar substitute

1 teaspoon vanilla extract

½ teaspoon grated orange zest

tip

Not all cheesecakes are baked in a water bath. Sometimes—particularly if a dessert has a cheesecake layer or topping—the cake is put into a hot oven and then the oven is turned off. The residual heat cooks the ingredients, but the heat isn't intense enough to cause curdling or cracking.

1 **For the brownie layer:** Heat oven to 350°F. Spray a 9-inch deep-dish pie pan or springform pan with cooking spray.

2 Stir together brownie mix, butter, water, egg, and cinnamon in a bowl. Scrape into pan, smoothing top. Bake until center springs back to the touch, about 20 minutes.

3 **For the cheesecake layer:** Meanwhile, beat cream cheese in a large bowl with an electric mixer until fluffy. Beat in eggs, one at a time, then egg white. Add sugar substitute, vanilla, and orange zest and mix until blended.

4 Scrape mixture onto hot brownie layer and return pan to oven. Turn off oven and let stand without opening the door until just set in center, about 20 minutes. Cool at room temperature for 1 hour, and then refrigerate until cold, about 3 hours.

Fresh Frozen Margaritas

2
3 4 Per serving: **NET CARBS: 2.5 GRAMS** ▪ Carbohydrates: 2.5 grams ▪ Fiber: 0 grams ▪ Protein: 0 grams ▪
Fat: 0 grams ▪ Calories: 105.5 ▪ **PREP TIME: 10 MINUTES** ▪ **SERVINGS: 4**

*If you've only had margaritas from a mix, prepare to be amazed. They're an entirely
different drink made with fresh lime juice (shown on page 293).*

1 teaspoon grated lime zest	6 ounces tequila (¾ cup)
1 tablespoon granular sugar substitute	¼ cup fresh lime juice
3 cups ice cubes	2 tablespoons fresh orange juice
	4 lime wedges

Place lime zest and sugar substitute in blender. Add ice, tequila, lime juice,
and orange juice, and blend until smooth. Pour into glasses and garnish with
lime wedges.

tip

Like salt on your margarita glass? Put a few tablespoons of kosher salt on a
small plate—no need to buy expensive margarita salt. Run a lime wedge
around the rims, then hold the glass at an angle and roll the rim in the salt,
coating just the outside. This ensures that you won't have salt dissolving
into your drink and altering its flavor.

On the Menu

Oysters Rockefeller with Blender Hollandaise

Edamame Dip with Crudités

Savory Turkey Strudel

Chocolate Martinis

oscar night

Chocolate Martinis

2 **3** **4** Per serving: **NET CARBS: 3.5 GRAMS** ■ Carbohydrates: 3.5 grams ■ Fiber: 0 grams ■ Protein: 0.5 gram ■
Fat: 5 grams ■ Calories: 191 grams ■ **PREP TIME: 15 MINUTES,** plus cooling time ■ **COOK TIME: 5 MINUTES** ■ **SERVINGS: 6**

Cocktail shakers are rarely large enough to make six drinks, but it's better to make a few in small batches in a shaker than it is to make one large batch in a pitcher. Vigorous shaking is necessary to melt enough of the ice to dilute the liquor sufficiently and blend the flavors in this luscious dessert drink. For photo, see page 303.

¼ cup heavy cream

1 (1-ounce) Atkins Endulge Chocolate Candy Bar, roughly chopped

1½ tablespoons chocolate extract

1½ cups vanilla vodka (12 ounces)

Ice

1 Heat cream in a small saucepan until scalding. Turn off heat, stir in chocolate, and let stand until chocolate has melted, about 2 minutes. Add chocolate extract and stir until well combined. Cool to room temperature.

2 Combine chocolate sauce with vodka in a large pitcher or measuring cup.

3 Fill 6 cocktail glasses and a cocktail shaker with ice. Pour about one-third of the martini mixture into the cocktail shaker; shake vigorously for about 30 seconds. Discard ice from glasses. Strain the martini into chilled glasses. Repeat with more ice and remaining martini mix.

Oysters Rockefeller

2 **3** **4** Per serving (with hollandaise): **NET CARBS: 8 GRAMS** ▪ Carbohydrates: 9.5 grams ▪ Fiber: 1.5 grams ▪ Protein: 6.5 grams ▪ Fat: 45.5 grams ▪ Calories: 467 ▪ **PREP TIME: 30 MINUTES** ▪ **COOK TIME: 15 MINUTES** ▪ **SERVINGS: 6**

Oysters can be difficult to shuck. They require an honest-to-goodness oyster knife and adequate protection; experience is also helpful. If you lack any or all of these, ask your fishmonger to shuck them—as close to serving time as possible. The type you use is less important than their condition: Be sure yours are impeccably fresh. For photo, see page 303.

1 (10-ounce) package frozen spinach, thawed, or 1 (10-ounce) bag fresh spinach

2 tablespoons unsalted butter

1 medium leek, trimmed, washed, and finely chopped (1 cup)

1 tablespoon Pernod or other anise-flavored liqueur

½ cup heavy cream

Salt and pepper

2 dozen oysters

1 cup Blender Hollandaise (Recipe follows)

tip
Fresh spinach is delightful in sautés and salads, but in cooked dishes frozen is easier to use, and it's hard to tell the difference between the two.

1 If using frozen spinach, squeeze to remove moisture and chop. If using fresh spinach, blanch in 2 cups boiling water until wilted, 1 to 2 minutes; rinse with cold water until cool, and then squeeze to remove as much moisture as possible; chop.

2 Melt butter in a medium skillet over medium heat. Add leek and cook, stirring occasionally, until tender, about 6 minutes. Stir in spinach, Pernod, and cream; cook, stirring occasionally, until thickened and creamy, about 5 minutes. Season with salt and pepper; set aside to cool slightly.

3 Heat oven to 400°F. Scrub oysters, shuck, and transfer to a small bowl. Arrange deeper halves of shells on a jelly-roll pan. Distribute spinach among shells and top with an oyster.

4 Bake until spinach and oysters are hot, 8 to 10 minutes. Top oysters with hollandaise and then run under the broiler, if desired. Transfer with tongs to 6 appetizer plates and serve immediately.

Blender Hollandaise

 Per (2-tablespoon) serving: **NET CARBS: 0.5 GRAM** ■ Carbohydrates: 0.5 gram ■ Fiber: 0 grams ■ Protein: 1.5 grams
■ Fat: 25 grams ■ Calories: 227 ■ **PREP TIME: 2 MINUTES** ■ **COOK TIME: 3 MINUTES** ■ **YIELD: 1 CUP**

Much, much simpler to prepare than traditional hollandaise, this sauce has only one requirement: The butter must be heated until it is bubbling hot because that is what heats the eggs and makes them safe. If you have a butter warmer or small saucepan with a spout, it makes pouring the hot butter into the blender less messy. You could also pour it into a heatproof glass measuring cup.

2 sticks unsalted butter	¼ teaspoon salt
3 large egg yolks	⅛ teaspoon white pepper
1½ tablespoons fresh lemon juice	

1 Melt butter in a small saucepan until it is bubbling but not brown.

2 Combine yolks and lemon juice in a blender. With the motor running, slowly drizzle in melted butter. Season with salt and pepper.

Save leftover egg whites in a tightly sealed container and refrigerate for three or four days, or freeze them for three to four months. Freeze whites in the compartments of an ice cube tray. When they're solid, transfer them to a freezer bag to use as you need them.

Edamame Dip

2 3 4 Per serving: **NET CARBS: 5.5 GRAMS** ■ Carbohydrates: 8 grams ■ Fiber: 2.5 grams ■ Protein: 7.5 grams ■ Fat: 13.5 grams ■ Calories: 175 ■ **PREP TIME: 5 MINUTES** ■ **COOK TIME: 5 MINUTES** ■ **SERVINGS: 6** (⅓ cup each)

Edamame, or fresh soybeans, can be found in some supermarkets (look in the organic foods section) and most natural foods stores in the frozen foods sections. They can be purchased in their pods or shelled—for this recipe, you'll want shelled edamame.

2 cups frozen shelled edamame beans, thawed

2 garlic cloves, peeled

⅓ cup mayonnaise

⅓ to ½ cup water

2½ tablespoons lemon juice

1 teaspoon salt

¼ teaspoon pepper

1 Bring a pot of lightly salted water to a boil; add beans. Cook until tender, about 3 minutes; drain.

2 Combine beans, garlic, mayonnaise, and ⅓ cup of the water, lemon juice, salt, and pepper in a food processor. Purée until smooth; add remaining water if dip is thicker than you prefer. Chill slightly before serving.

tip

To keep the carb count down, serve this dip and others with red bell pepper strips, endive leaves, or blanched cauliflower florets. Or look for low-carb flatbreads in your grocery store—be sure they're free of added trans fats.

Savory Turkey Strudel

Per serving: **NET CARBS: 14 GRAMS** ▪ Carbohydrates: 17.5 grams ▪ Fiber: 3.5 grams ▪ Protein: 34.5 grams ▪
Fat: 31 grams ▪ Calories: 485 ▪ **PREP TIME: 25 MINUTES** ▪ **COOK TIME: 40 MINUTES** ▪ **SERVINGS: 6**

3 4

This savory strudel can be made with chicken as well as turkey. For ease, buy rotisserie chickens at the market or use leftovers from a homemade bird; Smoke-Roasted Turkey (page 237) is particularly tasty.

6 tablespoon unsalted butter, divided, plus more for baking sheet

2 large leeks, trimmed, washed and chopped (2½ cups)

⅔ cup lower sodium chicken broth

6 ounces cream cheese, at room temperature

1 tablespoon fresh lemon juice

4 cups cooked shredded turkey or chicken breast

1 (10-ounce) box frozen chopped broccoli, thawed

Salt and pepper

2 slices low-carb multigrain bread

½ teaspoon herbes de Provence or dried tarragon

4 sheets (13 by 18 inches) frozen whole-wheat phyllo dough, thawed

1 Melt 2 tablespoons of the butter in a medium nonstick skillet over medium heat. Add leeks and cook, stirring, 2 minutes. Add broth; cover and cook, stirring occasionally, until leeks are tender, about 6 minutes. Stir in cream cheese and lemon juice until blended. Stir in turkey and broccoli; cook until heated through, 2 to 3 minutes. Season with salt and pepper to taste. Let cool.

2 Tear bread into pieces and pulse in a food processor to make ½ cup fine crumbs. Melt another tablespoon butter in a small skillet over medium heat; add crumbs and herbes de Provence or tarragon; cook, stirring, until toasted, about 3 minutes; transfer to a plate and let cool.

3 Melt 3 tablespoons butter in a small skillet and remove from heat. Lay a sheet of phyllo on cutting board; brush with butter and sprinkle with one-third of the bread crumbs. Top with another sheet of phyllo and repeat, brushing last sheet of phyllo with butter only.

4 Set oven racks so that one is in the center of oven; heat oven to 400°F. Butter a baking sheet.

5 Spoon turkey mixture lengthwise down center of phyllo, leaving a 1-inch border on each short end. Fold a long end over stuffing, then fold in short ends and roll phyllo snugly around stuffing to make a log. Carefully transfer to baking sheet and brush log with remaining tablespoon butter. If you like, make 11 shallow cuts, taking care not to cut all the way through the phyllo to the filling; the strudel will be easier to cut into 12 slices after baking. Bake strudel on center rack until golden and crisp, 25 to 30 minutes.

tip

You can make this strudel ahead; chill the rolled strudel for up to four hours, and add a few more minutes to the baking time.

star-studded snacks

From the moment the first star alights on the red carpet until the Best Picture winner is announced, movie aficionados are reluctant to leave their posts in front of the television. Even so, consider serving foods from a buffet at your Oscar Night bash. This way, no one's view will be blocked by someone reaching across the table for the dip, and no one will miss part of an acceptance speech should a guest ask for something to be passed.

When people eat in front of a TV, it's best to serve finger foods—wielding cutlery can be tricky when the plate is balanced on your lap. Canapés like Oysters Rockefeller or deviled eggs are preferable to drippy dips, though thicker ones like the Edamame Dip (page 307) in this menu are fine. Serve the dippers right next to the dip so guests can dunk while they're going through the line. Other tasty finger foods include cheese quesadillas (avoid chunky fillings) made with small tortillas (or make them with quartered tortillas, so each triangle has a folded edge to minimize leaks); satays or skewers (such as Vietnamese-Style Beef Skewers, page 219); or spread mustard on ham or aioli on Genoa salami; set a few asparagus spears on the meat and roll up.

On the Menu

*Salad of Endive and Boston
Lettuce with Pear and Goat
Cheese*

*Clementine-Glazed Duck Breast
with Green Beans*

Peach Melba

Pink Sunset Champagne Cocktail

valentine's day

Salad of Endive and Boston Lettuce with Pear and Goat Cheese

Per serving: **NET CARBS: 8.5 GRAMS** ▪ Carbohydrates: 12 grams ▪ Fiber: 3.5 grams ▪ Protein: 10 grams ▪
Fat: 24.5 grams ▪ Calories: 295 ▪ **PREP TIME: 10 MINUTES** ▪ **SERVINGS: 2**

3 4

What could be more appropriate for a romantic dinner than a salad that uses the hearts of the greens? This is exceptionally pretty with a red pear; choose one if they are in peak condition at your market.

¼ **cup walnut pieces** (1½ ounces)

2 **teaspoons extra virgin olive oil**

½ **tablespoon white wine vinegar**

¼ **teaspoon Dijon mustard**

¼ **teaspoon salt**

2 **cups Boston lettuce,**
   torn in pieces

½ **cup radicchio,** torn in pieces

1 **Belgian endive heart,**
   cut crosswise into ½-inch slices

½ **small Bartlett pear,** halved
   lengthwise, cored, and thinly
   sliced crosswise (½ cup)

1 (2-ounce) **log goat cheese,**
   crumbled (¼ cup)

Pepper

1 Toast walnuts in a small dry skillet over medium-low heat, shaking pan frequently, until fragrant, about 5 minutes. Let cool, then chop.

2 Whisk oil, vinegar, mustard, and salt in a medium salad bowl. Add lettuces and pear and toss to coat. Add nuts and goat cheese, season with pepper to taste, and toss again.

tip

It's wise to have a "wardrobe" of olive oils to choose from. Save the pure and refined oils for cooking, but pull out your best extra virgin one for salad dressings—particularly those with few other ingredients, where its flavor really comes through.

Peach Melba

Per serving: **NET CARBS: 16.5 GRAMS** ▪ Carbohydrates: 30.5 grams ▪ Fiber: 14 grams ▪ Protein: 3.5 grams ▪
3 4 Fat: 14 grams ▪ Calories: 228 ▪ **PREP TIME: 15 MINUTES** ▪ **COOK TIME: 10 MINUTES** ▪ **SERVINGS: 2**

If you can't find peach halves packed in juice, opt for peach slices and allow three per serving; serve the ice cream over the peaches (shown on page 311).

1 cup thawed no-sugar-added frozen raspberries

½ teaspoon fresh lemon juice

1 teaspoon unsalted butter

2 canned juice-packed peach halves, patted dry

1 cup low-carb vanilla ice cream

1 Purée raspberries and any juice in a blender. Set a strainer over a bowl and transfer berries to strainer. Press berries to release juice.

2 Melt butter in a small nonstick skillet over medium heat. Add peach halves, cut sides down, and cook until lightly browned, about 5 minutes. Turn with tongs and cook until browned, 2 to 3 minutes longer.

3 Scoop ½ cup ice cream into 2 small bowls or dessert cups. Top each with a peach half and 1 generous tablespoon raspberry sauce.

Pink Sunset Champagne Cocktail

Per serving: **NET CARBS: 4.5 GRAMS** ▪ Carbohydrates: 5.5 grams ▪ Fiber: 1 gram ▪ Protein: 0.5 gram ▪
3 4 Fat: 0 grams ▪ Calories: 100 ▪ **PREP TIME: 5 MINUTES** ▪ **SERVINGS: 2**

Pink and red grapefruit are sweeter than white. You can also use orange, pomegranate, or lime juice (use only 2 tablespoons of lime juice) instead. For photo, see page 311.

¼ cup raspberries or strawberries (quartered if large)

¼ cup fresh pink or red grapefruit juice

4 teaspoons sugar-free raspberry syrup

1 cup sparkling wine

2 mint leaves or sprigs

Divide berries, juice, and syrup between two champagne flutes. Top with sparkling wine and garnish with mint.

Clementine-Glazed Duck Breast

2
3 **4**

Per serving: **NET CARBS: 5 GRAMS** ∎ Carbohydrates: 5 grams ∎ Fiber: 0 grams ∎ Protein: 40.5 grams ∎ Fat: 16.5 grams ∎ Calories: 339 ∎ **PREP TIME: 10 MINUTES** ∎ **COOK TIME: 20 MINUTES** ∎ **SERVINGS: 2**

A cast-iron skillet is the ideal utensil for this recipe because it helps the duck to brown beautifully. If you don't have one, select another heavy skillet.

2 (7-ounce) boneless duck breast halves

Salt and pepper

4 teaspoons unsalted butter, divided

½ cup canned lower sodium chicken broth

½ teaspoon ThickenThin not/Starch thickener

¼ teaspoon granular sugar substitute

1 small shallot, minced (1 tablespoon)

½ teaspoon finely grated clementine or blood orange zest

¼ cup fresh clementine or blood orange juice

1 teaspoon balsamic vinegar

tip

Clementines are a type of tangerine; their thin, loose skins make them easy to peel and their deep orange-colored juice imparts a lovely color to the glaze. They're most readily available around Christmastime, when you're likely to find them in small crates. If they're no longer in season, look for blood oranges. They're wonderfully sweet, with a vibrant red juice and flesh.

1 Pierce duck skin all over with a fork; season duck with salt and pepper. Melt 1 teaspoon of the butter in a large cast-iron or heavy skillet over medium heat. Add duck, skin side down, and cook until skin is dark and crisp, 8 to 10 minutes. Turn and cook until done to taste, 4 to 5 minutes longer for medium-rare, 10 to 14 minutes for medium. Transfer to a plate and cover loosely with foil to keep warm.

2 Meanwhile, combine broth, thickener, and sugar substitute in a small bowl; whisk thoroughly to break up any lumps of thickener. Set aside.

3 Pour off all but 1 tablespoon fat from skillet. Reduce heat to low; add shallot and cook, stirring, until softened, about 2 minutes. Add zest, juice, and vinegar and cook until reduced by half, about 1 minute.

4 Increase heat to medium-high. Stir broth mixture again, then add to skillet and cook, stirring, until thickened, about 2 minutes. Stir in remaining 3 teaspoons butter and season with salt and pepper to taste.

5 Return duck to skillet and turn until heated through. Transfer duck to a cutting board and cut crosswise into thin slices. Transfer to plates and spoon sauce on top.

On the Menu

Spicy Tomato Refresher

Creamy Four-Onion Soup

Mustard-and-Pepper-Coated Ham

Spring Vegetable Barley Risotto

Asparagus with Toasted Hazelnuts

Creamy Lemon Bars (page 163)

easter

Spicy Tomato Refresher

2 **3** **4** Per serving: **NET CARBS: 6 GRAMS** ■ Carbohydrates: 6.5 grams ■ Fiber: 0.5 gram ■ Protein: 2 grams ■ Fat: 0.5 gram ■ Calories: 32.5 ■ **PREP TIME: 10 MINUTES** ■ **SERVINGS: 8**

This tomato drink (shown on page 316) is a nonalcoholic version of the bullshot. If you like, moisten the edges of the glasses with a lemon wedge and turn them in a dish of kosher salt or celery salt to coat the rims.

1 (32-ounce) bottle lower sodium tomato juice (4 cups)

1 (14½-ounce) can lower sodium beef broth

¼ cup fresh lemon or lime juice

1½ to 2 tablespoons prepared white horseradish

Few drops hot pepper sauce, such as Tabasco (optional)

Ice

8 thin cucumber spears or 8 celery sticks

8 lemon or lime wedges

1 Mix together tomato juice, broth, lemon or lime juice, horseradish, and hot sauce, if using, in a pitcher.

2 Fill 8 old-fashioned glasses with ice. Fill with juice mixture and garnish each with a cucumber spear or celery stalk and lemon or lime wedge.

tip

Prepare this up to a day ahead and keep in the fridge. Feel free to make this with vegetable juice, or with spicy versions of tomato or vegetable juice in this recipe. If you want to use clam-tomato juice, replace the beef broth with 2 more cups of clam-tomato juice.

Creamy Four-Onion Soup

2 3 4 Per serving: **NET CARBS: 7.5 GRAMS** ■ Carbohydrates: 9 grams ■ Fiber: 1.5 grams ■ Protein: 3.5 grams ■ Fat: 12.5 grams ■ Calories: 153 ■ **PREP TIME: 25 MINUTES** ■ **COOK TIME: 40 MINUTES** ■ **SERVINGS: 8**

Garlic, leeks, scallions, and onions are all part of the allium family. Leeks grow in sandy soil, so it is imperative they be washed thoroughly.

3 tablespoons unsalted butter, divided

1 **large onion,** halved and thinly sliced (1 cup)

2 **garlic cloves,** minced (1 teaspoon)

2 **large leeks,** white part only, trimmed, halved, and cut into ½-inch slices (2½ cups)

1 **medium (6-ounce) zucchini,** sliced

½ **teaspoon dried tarragon,** crumbled

¼ teaspoon salt

¼ teaspoon pepper

2 **bunches scallions,** thinly sliced, whites and greens divided (2 cups)

2 (14½-ounce) cans lower sodium chicken broth

1½ cups water

½ cup heavy cream

tip

Using a salad spinner to wash the leeks gives excellent—and easy—results, though it may take a few rinses to remove all the grit. Give them a good soak first. Spin the leeks dry before sautéing them.

1 Melt 2 tablespoons of the butter in a large, heavy saucepan over medium heat. Add onion, garlic, leeks, zucchini, tarragon, salt, and pepper. Cover and cook, stirring frequently, until softened, about 7 minutes.

2 Stir in 1¾ cups of the scallions, reserving ¼ cup tender green parts. Cover and cook until wilted, 2 minutes longer.

3 Add broth and water. Increase heat, cover, and bring to a boil. Reduce heat to medium-low and simmer until vegetables are very tender, about 10 minutes.

4 Remove from heat; with a potato masher or large wire whisk, mash vegetables in soup, thickening it a bit but retaining a chunky texture.

5 Return soup to medium heat; stir in cream and remaining tablespoon butter. Heat, stirring frequently, until soup is just boiling and butter has melted. Ladle into bowls and serve, garnishing with remaining ¼ cup scallion greens.

Mustard-and-Pepper-Coated Ham

1 2 3 4

Per serving: **NET CARBS: 0.5 GRAM** ■ Carbohydrates: 0.5 gram ■ Fiber: 0 grams ■ Protein: 42.5 grams ■ Fat: 28 grams ■ Calories: 438 ■ **PREP TIME: 10 MINUTES** ■ **COOK TIME: 2½ HOURS** ■ **SERVINGS: 8**

If you typically coat ham with a sugar-laden glaze to complement its salty, smoky flavor, you're missing out. Sharp mustards and spicy peppercorns pack a flavor punch that makes a sweet sauce pale in comparison. For photo, see page 317.

1 (7- to 7½- pound) fully cooked,
  bone-in, spiral-sliced ham or
  1 (4½- to 5-pound) boneless,
  spiral-sliced ham

3 tablespoons coarse-grain
  mustard

2 tablespoons Dijon mustard

1 teaspoon coarse-ground black
  pepper

1 Heat oven to 300°F. Line a roasting pan with heavy-duty foil.

2 Set ham face-down in roasting pan (this helps to keep slices intact). Bake until a meat thermometer inserted in the thickest part, not touching bone, registers 135°F to 140°F, 1½ to 2 hours for a bone-in ham, about 1 hour for a boneless ham.

3 Mix both mustards and pepper in a small bowl; stir in 1 tablespoon pan drippings. Brush over the ham. Increase oven temperature to 400°F. Bake until coating is lightly browned, 15 to 20 minutes longer. Let stand for 20 minutes before serving.

tip

Like other roasts, hams need to stand after you've removed them from the oven and before you slice them (even presliced hams). As the meat cooks, the juices move to the surface of the meat; when you slice the roast (or separate the slices) the juices are lost. Depending on the size of the roast, 10 to 20 minutes is enough time for the juices to redistribute throughout the roast, so less of the juices end up on your cutting board.

Spring Vegetable Barley Risotto

Per serving: **NET CARBS: 14 GRAMS** ■ Carbohydrates: 17.5 grams ■ Fiber: 3.5 grams ■ Protein: 3.5 grams ■
Fat: 4.5 grams ■ Calories: 122 ■ **PREP TIME: 25 MINUTES** ■ **COOK TIME: 1 HOUR** ■ **SERVINGS: 8**

This delicious barley risotto is prepared like an Italian risotto, stirring a bit of hot broth into the barley and letting it bubble away until the barley is tender and creamy. Barley doesn't demand the constant attention rice does, but stay near the kitchen.

2 (14½-ounce) cans lower sodium chicken broth

2 cups water

2 tablespoons olive oil

1 medium leek, trimmed, halved lengthwise, and thinly sliced (1 cup)

½ teaspoon dried marjoram or thyme, crumbled

Salt

¾ cup pearled barley

1 small carrot, cut into matchsticks (⅓ cup)

2 tablespoons chopped fresh parsley

Pepper

tip
Pearled barley is not a whole grain; the bran and the hull have been removed. Nevertheless, it's quite low in Net Carbs (13 grams per ½ cup cooked) and is an excellent source of B vitamins.

1 Bring broth and water to a boil in a medium saucepan over high heat. Reduce heat to very low and keep warm.

2 Meanwhile, heat oil in a large, heavy saucepan over medium-high heat. Stir in leek, marjoram or thyme, and a pinch of salt. Cook, stirring often, until wilted, about 2 minutes. Stir in barley and cook, stirring, until coated with oil, about 1 minute. Reduce heat to medium.

3 Add about 1 cup of the broth mixture (be careful, as this first addition will bubble up fiercely). Cook, stirring very frequently, until broth is nearly absorbed, about 4 minutes. Continue to cook, adding ½ cup broth at a time, stirring occasionally, until barley is creamy and tender, 40 to 50 minutes. (Barley can be a little soupy at this point.) Either finish the recipe or remove from the heat, cover, and let stand for 30 minutes.

4 To finish, bring ¼ inch of salted water to a boil in a medium skillet over high heat. Add carrot and cook until crisp-tender, 2 to 3 minutes. Drain. Stir carrot and parsley into the barley and season with salt and pepper to taste.

Asparagus with Toasted Hazelnuts

2 | Per serving: **NET CARBS: 2 GRAMS** ■ Carbohydrates: 3.5 grams ■ Fiber: 1.5 grams ■ Protein: 2 grams ■
3 4 | Fat: 7.5 grams ■ Calories: 82 ■ **PREP TIME: 10 MINUTES** ■ **COOK TIME: 15 MINUTES** ■ **SERVINGS: 8**

Thick asparagus are not overgrown, tougher versions of their thinner counterparts—they're a distinct variety and are fat from the time the spears poke out of the ground. In fact, thicker spears are actually juicier than skinny ones. How to determine whether the spears will be woody? Lift a bunch and look at the bottom. Round spears are more tender than oval or flat ones.

2 pounds asparagus, trimmed

Salt

3 tablespoons unsalted butter

⅓ cup coarsely chopped hazelnuts

2 tablespoons snipped fresh chives or scallion greens

2 teaspoons fresh lemon juice

1 Fill a large, deep skillet with 1 inch of salted water. Bring to a boil over high heat. Add asparagus and steam, covered, until crisp-tender, about 5 minutes, depending on thickness. With tongs, lift asparagus to a platter; cover loosely with foil to keep warm.

2 Meanwhile, melt butter in a small nonstick skillet over medium heat. Add hazelnuts and toast, stirring, until lightly browned, 4 to 5 minutes. Remove from heat and stir in chives, lemon juice, and a big pinch of salt. Pour over asparagus and serve.

tip

An easy way to trim asparagus is to bend the spears and snap off the ends, but that can be rather time-consuming when you're dealing with 2 pounds. If you're in a hurry, snap the ends off a few to see how much needs to be trimmed, then lop off the ends of the others with a knife.

all about alliums

Harbingers of spring abound. Some look for the first robin, others try to spy crocus or daffodil shoots. In the culinary realm, asparagus gets the good press, but those in the know look for alliums. This botanical family includes scallions (sometimes erroneously called spring onions), chives, shallots, leeks, garlic, and onions. Each has a distinctive appearance and taste, though some can be substituted for others.

Garlic contains potent antioxidants that develop after it is cut but do not form if exposed to heat. Chop or crush garlic, then let it stand for 10 minutes before you cook it. (0.9 grams Net Carbs per clove)

Leeks are mild in flavor and stately in appearance (they look like larger, thicker scallions). Leeks grow in sandy soil and can harbor considerable grit. Cut them as directed in your recipe, then rinse them thoroughly. (3.4 grams Net Carbs per ½ cup cooked)

Onions can be large or small, sweet or pungent, and range in color from creamy white to vibrant magenta. Unless another type is specified, use common yellow storage onions in these recipes. (5 grams Net Carbs per ½ cup cooked)

Scallions are long and thin, unlike spring onions, which have a slightly bulbous root. The sharply flavored white roots shine in stir-fries and sautés, but the milder green tops are often discarded (they're more perishable). Slice the tops to use in salads, as a garnish, or instead of chives in most recipes. They're a good source of beta carotene. (2.4 grams Net Carbs per ½ cup cooked)

Shallots are lobed, somewhat like garlic, but look like red-tinged onions. They have a pronounced bite; use them in lieu of onions. (3.1 grams Net Carbs per 2 tablespoons cooked)

Chives can be found with herbs, not vegetables, in most supermarkets, and indeed, they're typically used as a garnish. Add the stems and their lavender flowers to salads for a subtle onion flavor. You might find it easier to snip chives with a scissors rather than cut them with a knife. (0 grams Net Carbs per tablespoon)

Ramps are wild onions that grow primarily in the eastern United States and Canada; look for them in the spring and early summer at farmers markets and in gourmet groceries, especially those that specialize in produce. Ramps are between scallions and leeks in size, and their flavor is stronger than leeks but milder than some onions.

On the Menu

*Chicken Soup with Dilled
Mini Matzo Balls*

*Oven-Braised Brisket with
Horseradish Sauce*

Broccolini with Matzo Crumble

*Almond-Orange Macaroons
(page 157)*

passover

Chicken Soup with Dilled Mini Matzo Balls

3 4 Per serving: **NET CARBS: 5.5 GRAMS** ■ Carbohydrates: 6 grams ■ Fiber: 0.5 gram ■ Protein: 11.5 grams ■ Fat: 7 grams ■ Calories: 131.5 ■ **PREP TIME: 20 MINUTES,** plus standing ■ **COOK TIME: 2 HOURS** ■ **SERVINGS: 8** (2 cups each)

Don't bother to peel the garlic, onion, or carrot for the soup (shown on page 325); they're aromatic vegetables used for flavoring only. Do trim muddy edges so as not to add grit to the soup.

Soup:

1¼ pounds chicken thigh or
   2 (10-ounce) chicken legs, split

3 (14½-ounce) cans lower sodium
   chicken broth

4½ cups water

1 small onion, halved

1 small carrot, halved

1 celery stalk, halved

3 garlic cloves, smashed

6 parsley stems

2 dill sprigs

1 thyme sprig or ¼ teaspoon
   dried thyme

8 black peppercorns

Salt and pepper

Matzo Balls:

1 large egg

1 tablespoon vegetable oil

1 tablespoon snipped fresh dill

1 scallion, finely chopped
   (1 tablespoon)

¼ sheet whole-wheat matzo, finely
   ground in food processor (¼ cup)

tip

Make the broth a week or two ahead and freeze, or make it up to three days ahead and keep in the refrigerator. Don't make the matzo balls until the day you serve the soup, though.

1 For the soup: Combine chicken, broth, water, onion, carrot, celery, and garlic in a large saucepan. Bring to a boil over high heat. Skim off foam that rises to surface. Add parsley, dill, thyme, and peppercorns; reduce heat to very low and simmer gently until flavors develop, about 1½ hours.

2 Transfer chicken to a cutting board. Strain broth into a clean container; skim off fat, and season with salt and pepper to taste. Discard solids. Remove and discard skin from chicken; pull meat off bones and return to broth.

3 For the matzo balls: Combine egg, oil, dill, and scallion in a small bowl. Beat with a fork, then stir in matzo until well blended. Cover and refrigerate for 15 minutes.

4 Meanwhile, bring a large pot of salted water to a boil over high heat. With wet hands, shape matzo mixture into 16 balls, using 1 level teaspoon for each, and drop balls into water. Reduce heat to low; cover and simmer until cooked through, about 15 minutes. Reheat soup. With a slotted spoon, transfer matzo balls to soup and serve.

Oven-Braised Brisket with Horseradish Sauce

1 2 3 4

Per serving: **NET CARBS: 3 GRAMS** ■ Carbohydrates: 4 grams ■ Fiber: 1 gram ■ Protein: 57.5 grams ■ Fat: 24 grams ■ Calories: 473 ■ **PREP TIME: 10 MINUTES** ■ **COOK TIME: 4 HOURS** ■ **SERVINGS: 8**

Brisket really is best made the day before—its flavors develop, and it is much easier to cut cold, before reheating. If your schedule doesn't allow, let the brisket rest for 15 minutes after removing from the oven before slicing; let the juices stand for a few minutes and then spoon or pour off fat. Make the horseradish sauce while the meat stands.

2 tablespoons vegetable oil, plus more for pan

2 medium onions, halved and sliced

1 (14½-ounce) can lower sodium beef broth

3 garlic cloves, minced (1½ teaspoons)

1 tablespoon paprika

1¼ teaspoons coarse-ground black pepper

1 teaspoon dried thyme

¾ teaspoon kosher salt

1 (4½- to 5-pound) beef brisket, trimmed

2 to 3 tablespoons prepared white horseradish

tip

Whole briskets can weigh 10 to 15 pounds, so they're usually divided into first (flat) cut and front (point) cut. The front cut is fattier but more flavorful, and it is less expensive. Fattier cuts will shrink as they cook—ask your butcher how many you can expect to serve after cooking.

1 Heat the oven to 325°F. Lightly coat a large roasting pan with oil; scatter onions in pan and pour in broth.

2 Combine oil, garlic, paprika, pepper, thyme, and salt in a bowl. Rub over the brisket to coat thoroughly. Set brisket on onions. Cover tightly with foil. Roast until brisket is fork-tender, 3½ to 4 hours.

3 Transfer brisket to a baking dish; let cool, then cover and refrigerate overnight. Pour onions and juices into a bowl; let cool, then cover and refrigerate overnight. Remove any hardened fat.

4 About 45 minutes before serving, heat oven to 325°F. Slice brisket across the grain and return to baking dish. Pour 1 cup of onion and juices over brisket; cover and bake until heated through, about 30 minutes.

5 Bring remaining onion mixture to a boil in a medium saucepan; reduce heat to low and simmer 5 minutes. Stir in horseradish. Serve brisket with sauce spooned over.

Broccolini with Matzo Crumble

3 4 Per serving: **NET CARBS: 7 GRAMS** ▪ Carbohydrates: 8 grams ▪ Fiber: 1 gram ▪ Protein: 2.5 grams ▪ Fat: 3.5 grams ▪ Calories: 72 ▪ **PREP TIME: 8 MINUTES** ▪ **COOK TIME: 20 MINUTES** ▪ **SERVINGS: 8**

You can crumble the matzos with your fingers, but you'll get a finer crumb by pulverizing in a food processor; or place them in a plastic bag and crush them with a rolling pin. Use this topping over asparagus or cauliflower, too, or over a casserole.

2 bunches broccolini, trimmed, or 1½ bunches broccoli, trimmed and cut into spears

2 tablespoons vegetable oil

1 bunch (6 to 8) scallions, thinly sliced (1 cup)

1 garlic clove, minced (½ teaspoon)

1 teaspoon dried marjoram, crumbled

½ teaspoon salt

¼ teaspoon pepper

1 sheet whole-wheat matzo, finely ground

1 Bring ½ inch of salted water to a boil in a large skillet over high heat. Add broccolini; cover and cook, stirring frequently, until tender, 7 to 8 minutes. Drain and transfer to a platter. Cover loosely with foil to keep warm.

2 Wipe out skillet; add oil and heat over medium heat. Add scallions, garlic, marjoram, salt, and pepper. Cook, stirring frequently, until scallions are tender, about 2 minutes. Add matzo and cook, stirring, until crisp and lightly browned, 3 to 5 minutes. Spoon over the broccolini and serve immediately.

tip

Be sure to use whole-wheat matzo instead of its white-flour cousin. The flavor is more substantial, much like the difference between whole-wheat and white bread.

using up leftover matzo

Traditionally made from flour and water, matzo is the unleavened bread eaten during Passover. Matzo is crispy, like a cracker, and half of a plain matzo has 11.2 grams of Net Carbs—about the same as six saltine crackers. Matzo does come in a whole-wheat version; ask your grocer to stock it (enlist other controlled-carb consumers to ask, too— you might be surprised how willing grocers can be to accommodate requests). Here are some ways to use up leftover matzo. As with any grain, the key for those doing Atkins is to use it in small amounts.

The traditional use for leftover matzo is matzo brei. Crumbled matzo is tossed with egg and seasonings, then fried. The result is somewhere in between a pancake and French toast, and it's usually served with syrup or preserves. Top it with sugar-free pancake syrup or no-sugar-added jam, or make a savory version for lunch by adding sautéed onion and mushroom to the eggs.

Pulverize matzo in a food processor to a flourlike consistency and you have matzo meal, which is used to make matzo ball soup. Use matzo meal in meat loaves, or as a coating instead of bread crumbs.

Crumble matzo into pieces about ¼-inch square and you have farfel, which is eaten like cereal during Passover. You can also use farfel in lieu of croutons in a soup, or as a stuffing for chicken.

On the Menu

Shrimp and Avocado Salad with Lemon and Cilantro

Creamy Tomato-Cucumber Gelatin

Cheese Biscuits

Angel Food Cake with Raspberry Sauce

Iced Coffee Supreme

mother's day

Shrimp and Avocado Salad with Lemon and Cilantro

2
3 **4**
Per serving: **NET CARBS: 7.5 GRAMS** ▪ Carbohydrates: 17 grams ▪ Fiber: 9.5 grams ▪ Protein: 26 grams ▪
Fat: 44.5 grams ▪ Calories: 549 ▪ **PREP TIME: 15 MINUTES** ▪ **COOK TIME: 5 MINUTES** ▪ **SERVINGS: 8**

Avocados should yield to gentle pressure when they're perfectly ripe. Many markets will peel and devein the shrimp for you; it's often complimentary, but even if there's a fee, it's worth it when a recipe calls for this much. If you do it yourself, you'll add about 30 minutes to the prep time.

3 pounds medium or large shrimp, peeled and deveined

8 small Haas avocados, halved and pitted

2 medium red bell peppers, cut into ¼-inch dice (2 cups)

2 shallots, finely chopped (⅓ cup)

¼ cup fresh lemon juice

¼ cup white wine vinegar

⅓ cup chopped fresh cilantro

2 garlic cloves, minced (1 teaspoon)

1¼ teaspoons salt

½ teaspoon pepper

½ cup olive oil

Baby spinach leaves and lemon wedges, for serving

tip

To buy the best garlic, look to see that the papery skins are intact and that no sprouts are poking through. Choose heavy ones, too—those that are lighter may be past their prime.

1 Bring a large pot of salted water to a boil over medium-high heat. Add shrimp and simmer until opaque, 3 to 5 minutes. Drain and rinse under cold running water. Transfer to a large bowl.

2 Scoop avocado flesh from shells and coarsely chop; reserve shells. Add avocado, bell peppers, and shallots to shrimp; mix gently.

3 Whisk together lemon juice, vinegar, cilantro, garlic, salt, and pepper in a small bowl. Drizzle in olive oil, whisking constantly. Pour over shrimp-avocado mixture and mix gently to combine.

4 Line plates with spinach leaves. Set 2 avocado shells on each plate; spoon salad mixture into shells, allowing excess salad to spill onto plates. Serve with lemon wedges.

Creamy Tomato-Cucumber Gelatin

1 2 3 4 Per serving: **NET CARBS: 2 GRAMS** ▪ Carbohydrates: 2.5 grams ▪ Fiber: 0.5 grams ▪ Protein: 1.5 grams ▪ Fat: 11 grams ▪ Calories: 112 ▪ **PREP TIME: 10 MINUTES** ▪ **COOK TIME: 5 MINUTES**, plus chilling ▪ **SERVINGS: 8**

If you have a juicer, pull it out for this recipe, or stop at a natural foods store and pick up a small container of fresh tomato juice. Otherwise, use lower sodium prepared juice, preferably from a bottle. Prepared juices are often needlessly high in sodium, which dulls the tomato flavor, and canned juice can have a metallic taste.

¼ cup cold water

1 (¼-ounce) envelope unflavored gelatin

¾ cup lower sodium tomato juice

1 cucumber, seeded and cut into ¼-inch dice (1 cup)

1½ tablespoons fresh lemon juice

¼ teaspoon salt

¼ teaspoon hot pepper sauce (such as Tabasco)

1 cup heavy cream

tip
English cucumbers are longer and thinner than the common variety and have a less pronounced flavor. They are usually seedless. To remove the seeds from a common cucumber, cut the cuke in half lengthwise; if yours has seeds, drag a teaspoon along the flesh to scrape them out.

1 Put water in a large heatproof bowl and sprinkle with gelatin. Let stand for 2 minutes.

2 Meanwhile, bring tomato juice to a boil in a small saucepan over high heat. Pour over gelatin and stir until gelatin is dissolved. Chill until solid, at least 2 hours.

3 Meanwhile, combine cucumber, lemon juice, salt, and pepper sauce in a bowl. Stir into tomato-gelatin mixture.

4 Whip cream until stiff in a medium bowl, then carefully fold into cucumber mixture.

5 Rinse a 4-cup ring mold or bowl and shake out extra water. Spoon cucumber mixture into mold; tap mold on counter to remove air bubbles and level mixture. Cover loosely with plastic wrap and refrigerate for at least 3 hours or overnight.

6 To unmold, dip bottom of mold in a bowl of warm water or wrap in a warm, wet dish towel for 10 seconds; hold a platter over mold and invert.

Cheese Biscuits

1 2 3 4 Per serving: **NET CARBS: 2 GRAMS** ▪ Carbohydrates: 4.5 grams ▪ Fiber: 2.5 grams ▪ Protein: 8.5 grams ▪ Fat: 11 grams ▪ Calories: 146 ▪ **PREP TIME: 10 MINUTES** ▪ **COOK TIME: 14 MINUTES** ▪ **SERVINGS: 8** (2 biscuits each)

These comforting little biscuits are a snap to prepare. Developed to be spread with the Creamy Tomato-Cucumber Gelatin, they can also be served with Pork and Beef Chili (page 210), Quick Beef Stew (page 211) or Real North Carolina Barbecue Pork (page 230).

1 cup Atkins Quick Quisine Bake Mix	½ cup grated cheddar cheese (2 ounces)
1 teaspoon baking powder	¾ cup heavy cream

1 Heat oven to 425°F.

2 Combine bake mix and baking powder in a medium bowl. Stir in cheese and cream until well blended; dough will be quite stiff. Gather into a ball and knead in bowl once or twice to blend.

3 Transfer dough to a counter and press into a 6-inch square. Cut into 16 pieces. Set on ungreased baking sheet and bake until puffed and golden, 12 to 14 minutes.

tip

Feel free to experiment with flavored cheddar (try horseradish or herb) or try different cheeses; do choose one that's somewhat similar in texture to cheddar. Gouda and mozzarella (smoked or not) and manchego are ideal alternatives.

Angel Food Cake with Raspberry Sauce

Per serving: **NET CARBS: 10.5 GRAMS** ■ Carbohydrates: 13 grams ■ Fiber: 2.5 grams ■ Protein: 5 grams ■
Fat: 0.5 gram ■ Calories: 74 ■ **PREP TIME: 25 MINUTES** ■ **COOK TIME: 40 MINUTES**, plus cooling ■ **SERVINGS: 12**

Whole-wheat pastry flour has a slightly nutty flavor and makes for a cake (shown on page 331) that won't rise as high as a traditional angel food cake.

Cake:

1 cup sifted whole-wheat pastry flour

⅔ cup granular sugar substitute, divided

¼ teaspoon salt

12 large egg whites (1½ cups)

1½ teaspoons cream of tartar

1 teaspoon vanilla extract

½ teaspoon almond extract

Raspberry Sauce:

½ cup orange juice

1 tablespoon granular sugar substitute

1 pint fresh raspberries or 1 (12-ounce) package no-sugar-added frozen raspberries, thawed

tip

Don't wait till the last minute to make the raspberry sauce. It takes a while (and a bit of effort) to press all the juice through the strainer. Use a large spoon or spatula. It will keep for 2 days, refrigerated in an airtight container.

1 For the cake: Heat oven to 375°F. Sift flour twice. Add ⅓ cup of the sugar substitute and salt to flour and sift again. Set aside.

2 Beat egg whites in a large bowl with an electric mixer at medium speed until foamy. Add cream of tartar, vanilla extract, and almond extract. Increase mixer speed to medium-high and gradually add remaining ⅓ cup sugar substitute. Continue beating until egg whites are stiff but still moist.

3 Sift flour mixture over whites in 3 additions, folding in each addition thoroughly with a rubber spatula. Transfer batter to an ungreased 10-inch tube pan with a removable bottom. Bake until a toothpick inserted in the center comes out clean, 30 minutes. Invert cake over a rack until completely cool, about 1 hour.

4 For the sauce: Combine orange juice and sugar substitute in a small saucepan. Bring to a boil, then reduce heat to medium-high and simmer for 3 minutes. Stir in raspberries and cook until they begin to break up and release juice, about 2 minutes. Set a strainer over a bowl and transfer sauce to strainer. Press berries to obtain juice.

5 To serve, run a long, thin-bladed knife or metal spatula around edge of the pan and lift cake from the outer rim. Run knife along the center tube; then run it along the bottom. Invert cake onto a platter. Use a serrated knife to cut into 12 slices; top each slice with sauce.

Iced Coffee Supreme

2 3 4 Per serving: **NET CARBS: 3 GRAMS** ■ Carbohydrates: 8.5 grams ■ Fiber: 5.5 grams ■ Protein: 2.5 grams ■ Fat: 28 grams ■ Calories: 277 ■ **PREP TIME: 5 MINUTES** ■ **SERVINGS: 8**

Make a pot of coffee the day before your party so it will be cold when you need it. Remove it from the heat and cool right away; coffee becomes bitter if left too long on a warmer.

3 cups (24 ounces) cold brewed coffee or decaf

1 pint low-carb vanilla ice cream

16 ice cubes

2 cups heavy cream

1 teaspoon instant espresso powder (optional)

Put 1½ cups of the chilled coffee, ½ pint of the ice cream, and 8 ice cubes in a blender. Purée until smooth and thick. Add 1 cup of the cream and espresso powder, if using, and blend. Pour into 4 chilled glasses. Repeat to make 4 more drinks.

Root Beer Floats

2 3 4 Per serving: **NET CARBS: 2 GRAMS** ■ Carbohydrates: 13 grams ■ Fiber: 11 grams ■ Protein: 2 grams ■ Fat: 12 grams ■ Calories: 140 ■ **PREP TIME: 10 MINUTES** ■ **SERVINGS: 8**

Freeze the glasses for an hour before making the floats for a real soda-shop treat.

3 liters sugar-free root beer or birch beer

2 pints low-carb vanilla ice cream

¼ cup heavy cream, whipped (optional)

Fill 8 tall glasses with 6 ounces of soda each. Add ½ cup of the ice cream, then pour in an additional 6 ounces of soda. Top with 1 tablespoon whipped cream, if desired. Serve immediately with a long straw and spoon.

On the Menu

Best-Ever Beef Burgers

Better Baked Beans

Fried Onion Rings

Iceberg Wedges with Blue Cheese Dressing

German Chocolate Brownies

father's day

Best-Ever Beef Burgers

1 **2** **3** **4** Per serving: **NET CARBS: 0 GRAMS** ▪ Carbohydrates: 0 grams ▪ Fiber: 0 grams ▪ Protein: 37.5 grams ▪ Fat: 34 grams ▪ Calories: 470 ▪ **PREP TIME: 5 MINUTES** ▪ **COOK TIME: 13 MINUTES** ▪ **SERVINGS: 8**

Do you know the two secrets to super burgers? First, choose meat with a high fat content (80 to 85 percent lean) for burgers that are juicy and have great flavor. The second secret is to handle the meat as little as possible, so mix and shape the patties with a light hand.

4 pounds ground beef

2 teaspoons salt

1 teaspoon pepper

Pickles, raw onion slices, tomato slices, lettuce or spinach leaves, no-sugar-added ketchup, mustard (optional)

1 Mix meat with salt and pepper, being careful not to compress it. Shape it lightly into 8 patties about ¾ inch thick and 5 inches across.

2 Heat a gas or charcoal grill, or heat a large cast-iron or heavy skillet over medium-high heat until very hot, about 3 minutes. Add burgers and grill or pan-fry until done to taste, 5 minutes per side for medium to well done. If pan-frying, cook burgers in 2 skillets, or cook 4 at a time and keep the first batch warm in a 200°F oven while cooking the second batch. Serve with optional accompaniments.

condiment caution

Made properly, a burger has no carbohydrates at all. Topping and condiments can change that, sometimes dramatically. See how your burger stacks up:

Cheddar cheese, 2-ounce slice:
1 gram of Net Carbs

Tomato slice, ¼ inch thick:
0.5 gram of Net Carbs

Spinach or lettuce leaf, 1:
0 grams of Net Carbs

Hamburger relish, 1 tablespoon:
5 grams of Net Carbs

Dill pickle slices, 3:
0.5 gram of Net Carbs

Mustard (any type), 1 teaspoon:
0 grams of Net Carbs

Ketchup (low-carb), 1 tablespoon:
1 gram of Net Carbs

Ketchup (regular), 1 tablespoon:
4 grams of Net Carbs

Onion slice, ⅛ inch thick:
1 gram of Net Carbs

Better Baked Beans

Per serving: **NET CARBS: 22 GRAMS** ▪ Carbohydrates: 33 grams ▪ Fiber: 11 grams ▪ Protein: 15 grams ▪ Fat: 5.5 grams ▪ Calories: 239.5 ▪ **PREP TIME: 15 MINUTES,** plus standing ▪ **COOK TIME: 2½ HOURS** ▪ **SERVINGS: 8** (¾ cup each)

3 4

Full of molasses and often brown sugar, typical baked beans are verboten on the Atkins lifestyle. Substituting sugar-free pancake syrup makes them acceptable for the later phases.

1 (1-pound) bag great Northern beans, picked over

8 ounces thick-sliced bacon, cut into ½-inch slices

¾ cup chopped onion

⅓ cup sugar-free pancake syrup

½ cup no-sugar-added ketchup

2 teaspoons dry mustard

1½ teaspoons salt

½ teaspoon pepper

tip

If you don't have great Northern beans on hand use any small white bean except navy beans; they can be higher in Net Carbs. Most white beans have 12 to 14 grams of Net Carbs per ½ cup; navy beans can weigh in with 18 grams.

1 Put beans in a large pot and add water to cover by 2 inches. Let stand overnight. Alternatively, bring beans and water to a boil. Let boil 2 minutes. Turn off heat, cover tightly, and let stand 1 hour.

2 Drain and rinse beans. Cover beans with fresh water by 2 inches and bring to a boil. Reduce heat to low, partially cover, and simmer until not quite tender, about 35 minutes. Drain beans, reserving cooking liquid.

3 Meanwhile, cook bacon in a large skillet over medium-high heat until crisp, about 8 minutes. Transfer bacon to paper towels to drain, leaving drippings in pan. Reduce heat to medium, add onion, and cook, stirring frequently, until deep brown, about 15 minutes.

4 Heat oven to 350°F. Transfer beans to a 4-quart baking dish or Dutch oven. Stir in bacon, onion, syrup, ketchup, mustard, salt, and pepper. Add just enough reserved cooking liquid (and water, if necessary) to come to the top of beans. Cover dish with a lid or foil. Bake 1 hour, then uncover and bake until beans are thick and soupy, 30 to 60 minutes longer.

Iceberg Wedges with Blue Cheese Dressing

1 2 3 4

Per serving: **NET CARBS: 3.5 GRAMS** ▪ Carbohydrates: 5 grams ▪ Fiber: 1.5 grams ▪ Protein: 8 grams ▪ Fat: 27.5 grams ▪ Calories: 290 ▪ **PREP TIME: 15 MINUTES** ▪ **SERVINGS: 8**

This simple but classic combination is sure to please. Roquefort is the traditional blue cheese in salad dressings, but you can vary the taste by using other blues. Make the dressing a day or so ahead so the flavors have time to develop.

1 large head iceberg lettuce	2 tablespoons red wine vinegar
7 ounces Roquefort or other blue cheese, crumbled (about 1¾ cups)	Hot pepper sauce (such as Tabasco)
1½ cups sour cream	1 tablespoon finely chopped parsley
½ cup mayonnaise	½ teaspoon pepper

1 Core lettuce and rinse carefully with cold water to keep head intact. Cut into 8 wedges and set on paper towels to dry.

2 Combine blue cheese, sour cream, and mayonnaise in a medium bowl, mashing with a fork, making sure blue cheese remains lumpy. Stir in vinegar and add pepper sauce to taste.

3 Put each lettuce wedge on a salad plate. Pour about ¼ cup of dressing over each wedge. Sprinkle parsley and pepper over dressing.

tip

Don't buy into the myth that iceberg lettuce is nutritionally void. It's slightly more than 96 percent water, and although that doesn't leave a lot of room for vitamins and minerals, one-eighth of a large head supplies respectable amounts of folate, as well as some beta carotene and lutein and zeaxanthin, two carotenoid pigments that help protect against degenerative eye disease.

Fried Onion Rings

Per serving: **NET CARBS: 8 GRAMS** ■ Carbohydrates: 10.5 grams ■ Fiber: 2.5 grams ■ Protein: 6.5 grams ■

3 4 Fat: 22 grams ■ Calories: 257 ■ **PREP TIME:10 MINUTES,** plus standing ■ **COOK TIME: 30 MINUTES** ■ **SERVINGS: 8**

Onion rings (shown on page 339) are a sweet yet savory accompaniment to burgers—serve them atop, rather than alongside, for a twist. For best results, be sure the onions are very well coated with the cream mixture. Stir them often while they soak, then let them stand for 15 minutes to allow the batter to set before frying them.

2 Spanish, Bermuda, or other very large onions, cut into ½-inch slices	¼ cup whole-wheat flour
1 cup heavy cream	1 teaspoon salt
1 cup water	½ teaspoon pepper
1¼ cups soy flour	About 4 cups vegetable oil for frying

1 Separate onion slices into rings. Whisk cream and water in a large bowl. Stir in onion rings and let stand for 15 minutes, stirring frequently.

2 Shake soy flour, whole-wheat flour, salt, and pepper together in a gallon-size zip-close bag. Lift a few onion rings out of cream with a fork and add to bag; shake vigorously to coat. Set onion rings in a single layer on a baking sheet or jelly-roll pan and let stand 15 minutes so the batter can set. Repeat until all onions are coated.

3 Meanwhile, pour 1 inch of vegetable oil into a deep, heavy skillet, Dutch oven, or deep fryer. Heat over medium-high heat until oil reaches 365°F to 375°F. Fry rings in batches of 4 to 6, without crowding, turning once or twice, until golden, about 3 minutes per batch. With a slotted spoon, transfer to paper towels to drain. Serve immediately.

tip

In the case of onion rings, bigger is better. Instead of standard-size onions from the three- or five-pound bags, choose those that are closer to four or five inches in diameter.

German Chocolate Brownies

Per serving: **NET CARBS: 17 GRAMS** ▪ Carbohydrates: 22 grams ▪ Fiber: 5 grams ▪ Protein: 3.5 grams ▪
3 4 Fat: 36.5 grams ▪ Calories: 407 ▪ **PREP TIME: 20 MINUTES** ▪ **COOK TIME: 25 MINUTES**, plus cooling ▪ **SERVINGS: 12**

German chocolate cake is made of dark chocolate, layered with coconut in a caramel glaze, but it isn't from Germany. This rich, dark, and sweet chocolate was actually developed by an American named Sam German in the 1850s. The recipe for the cake was first published in the 1950s and was attributed to a woman from Texas.

Brownies:

1 (8.5-ounce) package Atkins Quick Quisine Deluxe Brownie Mix

½ cup (1 stick) unsalted butter, melted

⅓ cup water

⅓ cup oil

1 large egg

Topping:

1 cup granular sugar substitute

¾ cup heavy cream

2 large egg yolks

6 tablespoons unsalted butter, plus more for baking dish

½ teaspoon vanilla extract

1 cup unsweetened shredded coconut

¾ cup toasted chopped pecans

tip

Unsalted butter has a purer, fresher flavor than salted, which in comparison tastes muddled. Cut a slice of low-carb bread into three pieces, then spread one with salted butter and two more with unsalted; sprinkle one of the unsalted slices with a little salt from the shaker. Take a bite of each. Taste the difference?

1 For the brownies: Heat oven to 350°F. Line an 8-inch square baking dish with a 14-inch sheet of foil, wrapping overhangs around pan. Butter foil.

2 Combine brownie mix, butter, water, oil, and egg in a bowl, stirring until blended. Scrape into pan and bake until moist crumbs adhere to a cake tester inserted 2 inches from the edge of pan, about 25 minutes. Cool in pan, then unwrap foil and lift brownies out of pan.

3 For the topping: Meanwhile, combine sugar substitute, cream, yolks, butter, and vanilla in a medium saucepan over medium heat. Cook, stirring, until thickened and golden, 8 to 10 minutes. Stir in coconut and pecans, then spread over brownies. Let cool completely before cutting into 12 pieces.

On the Menu

Golden Summer Soup

Buttery Shrimp and Lobster Rolls

*Crudité Salad with Herbed
Ranch Dressing*

*Vanilla Fudge Ice Cream with
Berry Sauce*

Hibiscus Limeade

4th of july

Golden Summer Soup

2 3 4 Per serving: **NET CARBS: 5 GRAMS** ■ Carbohydrates: 6 grams ■ Fiber: 1 gram ■ Protein: 1.5 grams ■ Fat: 5.5 grams ■ Calories: 78 ■ **PREP TIME: 30 MINUTES** ■ **COOK TIME: 30 MINUTES,** plus cooling ■ **SERVINGS: 8** (1 cup each)

Yellow tomatoes impart a vibrant hue to this refreshing soup. If you can't find yellow tomatoes, use red ones; your soup will be a deeper gold. Serve this cold, if you like; chill after you've strained it. To skip the straining step, peel and seed the tomatoes.

1½ tablespoons extra virgin olive oil

½ pound (2 medium) leeks, trimmed and finely chopped (2 cups)

½ large celery stalk, chopped

1 garlic cloves, minced (½ teaspoon)

½ tablespoon ThickenThin not/Starch thickener

2 medium yellow bell peppers, cut into 1-inch pieces

¾ pounds (2 medium) yellow tomatoes, quartered

2 cups water

1 cup lower sodium chicken broth

½ teaspoon salt

⅛ teaspoon white pepper

¼ cup sour cream or crème fraîche

1 tablespoon chopped fresh basil or parsley

tip

Crème fraîche looks something like sour cream but isn't as sharp in flavor. You can buy it, but it's easy to make your own: Combine a cup of heavy cream and 2 tablespoons of buttermilk in a clean glass jar; let stand at room temperature until thick, about 12 hours. Stir and refrigerate for up to a week.

1 Heat oil in a large saucepan over medium heat. Add leeks, celery, and garlic; cook, stirring occasionally, until just beginning to soften, about 5 minutes. Stir in thickener, bell peppers, tomatoes, water, broth, salt, and pepper; bring to a boil. Reduce heat to low and simmer, stirring occasionally, until vegetables are very tender, about 15 minutes. Let cool 15 minutes.

2 Puree soup in saucepan using an immersion blender, or in a blender or food mill in batches; if you prefer a finer texture, press the soup through a strainer.

3 Reheat soup, if desired; ladle into shallow bowls. Top with sour cream or crème fraîche and basil or parsley.

Buttery Shrimp and Lobster Rolls

2 3 4 Per serving: **NET CARBS: 4.5 GRAMS** ▪ Carbohydrates: 9.5 grams ▪ Fiber: 5 grams ▪ Protein: 38.5 grams ▪ Fat: 16 grams ▪ Calories: 341 ▪ **PREP TIME: 30 MINUTES** ▪ **COOK TIME: 18 MINUTES** ▪ **SERVINGS: 8**

Feel free to use frozen shrimp in this recipe (shown on page 347), just be sure to thaw them well. Medium or large shrimp are best; don't spend extra money on jumbo shrimp because you'll be chopping them anyway. Remove the tails when you peel them.

1½ **pounds frozen lobster tails,** thawed

2 **pounds shrimp,** peeled and deveined

½ **cup (1 stick) unsalted butter,** divided

3 **garlic cloves,** coarsely chopped (1½ teaspoons)

¼ **cup chopped celery leaves**

¼ **teaspoon salt**

¼ **teaspoon pepper**

16 **slices low-carb white bread,** divided

2 **lemons,** cut into wedges

tip

If you prefer, you can make these with fresh lobster meat. You will need five 2-pound lobsters. To cook, fill 2 large pots two-thirds full with water and bring to a boil. Add 2 or 3 lobsters to either pot, cover, and simmer 12 minutes. Remove lobsters carefully with tongs and let cool slightly before splitting the lobsters and cracking the shells to remove meat.

1 Remove meat from lobster shells. Coarsely chop lobster and shrimp.

2 Heat 4 tablespoons of the butter in a large nonstick skillet over medium heat. Add garlic and cook until fragrant, about 30 seconds. Add lobster and shrimp. Cook, stirring frequently, until just opaque, 6 to 8 minutes. Stir in celery leaves, salt, and pepper. Transfer to a bowl.

3 Meanwhile, melt another tablespoon butter in a large nonstick skillet over medium heat. Add 4 slices of bread, cover with another skillet, and weight with cans; cook until toasted underneath, 1 to 2 minutes. Repeat with remaining bread and butter.

4 With bread butter-side up, use a slotted spoon to scoop about ⅓ cup lobster mixture onto bread; roll bread around filling. Serve warm, with lemon wedges on the side.

Crudité Salad with Herbed Ranch Dressing

Per serving: **NET CARBS: 6 GRAMS** ▪ Carbohydrates: 9 grams ▪ Fiber: 3 grams ▪ Protein: 2.5 grams ▪
3 **4** Fat: 8 grams ▪ Calories: 109 ▪ **PREP TIME: 15 MINUTES** ▪ **COOK TIME: 5 MINUTES** ▪ **SERVINGS: 8**

*For ease, make the dressing and prepare the vegetables except for the tomatoes up to
6 hours ahead. Layer the vegetables in a large bowl, cover with plastic wrap, and chill.
Add tomatoes and toss with dressing just before serving (shown on page 347). If you
don't use all the dressing, save any leftovers in a tightly sealed jar and use to dress
your favorite greens.*

Salad:

½ **small bunch broccoli,** broken
  into small florets (2 cups)

½ **small cauliflower head,** broken
  into small florets (2 cups)

1 **small cucumber,** halved, seeded,
  and cut into ¼-inch slices

2 **large carrots,** peeled and grated
  (2 cups)

8 **ounces romaine lettuce,** coarsely
  chopped

1 **pint grape tomatoes,** halved
  (2 cups)

Dressing:

⅓ **cup sour cream**

¼ **cup mayonnaise**

1 **tablespoon water**

2 **tablespoons white wine vinegar**

2 **scallions,** finely chopped
  (2 tablespoons)

1 **teaspoon finely chopped fresh
  thyme** or ½ teaspoon dried

½ **teaspoon salt**

¼ **teaspoon pepper**

tip
It's okay to boil
vegetables briefly,
as in this recipe, but
the longer they boil,
the more nutrients
are lost. Invest in
a stainless-steel
steamer, which
allows you to steam
vegetables above
the boiling water.
Alternatively,
microwave veggies
in a tablespoon of
water in a Pyrex
dish.

1 For the salad: Bring a large saucepan of salted water to a boil. Add broccoli and cauliflower. Reduce heat and simmer until broccoli is bright green,
about 2 minutes. Drain, then rinse with cold running water. Drain again and
transfer to a large bowl. Add cucumber, carrots, lettuce, and tomatoes.

2 For the dressing: Combine sour cream, mayonnaise, water, vinegar,
scallions, and thyme in a bowl, whisking until smooth; season with salt and
pepper. Drizzle dressing over salad and toss to coat.

Hibiscus Limeade

1 2 3 4 Per serving: **NET CARBS: 2 GRAMS** ▪ Carbohydrates: 2 grams ▪ Fiber: 0 grams ▪ Protein: 0 grams ▪ Fat: 0 grams ▪ Calories: 7 ▪ **PREP TIME: 20 MINUTES** ▪ **SERVINGS: 8**

Dried hibiscus flowers are also called jamaica, roselle, and flores de Jamaica. You can buy them in natural foods stores and Mexican grocery stores.

1 cup dried hibiscus flowers	¼ to ½ cup fresh lime juice
4 cups boiling water	10 packets sugar substitute
4 cups ice water	Ice cubes

Put hibiscus flowers in a heatproof bowl. Pour in boiling water and let steep 5 minutes, then strain into a large pitcher. Stir in ice water. When ice is melted, stir in ¼ cup of the lime juice and sugar substitute. Taste and add more lime juice if too sweet. Serve over ice in tall glasses.

a berry good fruit

Ruby red strawberries and raspberries and indigo blueberries are natural choices for the Fourth of July, but once you're out of Induction they should be part of your diet year 'round.

Berries are high in antioxidants that can protect against some cancers and prevent heart disease. They contain high levels of pectin, a soluble fiber that helps to lower cholesterol; they have also been shown to be effective in reversing age-related nerve disorders.

One-quarter cup of blueberries provides 4.1 grams of Net Carbs; one-half cup of whole strawberries contains 3.4 grams; the same amount of raspberries, 3 grams; and of blackberries, 5.4 grams.

Although berries find their way into baked goods, jams, and syrups, they're best eaten raw. Heat destroys vitamin C, so if you must cook them, do so only briefly. Using berries in low-carb recipes has an added benefit: Sugar can sap berries of their antioxidant power, so using sugar-free bake mixes preserves nutrients. Eating a handful of fresh berries is a summertime treat—just be sure to keep it to one or two "handfuls" to keep your carbs under control.

Toss berries into a green salad.

Whirl berries into a smoothie.

Sprinkle berries onto pancakes just before turning them (this keeps berries from sinking into the batter.

Vanilla Fudge Ice Cream with Berry Sauce

Per serving: **NET CARBS: 7 GRAMS** ▪ Carbohydrates: 11 grams ▪ Fiber: 4 grams ▪ Protein: 7 grams ▪ Fat: 50 grams

3 4 ▪ Calories: 572 ▪ **PREP TIME: 10 MINUTES**, plus chilling ▪ **COOK TIME: 8 MINUTES** ▪ **SERVINGS: 8** (scant ½ cup each)

Dark chocolate fudge pieces add an extra-rich indulgence in this delicious dessert paired with a fresh berry sauce. Look for bright, ripe strawberries.

Ice Cream:

1 quart heavy cream

⅓ cup water

7 large egg yolks

¾ cup granular sugar substitute

2 teaspoons vanilla extract

1 (2.11-ounce) Atkins Advantage Chocolate Decadence Bar, chopped

Sauce:

1 cup strawberries, divided

½ cup raspberries

1 For the ice cream: Bring cream and water almost to a simmer in a heavy medium saucepan.

2 Whisk or beat yolks and sugar substitute in a medium bowl until color lightens and mixture is thick. Gradually whisk half of the hot cream into egg mixture. Return to pan; cook over medium heat, stirring constantly, until thick enough to coat the back of a spoon or mixture registers 170°F on an instant-read thermometer, about 1 minute. Stir in vanilla. Cover and refrigerate until cold.

3 Pour mixture into an ice-cream maker and churn according to manufacturer's instructions, adding chocolate pieces during the last few minutes of churning. Transfer to an airtight container and freeze until ready to serve.

4 For the sauce: Purée ½ cup of the strawberries in a blender, pulsing and scraping until liquefied; transfer to a bowl. Dice remaining ½ cup strawberries and add with raspberries to the strawberry purée. Serve ice cream topped with berries.

tip

Keep berries fresher longer: Line a plate with a paper towel or two. Dump the berries onto the plate, then cover with another layer of paper towels.

On the Menu

Bones-to-Be

Blue Cheese Ghost

Spider Cupcakes

Green Gobs Soda

halloween

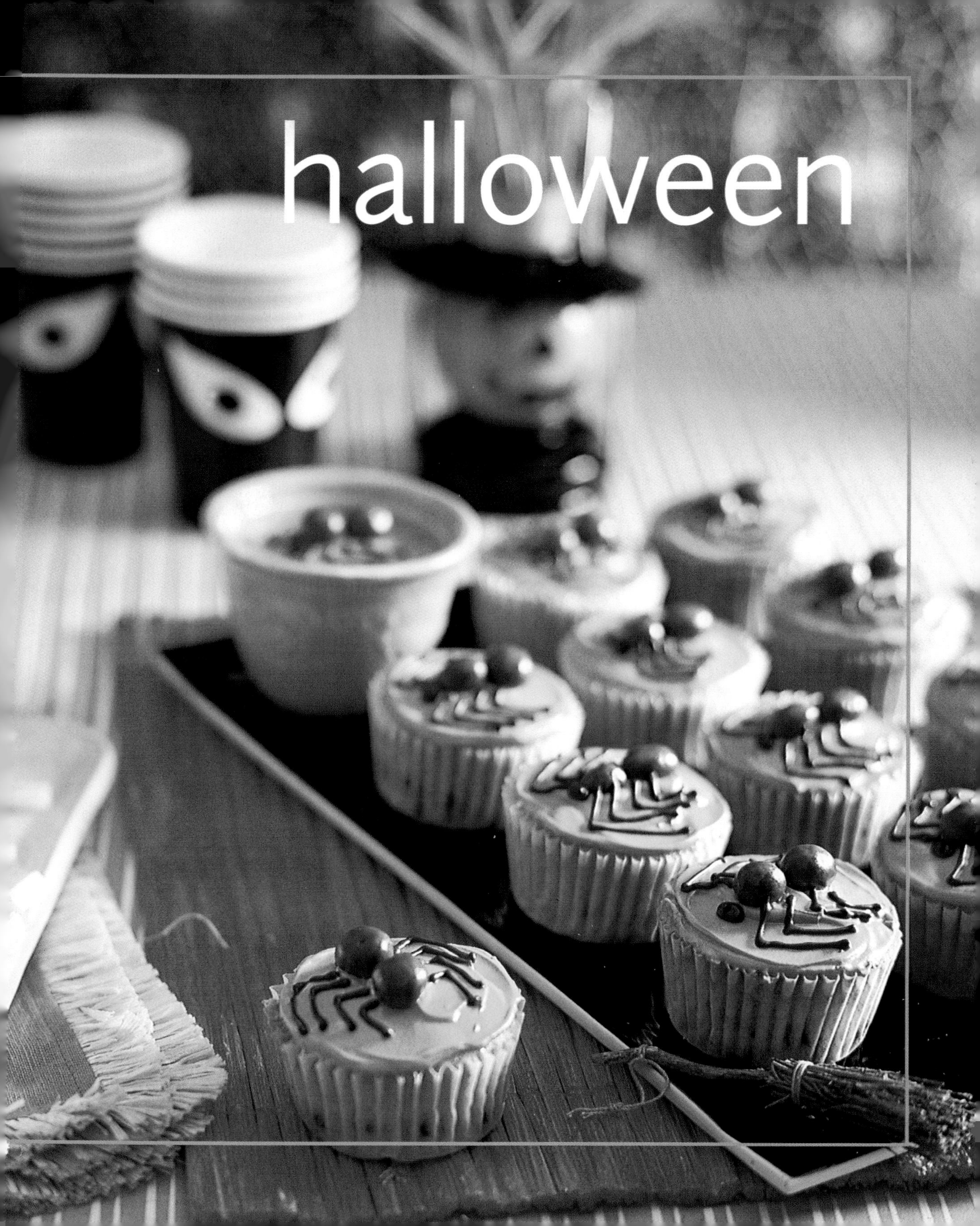

Bones-to-Be

1 2 3 4

Per serving: **NET CARBS: 1 GRAM** ▪ Carbohydrates: 2 grams ▪ Fiber: 1 gram ▪ Protein: 13 grams ▪ Fat: 9 grams ▪ Calories: 143 ▪ **PREP TIME: 10 MINUTES** ▪ **COOK TIME: 35 MINUTES** ▪ **SERVINGS: 8**

Wingettes range considerably in size, from 6 to 18 pieces per pound. If yours are smaller, they'll have a greater surface area and you may need to use more of the spice mixture. Use more or less cayenne depending on the heat tolerance of your ghouls—or guests. (For photo, see page 354.)

Cooking spray

2 tablespoons chili powder

2 tablespoons Atkins Quick Quisine Bake Mix

1 to 2 teaspoons cayenne pepper

2 teaspoons dry mustard

2 teaspoons salt

2 pounds wingettes, thawed if frozen, rinsed and dried

1 Heat oven to 450°F. Coat jelly-roll pan with foil and spray with cooking spray.

2 Combine chili powder, bake mix, cayenne, mustard, and salt in a large zip-close bag. Add half of the wingettes and shake to coat. Transfer to pan and repeat with remaining wingettes.

3 Bake, turning occasionally, until crisp, browned, and cooked through, 30 to 35 minutes.

tip

Chicken wings have three sections. For Buffalo wings, the two upper sections are used and the smaller wing tips are discarded. These are sold as wingettes or drumettes; prepackaged Buffalo wings usually come coated.

Blue Cheese Ghost

1 2 3 4 Per serving: **NET CARBS: 1.5 GRAMS** ■ Carbohydrates: 1.5 grams ■ Fiber: 0 grams ■ Protein: 5.5 grams ■ Fat: 15.5 grams ■ Calories: 165 ■ **PREP TIME: 10 MINUTES,** plus chilling ■ **SERVINGS: 8**

Ghostly shapes are everywhere around Halloween, but you can make this recipe (shown on page 354) in two one-cup molds any time of year.

1 (8-ounce) package cream
  cheese, at room temperature

4 ounces blue cheese, such as
  Roquefort or Gorgonzola

¼ cup sour cream

¼ teaspoon pepper

1 pimiento-stuffed olive

1 Line a 2-cup ghost-shaped mold with plastic wrap.

2 Mix cream cheese and blue cheese in a bowl until blended. Stir in sour cream and pepper. Fill mold, cover with plastic wrap, and refrigerate at least 2 hours. If you cannot find a ghost-shaped mold, use any seasonal mold.

3 Unmold ghost onto plate, then carefully remove plastic wrap. Cut olive into thin slices and place on ghost's face for eyes, or finely chop and sprinkle over mold.

crudité counts

Make this dip year 'round and serve with crudités. Although vegetables are low in Net Carbs, some are lower than others—check out this list. Net Carb counts are per ½ cup raw veggies, unless noted.

Broccoli florets: 0.8 gram

Carrots: 5.6 grams (blanched)

Celery: 0.8 gram per rib

Cherry tomotoes: 2 grams

Cucumbers: 1 gram

Endive: 0.4 gram

Fennel: 1.8 grams

Jicama: 2.5 grams

Peas in pods: 3.4 grams (blanched)

Radishes: 1 gram

Red bell pepper: 3.3 grams

White mushrooms: 1.4 grams

Zucchini: 1.1 grams

Spider Cupcakes

Per serving: **NET CARBS: 11.5 GRAMS** ■ Carbohydrates: 13.5 grams ■ Fiber: 2 grams ■ Protein: 3 grams ■

3 4 Fat: 20 grams ■ Calories: 233 ■ **PREP TIME: 45 MINUTES** ■ **COOK TIME: 20 MINUTES** ■ **SERVINGS: 13**

What could be spookier than a dozen spidery cupcakes? Why, 13 of them, of course (shown on page 355).

1 (8-ounce) package Atkins Quick Quisine Banana Nut Deluxe Muffin & Bread Mix

½ cup vegetable oil

1 cup water

2 large eggs

1 cup sugar-free chocolate chips

½ cup heavy cream

1 tablespoon granular sugar substitute

1 tablespoon sour cream

2 drops orange food coloring or 1 drop each red and yellow food coloring

26 sugar-free chocolate-coated peanut candies

1 (1-ounce) Atkins Endulge Chocolate Candy Bar

tip

If you can't find sugar-free chocolate chips (look for them in natural foods stores), chop a low-carb chocolate bar into chunks.

1 Heat oven to 400°F. Line 12-cup muffin tin and one 6-ounce custard cup with paper baking cups.

2 Combine bread mix, oil, water, and eggs in a bowl, stirring until moistened. Add chips and stir until combined. Divide batter evenly among muffin tin and custard cup. Bake until toothpick inserted in one of the inner cupcakes comes out clean, about 20 minutes. Cool in pans 5 to 10 minutes, then lift out cupcakes and transfer to a wire rack to cool completely.

3 Put cream, sugar substitute, and sour cream in a medium bowl and beat with an electric mixer at medium speed until soft peaks form. Stir in food coloring to blend.

4 Spread frosting over cupcakes. Set 2 peanut candies in center of each cupcake for spider's body. Melt chocolate bar in microwave on high for 1 minute. Transfer to a small plastic bag; snip off corner of bag. Pipe spiders' legs with melted chocolate.

Green Gobs Soda

Per serving: **NET CARBS: 1.5 GRAMS** ■ Carbohydrates: 1.5 grams ■ Fiber: 0 grams ■ Protein: 1.5 grams ■ Fat: 0 grams ■ Calories: 11 ■ **PREP TIME: 5 MINUTES,** plus chilling ■ **COOK TIME: 5 MINUTES** ■ **SERVINGS: 8**

Globs of green "slime" floating in yellow fizz are sure to appeal to the children on your guest list (as well as adults with a flair for the macabre). For full effect, serve in clear glasses.

¼ cup fresh lime juice

2 (¼-ounce) envelopes unflavored gelatin

1¾ cups water

¼ cup granular sugar substitute

2 liters sugar-free ginger ale, chilled

1 Put lime juice in a heatproof bowl and sprinkle with gelatin. Let stand for 2 minutes.

2 Meanwhile, bring water and sugar substitute to a boil in a small saucepan over high heat. Pour over gelatin and stir until gelatin is dissolved. Chill until solid, at least 2 hours.

3 Scoop out handfuls of gelatin and squeeze through your fingers into a punch bowl. Pour ginger ale over gelatin.

nutritional powerhouse: pumpkin seeds

Whether the jack-o'-lanterns you carved smile or scowl, don't toss the seeds you scoop from them. They are extremely high in nutrients. One ounce of hulled seeds supplies more than half of the recommended daily amount of iron and about 20 percent of the vitamin E and zinc. The seeds are also high in monounsaturated and polyunsaturated fats.

You can buy pumpkin seeds year-round, but they go rancid very quickly; so consider making your own: Rinse the seeds thoroughly in a colander, pulling and rubbing off the orange pulp. Rinse them again and dry them well. Toss with a bit of oil and a little salt mixed with chili powder or curry powder. Roast in a 375°F oven, stirring three or four times, until golden, about 45 minutes. Store in an airtight container. Enjoy them as a snack, in salads, or sprinkle over yogurt.

acknowledgments

All books are team projects, but cookbooks—and particularly illustrated cookbooks—require a larger team and one composed of individuals with a myriad of talents. The development of *Atkins for Life Low-Carb Cookbook* was overseen by Olivia Bell Buehl, vice president and editorial director of Atkins Health & Medical Information Services, a division of Atkins Nutritionals. Executive editor Christine Senft, M.S., who is also a nutritionist, managed the team of freelance contributors. Managing editor Jenny L. Moles diligently oversaw the editorial review process. Senior food editor Allison Fishman carefully reviewed all the recipes and oversaw the photography. Assistant food editor Amanda Dorato lent her savvy low-carb palate to tasting as many recipes as possible. Nutritionist Colette Heimowitz, M.S., vice president and director of education and research, reviewed the recipes for compliance with the Atkins Nutritional Approach and made helpful suggestions.

Without a large team of talented freelancers, this book would not have seen the light of day. First, I owe a special debt of gratitude to Stephanie Nathanson, my coauthor, who is a skilled low-carb cook and a contributing editor to The Atkins Kitchen. She was instrumental in creating the editorial concept for this book and overseeing the development of the recipes to make them appropriate for the home cook. The ever-capable Martha Schueneman served as project editor and oversaw the recipe testing. She also wrote the tips and sidebars that enhance the book's usefulness.

The exquisite photographs were produced by a dynamic team headed up by photographer Ben Fink. Food stylist William Smith made and beautifully arranged all the food for the photo shoots. Stylist Cathy Cook brought life into the table settings, providing everything from forks to flowers.

Renata De Oliveira and Alison Lew, principals of Vertigo Design, created the book's inviting graphic design. Renata also art-directed the photography.

A special thank-you to recipe developers Cynthia DePersio, Tracey Seaman, Susan Jaslove, Wendy Kalen, Miriam Rubin, Elizabeth Fassberg, Anne Bailey, Grady Best, and Fred Thompson. We owe a similar nod to our recipe testers, Becky Billingsley, Mary Donovan, Donna Hammond, Susan Hanemann, Robin Kline, Paul E. Piccuito, Sarah Reynolds, Dina Ronsini, Charlie Schaffer, and Belinda Treu.

Other helping hands include the army of assistants who helped make the photography happen. Shannon O'Hara assisted photographer Ben Fink. Working with Cathy Cook were Erica Shires and Tammy Schoenfeld. In the kitchen with William Smith was Matthew Vohr.

The team at St. Martin's Press pulled out all the stops to get this book done in record time. Special thanks to Sally Richardson, publisher of the trade division, Matthew Shear, publisher of the paperback and reference group, Lisa Senz, associate publisher, Amelie Littell, managing editor, and the rest of the team for their faith in this project and support under daunting deadlines.

index